D1196769

Errant Selves

Errant Selves

A Casebook of Misbehavior

edited by

Arnold Goldberg

THE ANALYTIC PRESS

2000   Hillsdale, NJ   London

© 2000 by The Analytic Press, Inc.
All rights reserved. No part of this book may be reproduced in any
form: by photostat, microform, retrieval system, or any other means,
without the prior written permission of the publisher.

Published by
The Analytic Press, Inc., Publishers
Editorial Offices:
101 West Street
Hillsdale, New Jersey 07642

www.analyticpress.com

Designed and typeset by Compudesign, Charlottesville, VA

Index by Leonard S. Rosenbaum

Library of Congress Cataloging-in-Publication Data

Errant selves : a casebook of misbehavior / edited by Arnold Goldberg.
p.   cm.
Includes bibliographical references and index.
ISBN 0-88163-333-X
1. Compulsive behavior—Case studies.   2. Psychology,
Pathological—Case studies.   3. Psychoanalysis—Case studies.
I. Goldberg, Arnold, 1929–
RC533.E774 2000
616.85'227-dc21
00-057603

Printed in the United States of America
10 9 8 7 6 5 4 3 2 1

Contents

Acknowledgments

The editor and contributors are grateful for the support of their families, friends, and patients. In addition to the authors of these cases, our study group was composed of Constance Goldberg, Dr. Robert Gordon, Dr. Robert J. Leider, Dr. Sheldon Meyers, Ms. Judith Newman, Dr. David Solomon, and Dr. Ruth Yanagi. Financial support for our work was given by the Psychotherapy Fund of Rush-Presbyterian-St. Luke's Medical Center in Chicago. Editorial and secretarial assistance was provided by Ms. Christine Susman. She and all of those listed were supportive and encouraging throughout this project and we are all indebted to them.

Introduction

This book evolved over time. A group of analysts was formed in order to collect and study cases of perversions, delinquencies, and addictions for a casebook. We met to discuss these cases, and we hoped ultimately to publish the clinical data we felt were all of a piece, that is, the cases in which behavior disorders shared similar characteristics, a similarity that deserved a detailed presentation. One of the features common to all cases was that the noteworthy behavior (of whatever sort) served primarily to ward off or obliterate painful affects or states of dysphoria, and in doing so to make for a feeling of self-strength or consolidation. Just as a long run for exercise or a comic movie for fun helps one temporarily both to forget reality and to live in another world, so too did these behaviors enable our patients to step away from their everyday and often unhappy lives and to experience relief and (sometimes) pleasure. That some or most of these behaviors were more appropriately termed *misbehavior*, such as seen in the sexual perversions, was considered to be an added ingredient to that first basic and fundamental characteristic: the behavior was necessary. One could, of course, think of this misbehavior as defensive or as a weakness or even as a communication to others. But all of that came later. We began with the understanding that it made no sense to try to suppress or eradicate someone's needs, no matter how offensive the needs may seem to others. With our commitment to understanding the symptom rather than treating the behavior, we saw it primarily as necessary for achieving a sense of self-consolidation in our patients.

The second feature assigned to this fairly large and (at first) poorly delineated category of misbehavior had to do with the degree of offensiveness. Most if not all of our patients seemed to share much the same dislike of what they did as did the rest of us. Although it became clear to us that our patients could make no claim to being run of the mill criminals, perverts, or addicts, we could not conclude that they were much different from what is commonly considered as antisocial, save that they regularly joined with us in contemplating the awfulness of and disdain for their actions. This in itself soon became a significant, if not essential, component for better definition and delineation of our own categorization and a critical issue in the consideration of treatment, inasmuch as the negative appraisal of the behavior was regularly the launching pad for its later understanding and subsequent control or eradication. Here is one beautiful example of this kind of negative appraisal, its appearance and disappearance.

> Henry Jekyll stood at times aghast at the acts of Edward Hyde; but the situation was apart from ordinary laws, and insidiously relaxed the grasp of conscience. It was Hyde, after all, and Hyde alone, that was guilty. Jekyll was no worse; he woke again to his good qualities seemingly unimpaired; he would even make haste, where it was possible, to undo the evil done by Hyde. And thus his conscience slumbered [Stevenson, p. 87].

Robert Louis Stevenson's classic fictionalized study is of a man who ingests a magical potion to become someone else—although only temporarily, and regrettably, regularly. Dr. Jekyll can be said to be transformed into Mr. Hyde or seen as both men with different claims for recognition. Mr. Hyde does demonic things and Jekyll claims innocence; while Stevenson lets us know that Jekyll initiates and enjoys everything that Hyde does. Jekyll is of two minds and literally embodies what we call a vertical split. This split is not the horizontal split of repression but rather that of disavowal and so is a division available to consciousness and self-appraisal.

Such a split, of one person living parallel lives with different goals, aims, and values, is a hallmark of our overall category, which now can be seen as a pathological group: a group that (as Jekyll) is aghast at what they (as Hyde) do. The moral component in the evaluation of one's parallel and aberrant behavior is a powerful incentive to its delineation as pathology. How differently we judge a person with a symptom such as depression versus (say) one who exhibits his genitals to small children. Of late, some think that depression is something so basic and biochemical that the sufferer may indeed be an innocent victim; rarely, however, do we believe that a periodic thief can lay equal claim to an affliction beyond his control? Shoplifters are caught and punished; bipolar disease and depression are pitied and medicated. This moral stance is, not surprisingly, adopted by that same misbehaving patient who, because of this split, can treat his or her actions as if they were misdeeds of another. Our patients—in order for them to become patients—to some degree or other hate that other self. But just as Jekyll enjoys what Hyde does, so, too, do our patients—to the detriment of their treatment—enjoy their own misdeeds. The psychological state of disavowal of a parallel person is a sine qua non for our categorization of *narcissistic behavior disorders,* a phrase that joins together the use of disordered or offensive behavior with the treatment goal of self-cohesion. Our patients were neither unitary selves nor persons with an easy ability to bolster or reconstitute themselves in socially acceptable ways. Rather they utilized all manner of deviant, immoral, aberrant efforts to gain their sense of solidity, and in so doing they were rent in two.

No doubt much of the richness of a depth psychology lies in the content of the life stories that unfold; however, our initial two elements of describing our patient population had to do not with content but with form: the halt to disintegration and the disavowal that ensued. There are no stories here—not yet.

The cases that are discussed in this book are representative of those that were presented to our group over a period of years. Several of the cases we discussed may have been more illustrative of points that we wished to present, but they could not be included in this book because of issues of confidentiality. Some could not be properly disguised, whereas others were vetoed by the patient who had been invited to read the writeup for an agreement to publish. Surely case presentations need to be at the heart of our scientific study, but we are necessarily constrained by our obligation to protect patients. We are fairly confident that nothing extraneous or misleading has been added to these cases that would in any way significantly alter the essential content of the material.

For the most part, patients who become involved in unlawful behavior are sent for treatment rather than seek it out for themselves. Similarly, those whose misbehavior is ordinarily seen as distasteful or aberrant, although still not quite illegal, do not present themselves for the treatment of problems unless these problems cause psychic discomfort. Indeed, many such sorts of behavior are felt to be themselves relieving of psychological dysphoria and are looked on as negative only after the fact. Thus a person who masturbates while watching pornographic movies does not become a patient until he finds himself unable to enjoy sex with a partner and/or uses this outlet in an uncontrolled manner. The passage from a mild pastime to a significant form of deviant behavior is often an unclear one; only when the person himself considers his action as offensive can one hope to see this activity as symptom rather than as an innocent quirk.

The technical interventions of any depth psychology deal with that special adjective of depth and do so by interpreting the unconscious and bringing the hidden to the surface. Because all of the contributors to this book are psychoanalysts, we are devoted to understanding our patients by way of analytic concepts and analytic theories, but primarily with the utilization of psychoanalytic self psychology. One cannot, of course, offer a comprehensive review of our theories here, and so the reader we imagine and hope for has some familiarity with self psychology and, in particular, with the forms of selfobject transferences. We refer to idealizing, mirror, or twinship transferences rather than to maternal, paternal, positive, or negative ones. Psychoanalytic self psychology is an elaboration of psychoanalysis that is particularly helpful in the explanation of disorders of narcissism. The references to the way we talk and think are listed in the back of this book for the interested reader and, for some, may be a prerequisite for a full group of the cases to be presented. For others, the cases are certainly described with a minimum of jargon, and the theoretical baggage may not be essential. However, for a start, we do propose that all of our cases of behavior disorders have problems in twinning, idealization, and grandiosity. Thus, the content of our stories lies within these forms.

If one thinks of the self as the experiencer of a heterogenous group of regulatory functions that are realized and maintained by way of connections with others or selfobjects, then this relatively cohesive and coherent psychic structure may be described as organized along poles of grandiosity, idealization, or twinning. When we study any individual, the development of the self-organization is posited as formed by his or her significant parental selfobjects. A person becomes stabilized around a complex configuration that essentially reflects that person's best adaptation with his or her selfobjects; and so the self is as varied and variable as individual experience can be. In those whose childhood selfobjects were unavailable and/or unable to aid proper growth and development, we see either the intense preoccupation with self-esteem regulation so characteristic of narcissistic personality disorders, or periodic efforts to maintain self cohesion by way of acting out as we describe in narcissistic behavior disorders. The personality disorders, on the other hand, usually find some sort of stability in a particular set of distressing symptoms such as in empty depression, hypochondria, or shame of narcissistic vulnerability. The behavior disorders seek stability by way of action. The personality disorders are primarily organized around one single pole of self-development, whereas the behavior disorders seem unable to manage such a psychological commitment and so are divided or split between a self of stability and one of behavior utilized to restore stability.

Disavowal is the predominant developmental problem in behavior disorders, so our treatment efforts are often concentrated on this aspect of the patients' lives. The dynamics that one regularly encounters in the scrutiny of the content of a patient's life are regularly seen by psychoanalysts to unfold in an oedipal drama or a preoedipal narrative. Whether dyadic or triadic, we tend to describe individuals as autonomous and unified, albeit in depth. The struggles are described as conflicts: first those between parents and child, and then those within the child. The contributions of so-called relational schools have given us a further perspective on the reliving of these dynamics in treatment as our consciousness has been raised in terms of the analyst's presence. However, the intersubjective or interpersonal or relational outlooks also are locked into thinking of and seeing *persons* which is a term pertaining to social beings and so conceptualizing such persons as unitary individuals. Current schools that speak of interaction, intersubjective fields, and internalization and externalization of relations, all presume a person that, as complex as he or she may be and as significant the unconscious determinants of that person may be, remains as and retains the premise of an individual. This premise did not serve us well in our study of our patients with behavior disorders. A concentration in the quality of the selfobject transferences enabled us to see and understand that a split lived in these persons and soon became alive as well in those of us who treated them.

The concept of *borderline personalities* or the use of splitting in describing many patients said to have multiple personalities often has a therapist involved in a myriad of interactions, even to the point of giving names to these personalities. As our case material will show, this picture of continual and diffuse disorganization and/or occasional acts of splitting is inapplicable to our study.

The psychodynamics of our patients become narrated and/or reconstructed by us as a biography and, as with any redescription of events, is necessarily a selective and coherent one. Our patients' stories revealed a very fundamental dissonance, which we saw best described as a vertical split. These are individuals dealing with divided parallel selves and different values, goals, and ideals. Our group's selectivity insisted on an omission of other significant material. As we focused on the split of our patients, we may have closed our eyes to other factors. Not surprisingly, that fact allowed us to see that a vertical split exemplifies that very act of unseeing. Thus, the next point of our case presentations became that of showing our colleagues what they (and we) have been blind to in the past. The following cases therefore are revealing both of our patients and ourselves.

John Alter

In the case of John Alter, correcting our vision was not easy to accomplish. It seems fair to say that our group knew about our blindness and yet had no idea of what it meant to fully know it. This case wrenched us out of our innocence and complicated our mission. The case was offered as that of a thief but soon became one that included another as well; the analyst became an equal object of our study. We followed the often painful emergence of the pattern of a divided person matched with that of the analyst who insisted on his unwitting rationalization of a behavior that mirrored his patient's. Our group soon learned what the analyst had been doing, took an immediate moral stance of condemnation, and attempted to banish him from the project. We have since realized that this act of correct conscience is one that is both the easiest to assume and the least likely to do any good. John Alter's therapist (the change from "therapist" to "analyst" as the story unfolds begins to make sense) initially could not comprehend what he heard from his colleagues, and he defended himself in a manner familiar to anyone who reads case reports justifying any and all therapeutic intervention from hugging to yelling, from silence to threats. When at last our colleague, the chastened therapist, did hear, he grew depressed, sought consultation, changed the treatment, and the case was successfully terminated. In one sense, it was simply a case of group supervision but I think of this case as our "baptism of commitment." Not all members of the group became believers, although all could see the nature of the split transference and the corresponding split in the analyst. However, some felt that such a disavowal on the analyst's part could be noted but contained without action. Some therapists feel to this day that such splitting occurs only in others. We came to realize that the power of disavowal is an ever-present lure to one's insistence on the unity of the world that allows one to sit silently and not notice "the stranger beside you."

Once aware of the split transference appearing in the treatment situation, we could puzzle over how and when the analyst participated in its realization. The part of the patient that was pathological was one that could easily be circumscribed and studied as the analyst reported the incidents of misbehavior. The response of the analyst would seem equally accessible but that is not the case and often is the major stumbling block.

Kool

Our next case is one of a complete failure of the analyst to recognize his disavowal. He failed in the realization of that deficiency until sometime later. This treatment is a dramatic one of a male cross-dresser struggling to become a woman. The patient needed a response from an analyst who knew of that struggle as well. The analyst reports this case with incredible candor, but his personal uncertainty about the patient's commitment to analysis was extended to every facet of the treatment in terms of the patient's own reciprocal uncertainty as to whether he was to be entirely a man or both a man and a woman. The reader may feel an immediate sense of futility about the conduct of the case from its onset to its ending, but one must go further than merely throwing up one's hands in despair. The analyst of the case reports that he did just that and saw that fundamentally he could never see himself—even for a moment—as a woman. And all his quite sensitive communications to the patient about understanding the patient's need to cross dress betrayed his own personal message of reluctance and repugnance. There is no doubt that this case enabled all of us to move a little closer to seeing the nature of the split state in the analyst.

Bert

The case of Bert depicts an analyst's being pulled into a variety of enactments with her patient and an expanding awareness of the very difficult set of decisions about doing things differently. It is important here to underline that fact that the particular forms of enactment have shown themselves to be of minor significance. Aside from the moral issues involved in so-called boundary violations, our group felt that the only point of therapeutic significance was that of not recognizing and bringing the acts into the analysis and thereby interpreting them. We felt that the host of contributions of other writers that insist on either allowing or forbidding all sorts of therapeutic behavior may miss the point. Indeed a concern about boundaries may well substitute judgment for understanding. The case of Bert is best seen as a struggle over all of the terrain of enactment as the therapist worked to a better position for herself. The reader may well feel that the case could have been handled quite differently and one may have made sense of it in a different way. We all felt that way about almost all of our cases, and we expect the same of the reader. The aim here is not to demonstrate a correct way to see and treat patients as much as it is to call attention to the division in the patient and its subtle and often unrecognized expression in the analyst.

Janie

The case of Janie encompasses a range of enactments up to and including a patient who had searched through the analyst's garbage and finally brought her collection of refuse to the analyst. Our group had what might be called an expectable range of responses to this singular act. We hope that our own discussion will be mirrored in our readers, because it should demonstrate the crucial point of what an analyst can both tolerate and understand. Sometimes toleration is most needed in cases of repugnant, offensive, or antisocial behavior. Sometimes the search for understanding dominates as one puzzles over peculiar or weird behavior as is nicely illustrated in "the garbage collector." In this case discussion, the analyst seemed quite honest and open in her curiosity about these acts, whereas others of us were more guarded from and frightened by them. Here, once again, was a critical opportunity for an examination that required a full study of the complexity of the transference, a study that may well be ignored if one merely subsumes everything under a convenient term such as *the relationship* and/or the countertransference contribution of the analyst.

Peter

Although some of these patients present obvious symptoms such as stealing or stalking, others are much quieter and may easily lull the analyst into a conspiracy of inattention. Peter did just that with his first analyst. His behavior of "not mentioning" became a striking feature of this second treatment. The patient had never mentioned his symptom of compulsive masturbation to his first analyst, and when he resumed treatment with a new analyst she had a personal and private "scene" of not mentioning. Her own story, which she reveals to us, could be seen as having nothing to do with the patient, or else it could have been the essential factor of the treatment. Working through these matched positions demanded a careful and detailed effort of integration. It may be seen in the case presentation more or less as a highlight. It should, however, be best considered as reflecting a guiding theme for the entire analysis, inasmuch as it exemplifies the parallel split in the analysis.

Alice, Rashid, and Alexander

The next three cases were presented to our group by analysts who, in their openness and ability to share their countertransference feelings with us, insisted they were able to be aware of the split in the patient but denied any sort of acting out of their own that was not recognized or brought into the treatment. The skepticism engendered in our study group by the first cases in this collection could not easily be dissolved by the righteous stand of these presenters. Yet the patients did seem to do well and we detected no paucity of intense feelings on the part of their therapists. We had to rethink our conception of a matching of the vertical split. In our original recognition of a split in patients with narcissistic behavior disorders, we initially thought that effective treatment of these patients required a reciprocal split in the therapist or analyst. We next concluded that certain forms of split-off behavior could remain entirely outside of the treatment with the implicit agreement of the analyst, or else could participate in the treatment with the implicit acceptance and corresponding blindness of the analyst. Each possibility demanded a collusion with the analyst and could be effectively treated only by integrating the disavowed material into the treatment and interpreting the underlying unconscious content. We now advanced our conditions for therapeutic effectiveness to include a match with an analyst who could struggle with both sides of the split without condemnation or acceptance. Perhaps this match and the ensuing concealment could explain these cases better than the skeptical view of concealment. Such a collusion is a proper question for all of us to pursue. The case of Alexander is a psychotherapy case that strikingly illustrates the puzzle of therapist participation.

Rashid is the patient who brings us full circle. He is a thief sharing only that misbehavior, as did our first patient. The analyst ends with the query of where he was in "all of this." Our book addresses this issue and more specifically asks how we can possibly comprehend and contain all that we are and come to be in the treatment of those people who are themselves not all of a piece.

The most difficult part of turning our work into a book was not at all the back-and-forth discussions about these cases, which turned out to be fun. Rather, it was the very daunting project of presenting our work to others. In particular, it was the worry and concern over protecting our patients. I remain convinced that it is an unsolved and perhaps insurmountable problem. Some of our cases were not reported because the analysts felt that the patients might read the book and become upset. Although all the patients are disguised, a high probability remains that a patient will recognize himself or herself. Some authors have taken this risk but not without a good deal of apprehension. Several cases were disguised and then presented to the patients for discussion and approval. One should be extremely wary of this as a regular procedure despite a suggestion by some (e.g., Stoller, 1988) to make it routine. At least one of our patients refused outright, and, though others agreed, it was often after a stormy period of negotiation that concluded with the author convinced never to do that again. In the long run, open discussion with the patient did little good. In terms of the disguise, we all agreed that this resulted in an inevitable alteration of the case material, which was often distorting and potentially misleading. It is not surprising that an effort to mislead the reader as to the identity of the patient will very likely misrepresent other realities as well. On a few occasions, some extremely telling and important material could not be disclosed for reasons of confidentiality.

Our study group is convinced that work will advance only through the careful study and discussion of cases and that it is an obligation for all members of our scientific enterprise to help one another to be as open and available to case presentations as possible. There may be several solutions to this conflict of confidentiality and scientific advancement and we hope this book is a step in that direction. The present climate of hypervigilance over ethical and legal missteps in case presentations seems to inhibit many writers from offering such material to the public. There is no dearth of readers and listeners offering criticism and suggestions to those few beleaguered authors who do come forth.

A final caution is in order. The cases in this book are offered for study with no claim whatsoever that they are guides to the proper treatment of behavior disorders. They, like many cases for all of us, are messy, erratically understood, periodically mishandled, and never completely cured. The cases presented are meant only to demonstrate the difficulties in treating such errant selves and the possible potential for improving such treatment.

1

The Case of John Alter
To Catch a Thief (or Two)

John Alter came for treatment when he was 36 years old, having been referred to me by one of his colleagues, a former patient of mine. He had been in treatment for about a year and a half with a respected analyst prompted by drug abuse and feelings of inadequacy. The analyst contracted with the patient to stop using drugs in return for continued treatment; the patient complied and has always felt that this analyst enabled him to stop his drug abuse. Additionally, the patient was in panic over his financial position. Prior to seeing the first analyst, Alter did very well practicing corporate law. After a few months of treatment, the analyst established another contract requiring Alter to stop practicing in this legal arena because it was too stressful (the demands for "immediate" responses were intense). The patient agreed that his practice placed too many demands on him and contributed to the panic and the drug abuse; he decided to give it up in favor of a less demanding practice. Because his insurance policy was predicated on his being a corporate lawyer, he applied for and obtained disability. However, the analyst felt that the disability payments, substantial at $3000 a month, precluded clinical improvement because they would diminish his incentive, and he so informed Alter, who sought consultation with another respected and more senior analyst, who agreed with the first. The patient was unwilling to give up the disability; he felt that it was worth $600,000 over the life of the policy. Furthermore, a friend in a similar situation had recently settled with the insurance company for $200,000. Alter had been offered a settlement 6 months before contacting me and had rejected it, but was reconsidering after his friend's settlement. He felt that his previous

1

analyst did not believe him about the future value of the disability policy, and the consulting analyst, whom he also saw, felt it was part of Alter's grandiosity. (He ultimately collected $36,000 a year for over 14 years for a total of over $500,000.) Because he needed a physician's monthly signature to continue receiving the payments, Alter decided to find another therapist, and found his way to me.

The patient was forthcoming about these issues with me from the start. It happened that I was in private supervision at the time with the same consulting senior analyst, and we talked about the situation. He reiterated his misgivings about the prospect of clinical progress under the circumstances. I saw the patient several times before making a decision as to whether to treat him. I finally decided to do so despite my misgivings and against the advice of both analysts, whom I respect, because I was not convinced that the disability payments precluded a successful outcome. Further, the patient told me that his previous analyst was like his stern and critical father—"soft," according to Alter, but also "tough and confronting." He felt "betrayed" by the previous analyst, who saw him as an "addictive personality." It was soon apparent that he had many grievances against his father, and that the disability issue seemed to have locked the transference configuration into the same pattern with his previous analyst. Because I was not so rigid about the disability crippling the treatment, perhaps things would be different with me. I also knew that he could find someone else to treat him and to sign the disability forms, which simply required my indication that he was unable to perform the functions of his previous job, a fact to which I felt I could attest. Although I had problems with the disability, I liked him well enough and felt I could help him. I decided to begin treatment and see what happened, hoping that at some point he would come to feel that he no longer needed the disability despite its legality. Aside from the clinical considerations just noted, I needed patients at the time. And so we proceeded.

Alter was the youngest of four boys, the older ones more troublesome and rebellious. John was considered the "love child," whose job was to bring joy to his parents by being good and compliant. They called him by the diminutive, "Johnny." Mother was endlessly loving; sitting in father's lap, Johnny relished the warmth of his hugs and kisses. Mother helped him with his homework, and he was a top student.

Things changed when he was put into special classes for brighter students in late grammar school. He did less well in school and began retreating to his secret world in his room to read pornographic magazines and masturbate. Now father was not around much. Mother's ministrations and occasional intrusions into his secret world to ask him what he was doing became embarrassments for the boy, for he found her very sexy and feared being a mama's boy. He wanted his father's continued approval and love, but instead got paternal temper and criticism. His father took him fishing on a charter boat. Johnny was helping the mate when his father suddenly hit him; to this day he does not know why. He had helped out on occasion at his father's grocery store with chores like sweeping. One day, his father angrily took the broom from him, shouting, "Here's how you sweep!" Although he continued to receive love and support from his mother, Johnny was disappointed that when he came to her for solace, she usually took the father's side. If mother intervened on his behalf, he was embarrassed. His brothers often stood up to their father and Johnny witnessed terrifying shouting matches; he was very afraid of his father and ashamed of his fear.

Only late in the analysis did Alter come to understand how self-centered his father was, being another youngest child who usually got his way. As a father, he organized his life and his household to his liking "or else": when he came home, Johnny had to bring him his drink and his slippers. The persona of Johnny was valuable to Alter because it got him special treatment (such as his mother doing his homework for him) thus sparing him his father's anger, but he felt increasingly ashamed of Johnny and his cowering, infantile stance.

These preadolescent and early adolescent circumstances may have exacerbated the split in Alter's psyche. School, social life, and his relationship with his father changed. He was no longer the adored Johnny. Turning to his father was too dangerous and turning to his mother too embarrassing, so the secret world of his room was his solace. He disavowed or split off the painful affects experienced with his parents and focused on pornographic literature and masturbation.

Alter developed a significant interest in baseball and for a while spent much of his free time on the diamond, although he was never a participant on his school teams. A few double promotions at school made him younger than his classmates, and he was terribly naive, especially about girls. He was fat and self-conscious about it. When he was 12 years old at camp, he was reduced to asking a girl some boys called "pigface" to dance. Only after high school did he trim down, eat healthy foods, and begin to date girls under the tutelage of an admired older boy.

When Alter stole cigarettes from his father's grocery store a few times, an employee told him that if he did not stop, his father would be told. In college, Alter was caught stealing a book from the campus bookstore and was suspended. When he reported this suspension to his parents, his father's response was, "You're not my son!" This comment stung terribly, and in treatment became the prototype for rejections he bore from his father. Alter went to see a psychiatrist and felt it was the first time in his life he could open up to anyone.

Years later, while vacationing in Morocco, Alter was arrested and jailed for possession of marijuana, and perhaps other drugs. When he returned home, his father criticized him but his mother never mentioned it.

Eventually thrown out of college, Alter asked an employment agency to "get me a job in a law firm." Starting in the mail room, he developed sufficient interest to pursue a law degree. His father once again carped, calling him a shyster.

Alter married a woman who pleased his mother and delighted him by assuming his social role with her, thereby relieving him of the responsibility of talking to his mother. The women could talk together endlessly. He was shyer and more reticent than his more social wife, although she too had her limitations in this regard. Unfortunately, within 6 months of their marriage she developed gynecological tumors that required constant monitoring. As a result, her conflicts about sexuality intensified dramatically and their marriage became relatively asexual. Their sexuality consisted primarily of foreplay; intercourse was rare and there were no children. During a 2-year separation early in the marriage, Alter partied extensively with women and drugs. His wife was depressed and made one minimal suicide attempt, but did not enter psychotherapy for many years. Their marriage was not good; communication between them was inadequate; nor were they open with their feelings; while they withdrew from one another, resentments built up.

The disability issue colored the treatment from the beginning: Alter said he was sick of talking about it, that at times he felt he was not entitled to it, but that he felt he needed it because he lacked confidence in his earning capacity and in his general stability. At first he could not ask me about my fee because he feared I might not like him. His previous analyst had balked at signing the disability forms after 4 months, but Alter persuaded him that his current legal work was quite different from his previous corporate practice. A few months went by, the analyst balked again, and the patient began to fall silent, feeling mistrust and anxiety because of the analyst's power over him. Alter was unsure in his new job and felt he could not risk the loss of the disability.

Although Alter admired his previous analyst's rigidity and integrity and felt both characteristics helped him, he readily likened the experience to the one with his father, which was ultimately a betrayal. His father, having retired 10 years earlier in Arizona on an annuity, was passing himself off as a rich man. Having discovered in his earlier treatment (confirmed by his friends) that his father was a "big bullshitter"—that his big paunch, big cigars, and big cars signified a sham—Alter realized that when his friends had called his father "Doc," it was not out of respect but in derision. When his father said he thought Alter was as good a husband as he had been, the patient responded, "I learned from your mistakes." His previous treatment also taught Alter that he had (idealized) fantasies about his father, but reality was different. Alter thought that he could be easily influenced but longed for an ideal father nevertheless.

Not surprisingly, Alter developed an idealizing transference to me. I was the "good" therapist who could understand and empathize with him, in contrast to his previous analyst who betrayed him, and in contrast to his wife, who was unavailable or critical. From time to time, Alter made associations to the disability or to the insurance payments he also received, which enabled him to pay for therapy. I grew irritated with him and with what I considered his dubious morality; because of the disability and health insurance payments, Alter was making money by being in treatment. My comments betrayed my irritation. More than once, I hoped aloud that at some point he would be confident enough in his money-making abilities to no longer feel the need for the disability payments. His response was, typically, "The insurance company made a bad deal and people tell me I'd be crazy to give it up," and a reiteration was made of the difference between the two kinds of law practice and his entitlement to the payments because he was no longer a corporate lawyer. I agreed that the demands of his earlier practice were certainly not in his best interest. When these "crises" occurred in the treatment, Alter's anxiety and hesitance to tell me his feelings and thoughts increased, but once I either realized or was reminded by him that I was being moralistic and I managed to convey my feeling that I could accept and understand his position again, he felt better about me and our relationship.

As he had indicated from the outset, he was easily influenced by a propensity to idealize certain men. In a series of these relationships during the years of therapy, the most dramatic was probably with Mr. Barker. All of the events detailed in the patient's relationship with Barker occurred during treatment with me.

When we started treatment, Alter was working for a man who subsequently left the practice. The patient then became a partner of Barker, a man with significant psychopathic tendencies. Barker had already served a suspension from the bar when he joined forces with the patient; Alter knew this fact but rationalized that Barker had "cleaned up his act" and could make him lots of money. Alter knew himself to be a good lawyer, but not good at getting clients; Barker was very good at that.

For a while, things went well. But when clients were few, the partners were responsible for covering overhead and meeting a payroll. For some time they lost money, a serious problem given the small scale of the practice. Alter panicked when he had to write the monthly checks, then looked for money from any source. Escrow funds were sometimes available, so he "borrowed" them. When Alter told Barker what he was doing, Barker was encouraging. Alter clearly idolized Barker, saw him as confident, bright, with a golden touch, and he very much wanted to be liked by him. Because Alter had few friends, he hoped their professional relationship would evolve into a solid friendship.

Then Barker's wife was killed in an accident. Alter felt she had helped to keep Barker on track, but now Barker began spending less time with the practice and began dating a woman whom Alter did not like. Barker bought a lease on a Mercedes and because he did not have a good credit rating, persuaded Alter to cosign the note. When Barker sold his part of the practice to a Mr. Crone, Barker and Crone agreed that Crone would pick up the cost of the lease, $3000 a month; but soon Crone discovered that the practice was not making much money and, pleading poverty, backed out, reneged on the lease payments, and left Alter with 3 years of payments remaining. Barker refused to help in any way, infuriating Alter and bringing about his realization of what a sucker he had been to idolize Barker.

Alter's wife was initially furious and threw her hands up in despair, saying it was her husband's problem. He had always felt that she expected him to be strong, had not wanted to hear about his problems or his needs, and in that respect was like his parents, who were fine as long as he was Johnny the love child, but were critical and unhelpful when he had needs or when he attempted to assert his independence. But now Alter turned to his wife for help, and found her advice and stabilizing influence very helpful. Alter arranged to repossess the car, sold it, and recouped some of the money. Barker then sued Alter and the matter dragged on for years, culminating in a decision in favor of Alter that required both Barker and Crone to pay Alter in full for all of his costs. The "hold" over both was that neither could practice law until Alter was reimbursed. Over the years, Barker paid off Alter in full, but Crone has not.

Paradoxically, Barker's charges against Alter exposed Alter's practice to increased surveillance. Alter was asked for all his records going back a few years. Alter knew he was in trouble because he had been "borrowing" escrow funds to meet the expenses of the law practice. His career was in jeopardy. He was ashamed and guilty, with none of the familiar rationalizations from his discussions of the disability. Further, Alter was afraid of what his wife might do, and what I, too, might do. His wife was furious, devastated, and afraid, and ultimately sought treatment (detailed later).

My own reaction was mixed. Alter had discussed the escrow funds with me from time to time. I alternated between trying to analyze his motivation and warning him of the potentially severe consequences, particularly as he continued to use the escrow funds while the investigation was ongoing. At some level, I was clearly glad he had been discovered. My own sense of justice was satisfied, but Alter might also benefit by the added external pressure from the authorities on his incompletely developed inhibiting and controlling mechanisms. I felt it crucial for his internalization of these mechanisms that I try to be empathic without exonerating him or taking too moralistic a stance. It was not easy. On at least one occasion, I spoke of an attorney I knew who had been jailed for bribing a judge and whose life was dramatically changed for the worse; it had clearly affected his wife and children very badly. Alter alternately felt ashamed or protested my attitude, claiming to know suspended lawyers who had returned and managed to achieve some success.

Alter's lawyer advised him to continue to work as before, and to deny any wrongdoing if asked by anyone. Alter, in turn, stalled the authorities for as long as possible. He was clearly having a rough time, both emotionally and financially. After the disasters with Barker and Crone, he decided to go to work for another attorney, and in general things improved, but he did not make as much money.

After 3 years of not knowing what to expect from the authorities and waiting for the most probable outcome of a 6-month to 2-year suspension and a $50,000 to $100,000 fine, Alter was fined $25,000 and suspended for 3 months for misusing the escrow funds.

His problems with Barker and the authorities were central to the treatment for a long time. Although I made attempts to question whether turning to Barker or misusing escrow funds were related to vicissitudes in the transference, I have no clear recollection of these interpretations bearing much fruit. Alter's stealing seemed at the time to be so focused on the fluctuation of the firm's finances that I may have overlooked any connections. But my transference interpretations must have had some impact during the approximately 10-year middle phase of treatment within the silent idealizing transference. In more recent years, in the second couch hour (after agreeing, finally, to move to the couch), there was a definite sense of loss when John was unable to see me and had the impulse to do some "borrowing" as a result.

A vignette from a session during the middle phase of treatment, prior to his going to the couch, illustrates work with Alter that resulted in his feeling "connected" to me, a term that has come to be a code for the good feelings he had when he felt understood by me. He arrived to report that he had surprised his wife at the doctor's office by coming in during her cancer check. Though previously she was annoyed when he showed up, this time she was pleased. Then he reported that he had successfully drummed up some law business on his own as a result of a course he was now teaching at a night school. He was particularly pleased because he rarely brought in clients. Teaching had not been easy in the beginning, but he now felt he was mastering it. Suddenly he asked me what I thought about the Chicago Bulls' most recent game—something about which we occasionally talked. My perfunctory comments on the game were followed by my asking him if he had asked me about the Bulls in an effort to connect with me because he felt that I had not connected with him. He said he thought I was bored as he had caught me looking at the clock (probably true—he was the last patient of the day and I do not know if I was fully attending).

I replied that he did some things of which he felt proud, and it was just as important to have his triumphs acknowledged as his needs and difficulties. I associated aloud to his suspension from college for stealing books from the store, and to his father's "You're not my son," and to the initiative he had shown at the beginning of his career, still without acknowledgment from his parents, particularly his father. Even now, under threat of suspension and fine and with his practice endangered, he managed to continue functioning, to make a living and to be a husband. And if his wife was often cold and critical, or at least ungiving, at such times those people who noted his dilemmas and achievements were important to him, so that my seeming unresponsiveness was not helpful. Alter responded that other friends to whom he often turned and who had usually been helpful had recently withdrawn support ever since he told them about his troubles with the authorities. He teared up during our discussion, noted it explicitly, and was visibly moved by the interpretation and interchange. (Some readers of this case felt that my being so forthcoming about my "unresponsiveness" belied my guilt for not being fully attentive. Nevertheless, the patient was moved by it.)

During the investigation into Alter's practice, his marriage was under more than the usual strain. The patient's wife suddenly asked about marital counseling, which she had refused for the first 10 years of her husband's treatment. They both wanted to see me, and I agreed. (I had met with other patients and their spouses in the past when there were marital difficulties with what I thought was considerable success.) I saw them together for some months on a weekly basis, Alter cutting down to twice-weekly sessions. Their hours with me helped them be more honest and open with each other, to relieve misgivings and fears of being wounded or of wounding the other. Then, to the surprise of both

Alter and myself, Mrs. Alter expressed her wish to be in individual treatment with me as well. After the three of us explored the implications, Mrs. Alter remained adamant in wanting to do this. We had already established a relationship. I began seeing Mrs. Alter twice a week sitting up, but after some months she wanted to come three times a week and to move to the couch, and I agreed. Although I was certainly aware of the proscriptions against such a practice, I rationalized it for a variety of reasons. I had not seen the negative consequences myself because I had never treated spouses in intensive psychotherapy or analysis. I thought there might be certain advantages in knowing both spouses and I knew of other respected analysts who had done it or were doing it. But more about this in the discussion at the end of the chapter.

Mrs. Alter had probably been somewhat depressed for much of her life. Her father was chronically ill from her infancy and did not work, finally dying when she was 8 years old. Her mother was overburdened, and with her own narcissistic problems could not attend optimally to Mrs. Alter's needs. Mrs. Alter developed a substantial capacity for disavowal and a propensity to hope that men might rescue her alongside an expectation that they would disappoint her. She had, for her part, given Alter far less of herself than was optimal. Psychotherapy, analysis, and Prozac helped her enormously. She started working, did well in her job, and her relationship with her husband improved.

Alter moved to the couch within a few months of his wife, but did not want to come to sessions more than twice a week. I had been encouraging him to come into analysis from early in the treatment, but he had consistently refused. Although he agreed to the couch, he refused for a year to come more often, until I told him, once again, that he needed analysis. After some weeks of hesitation and discussion, particularly about whether he would be doing it simply to please me, he asked to come a third time each week.

Alter saw me for 11 years before I began participation in the casebook discussion group. During this period, there was considerable diminution in his grandiosity on the unstructured side of his vertical split. There was no longer as much excitement and stimulation in his secret world of stealing, drugs, sexual affairs, drinking, and masturbation to pornographic material. As this behavior diminished he experienced the emptiness, isolation, and loneliness this behavior was designed to combat, affects he later attributed to the shift in his relationship to his father in preadolescense. This shift deprived him of his father's pride and joy in him, or the requisite mirroring. His father was good at being the recipient of idealization, but was not so good at mirroring. The patient's feelings of emptiness were above the repression barrier on the structured side of the split; as he gave voice to them over a period of sessions, he felt that his unfulfilled needs for recognition, understanding, and mirroring beneath the repression barrier were being expressed and understood. "I'm flying, really flying," he said—an indication of his excitement at finally being understood and at the consolidation of his grandiose self.

Having read Goldberg (1995) and having entered the casebook discussion group, I bided my time and waited to make integrative interpretations. Before long, an opportunity presented itself. The insurance company asked for a meeting with the patient to discuss the disability. Alter told me of the request following his report of a meeting with his bosses in which they indicated their pleasure with him and his capacity to get things done "because of who I am. They recognize that." "Great," I said. "Got a call from the regional claims adjustor, we'll meet tomorrow after work. I don't feel stirred up—relief, a little. They probably want to settle. Seven years left on the contract. Insurance agent said 50% to 60% of the balance is what I should consider . . . It could affect what we do here . . ." "How could it?" I asked. He said, "I know we could handle the loss of reimbursement from the health insurance policy. We'd make ends meet elsewhere. If there is no more disability it might be tough." "To continue to come to therapy?" I asked. He was silent. "You don't like talking about this because you don't like talking with me about the idea of not being able to continue with therapy," I prompted. He replied, "I don't know how you feel about the disability, you haven't said anything bad. This is something I haven't heard from you for a long time, where you stand vis-à-vis the insurance. Lately you've been helpful with the company. Back of my mind you always said you thought it would be best for me to get off the disability. Not for a long time; but you've said it. Part of me feels there's still a part of you that reserves judgment of me, you might still think badly of me. Still see the disability as an issue. It's difficult for me to bring it up because

I'm afraid of what you might think. Usually when I brought it up in the past, part of me would say, "Why did I bring it up? A self-destructive tendency? Need to fuck it up?"

Here I made an effort to illustrate his split to him: "You know, this is complicated. I think there are two sides of you. One is the moral, honest, competent guy who does a good job, takes care of his family, and so on, the guy who just said that his bosses recognize his competence. The other side of you, because of shame, or panic, or whatever, has this secret world that includes stealing, porn, masturbation, activities you sometimes tell me anyone would resort to in your position but at other times you're clearly ashamed of. That part of you may be like your father, the little man with the big cigars and big cars who you came to feel was a phony. It would be wonderful if we could bring those two sides of you together. That is, if we could take the behavior from your secret world and bring it into the light of day where the other part of you could take a more direct look at it."

(One reader of this case history felt that at this point I may have been projecting my own complicated feelings apropos the disability payments, that is, my own split, thus complicating the treatment. Although this is possible, it may have been an indication that I was beginning to engage my own split, a prerequisite for successful treatment of the patient.)

In a later session, Alter expressed more anger toward his father and me than ever before, to great relief, "because I need you!"—a need exacerbated by continuing inquiries from the insurance company about the disability and his fear of my criticism. I once again talked about his two sides and his wish to know that I felt it was okay for him to have these two sides. (This was a more integrative interpretation than the aforementioned one because it implicated the transference.) His reaction was dramatic: "Oh boy! There never was a middle ground in my house . . . Either did it his way or not at all." He spent considerable time recalling his childhood humiliation and shame, his embarrassment before his peers, being laughed at, feeling like he was under a microscope. I, like his father, felt he was a failure, or he came running to me like he ran to his mother.

Working through his feelings about his father and his ambivalent feelings about Johnny continued. He addressed his feelings of grandiosity engendered by my opinion on the insurance company questionnaire that he should not return to his previous kind of practice, an opinion that came from him. "Sometimes," he said, "I feel like I can. I can do anything in my secret world . . . I used to have the recurring dream I could fly. Not like Superman but I could levitate over trees and buildings. I was real small. I could do anything." During the next year, he delayed taking a much needed class, postponing course work and study, fearing a comedown similar to his preadolescent woes in "gifted" classes. When he ultimately decided to proceed and passed the test with flying colors, it was a great triumph. Later he realized that, although I had adequately acknowledged his success on my return from vacation, I had not acknowledged his overcoming his grandiosity.

As his self flowered, he more readily asked me and others for help, including his wife and his colleagues at work. The improvement in his relationship with his wife brought to the fore his sexual history of adolescent embarrassment, his experimentation after high school and subsequently during a marital separation, and the specifics of the sexual relationship with his wife. As a boy, he felt guilty for not telling his mother everything, but clearly did not want to, and now thought that this conflict led to his acting out. He may be right in that in his preadolescence and early adolescence, he began to find that he could not turn to either parent. By itself, that is not so unusual, but we still did not understand how and why the split in his self developed.

As he deepened his exploration of his intense feelings of humiliation and shame, starting with his Johnny persona through his painful adolescence of constant embarrassment before his peers, and continuing to the present, we both came to better understand his need to steal and resultant legal problems. He realized he never treated his previous stressful practice merely as a business. "There were big swings. My manhood was always at risk. What I'm doing now is just a job. Before it was a big ego thing." He had to adjust to working in a "scaled-back" situation, safer but much less exciting.

And in an ironic response to his secret world, he fixed up a room in his basement where he could study, and where he and his wife could exercise. If this room contained elements of his secret world, it was also the world of a man whose two sides were better integrated, and he used it not so much to escape into grandiose fantasies and activities, as to study for his class, a realistic response to his need to pass the test.

I presented Alter before the casebook group twice, about two and a half and one and a half years prior to the termination of the analysis. My first presentation was intended to illustrate the propositions of Goldberg's (1995) work on perversions, using another behavior disorder. These propositions seemed persuasive to me.

But I was surprised by, and unprepared for, the severe criticism by my colleagues for both taking on a patient whose disability payments were dependent on monthly signatures from a psychiatrist attesting to the disability, and for my simultaneous treatment of the patient and his spouse. It was not until after the second presentation of the case that I had something of a breakthrough. To quote from a letter I wrote to the casebook discussion leader:

> I was pretty down in the dumps after the last presentation of my case. I felt like I took something of a beating. I wondered what possessed me to think that I wouldn't, given my handling of this case, and realized that the same disavowal which was undoubtedly present when I decided to start with Alter in the first place was probably still active. There was, I think, something of a denouement as a result of that meeting, and I felt awful for a few weeks while on vacation . . . I thought of withdrawing the case from consideration. Subsequently . . . I thought that if I could handle this well perhaps it could still be a useful lesson about the split within the analyst needing to be healed before the split within the patient can be dealt with.

By this time, Alter had begun speaking about a subject I had totally missed, an indication of the internal struggle that had begun in me, probably since my first presentation earlier that year. (One of my group colleagues called my stance toward the patient "mushy" and doubted Alter could heal his split while I was so unclear in what I communicated to him about my feelings about his disability.) Alter was beginning to talk about termination, talk I ignored perhaps because my colleagues' responses to my initial case presentation intensified questions in my mind (not for the first time) about the ethics of the disability signatures (from me) and payments (for him); I wanted him to issue a mea culpa, to give up the disability payments, and then to terminate.

When he began to talk about terminating without having talked about or dealt with his sense of entitlement to the disability payments, it meant to me that he was not going to terminate in the way I wanted him to, that is by vindicating both my early judgment in accepting him as a patient, and my hoping that our work together would so solidify him that he no longer wanted or needed the disability.

After my second case presentation, in my intense self-doubts, in my despair and desperate efforts to fix things, I decided to follow the advice of a consultant. I could not continue to sign off on the disability forms, and I could not continue to treat both spouses. On return from my vacation I called the Alters in together and told them of my decision. Afterward, I felt horrible. In subsequent sessions, it was apparent that I had never heeded Alter's allusions to termination, as he reminded me, and that Mrs. Alter had understood me to mean that I wanted her to seek therapy with someone else. Alter indicated that he and his wife had discussed his desire to terminate in about 6 months. These discussions had begun 6 months earlier, and the Alters had decided together that, although he had to give up the disability payments he was entitled to for 7 more years, he felt good about what he was planning to do.

I finally realized that in pursuing my own agenda of wanting Alter to give up the disability payments as a measure of his progress, I had disavowed the fact that he was planning to do something quite similar, but in his own way; and, paradoxically, that he was feeling good about doing so. He was exhibiting the very idealization of the contents of the superego that we had been working toward; he was doing the right thing because he wanted to and feeling good about doing so. But, in my fragmented and confused state, I was ignoring both Alter and his wife by issuing my decrees about no longer signing the disability forms, and no longer seeing both of them. I felt I had betrayed them both, especially Mrs. Alter, and quickly reversed my decision. If Alter was going to terminate so soon, both goals would be achieved in any case.

Although this was a turbulent period for me and iatrogenically for both patients, it may have been crucial for further progress with Alter. Continued pressure from my colleagues made me sufficiently confused and fragmented to break through my rigidly held disavowal, or split, which had been continuously active for more than a decade in the management of this case. Paradoxically, the reaction of both patients to my "intervention," as it came to be known, helped me to repair my fragmented state. It took only one or two sessions with each of them for me to realize how I had erred in impulsively following the consultant's recommendations that I could not continue to sign off on the disability forms and could not continue to treat both spouses. These were not appropriate recommendations at this late stage of both treatments, particularly because of Mr. Alter's decision to terminate soon. I quickly reversed my decision. It was then not difficult to get both analyses back on track. In Mr. Alter's case, we quickly resumed the conversation about termination and continued work on healing the split.

Things appeared to be moving along nicely for a few months when the insurance company served Alter with a subpoena, suing him for fraudulently receiving disability payments during some months while engaged in his former type of legal work, and cutting off any further disability payments. This prompted weeks of intense obsessing over, and discussion of, what action he should take. His feisty lawyer encouraged him to go for the pot of gold, and did not understand why Alter should have to give up the disability payments just because he was giving up therapy. He would still be disabled from practicing corporate law, wouldn't he? Alter vacillated between wanting to complete his treatment and getting the insurance company to pay for the few more months he had left, or going for the pot of gold. At times, he was angry with the insurance company for suing him, for making him defend himself yet again.

He worried that I might have to sign an affidavit and what I would say, because I had so recently refused to sign the disability forms. He wondered about the genuineness of his good feelings a few months earlier about planning to terminate. Had he really been feeling good or had he simply complied with what he felt I wanted him to do? For some months, he struggled with his feelings and waited for some response from me (my absence for a few weeks merely intensified his anticipation). I justified not responding to him by telling myself that it was important for him to do what he felt was right for him, and not to comply with me, yet finally realized that in not talking with him about what I felt, I was once again betraying my "mushiness," evidence of my own split. I thereupon told him I had never felt he deserved the disability payments. Surely the insurance company had written a bad contract, from their standpoint, but he had not been disabled from working and had continued to earn a good living. I thought of him as once again at risk of being seduced by a man he idealized (now the feisty lawyer, "a professional, for God's sake," as Alter put it). His split had been healing nicely—to wit his decision to terminate and to give up the disability—but now was at risk of being opened wider again. The healing split was a new structure in his personality and understandably vulnerable. Telling him how I felt was not nearly as important as my willingness to discuss both my feelings and his about this difficult topic, to help him to cope with the two views of reality with which he had been struggling for many years.

That weekend he decided to readopt his original plan. He would terminate as he had intended, and he would get the insurance company to pay for the remaining months, as well as for his legal costs—and of course drop the fraud charges. John did not want to be greedy in trying for a larger settlement; he felt good about his decision. But the insurance company lawyer stood firm in his unwillingness to settle. As the termination process proceeded in the usual way, with misgivings and excitement sharing the field, he struggled with his decision about the lawsuit. Finally, within a couple of weeks of termination, he decided to stop fighting the case, and to "walk away from the insurance company." It had cost John Alter $20,000 in legal fees but, once again, he felt good about his decision. He had taken considerable risks in talking through his feelings with his wife: "I feel good that I can take risks and verbalize it with her . . . also, I'm much better with the seduction of the split, with someone like Barker . . ." He knew that although he was still vulnerable to looking for someone to lead or rescue him, he was much better at resisting and standing on his own two feet. Within months of termination, he decided to return to school to obtain a degree in teaching. He had enjoyed teaching at night school and wanted to see where it would lead. As we terminated this lengthy treatment, he felt good about what he had accomplished and hopeful about the future.

Discussion

This case shows that an analyst functioning with an unrecognized vertical split in his psyche cannot hope to heal a similar split in a patient. An important corollary is that patients with narcissistic behavior disorders specialize not only in vertical splits but in inducing such splits in the analyst. Many self psychologists avoid the words "evoke" or "induce" because these words imply an interactional or transactional motivational system or causality, which is inconsistent with Kohut's (1971) emphasis on the intrapsychic nature of the selfobject. However it is to be labeled, something appears to be communicated from patient to analyst that induces a split; Goldberg (personal communication 1999) thinks this communication is probably largely nonverbal. An additional hypothesis, with which many theorists influenced by Racker (1968) might agree, is that successful treatment may require the patient to recruit the analyst into exhibiting a split.

John Alter was an attorney caught "borrowing" his clients' escrow money. He served a 3-month suspension for his errant ways, paid a $25,000 fine, and subsequently returned to work as an attorney.

As evidence of a significant vertical split in his psychic structure, one of the crucial phenomena described by Kohut (1971) and subsequently elaborated by Goldberg (1999) in behavior disordered people, the patient had a secret world of which he had been aware since early adolescence, and in which he engaged in behaviors such as masturbation, perusing porno literature, sexual fantasy, and fantasies of "levitation over buildings" otherwise uncharacteristic of him. He was quite conscious of such behavior, engaged in it willfully and repeatedly, and often found in it some measure of excitement; but it did not feel like it emanated from another person, nor did it feel "unreal" to him.

John Alter's sexualization, his perverse behavior, was not a major part of his story. But just as sexualization is crucial to an attempt to handle structural deficiency in some perversions, so is illicit behavior in other behavior disorders.

John Alter's experience would seem to illustrate this point. Toward the end of the analysis, tracking his feelings when he "borrowed" money, he clearly remembered his sense of humiliation when unable to pay some of his bills (humiliation analogous to his boyhood experience of his yelling father, and often precipitating entrance into his secret world) and a sense of panic as he worried about where he would get the money, which was usually what prompted the borrowing. Not only did the borrowing rectify his immediate financial problem, it also temporarily filled his structural defect through an idealized merger with his grandiose father. Although he might feel some shame for his actions, he might simultaneously feel excitement at what he had managed to accomplish, ignoring the consequences as if saying, "Rules don't apply to me; I can do anything I want to". The shame reflected feelings on the structured side of the split, the excitement occurred on the unstructured side. His structural deficiency gained expression in an inability to temper the profound feelings of humiliation and panic attendant on his awareness that he was short of money, an inability to soothe himself so common in such disorders.

Since splitting is the most significant feature of the pathology in a case like this one, the most intriguing question is how it developed. Goldberg (1995) nicely outlined how the two versions of reality that constitute splitting originate in a childhood construction with one or both parents. That certainly seemed to be the situation here. In early childhood and as the younger son, Johnny was his parents' favorite. He remembered changes at preadolescence when he began attending a different and more difficult school, but the comedown probably began much earlier, when he began to have a will of his own. How could the boy who had been the center of his parents' world be subject to such humiliation? How could mother, who witnessed her husband's irrational explosions, not have come to John's aid? Here were the two versions of reality John had to live with: reality as he understood it, with concomitant ideas of fairness and justice, and reality with father, supported by mother, as its arbiter. His adaptive response was to "go down the hall and turn left" into his room, to attempt to soothe his painful feelings of humiliation in grand fantasies of "levitation over buildings." These grandiose fantasies may have served two functions. First, they relocated him in the world of earlier childhood where his grandiosity was more syntonic with parental imperatives and the selfobject bond was intact. Second, the fantasies may have created a merger with his grandiose father, and so repaired the ruptured selfobject tie in fantasy.

The most recent derivative of such grandiose fantasies appeared only a few months prior to termination when, in response to the humiliation and anger he experienced when sued by the insurance company, he once again felt "I have to stand up to them" and fought the suit instead of simply giving up the insurance in return for the company's willingness to drop charges. He spent $20,000 in legal fees before ceding the war. But in the process he came to understand more clearly the dynamics at work in fomenting "my greed."

A likely source of his split was lack of parental help in reconciling or dealing with their two views of reality, as evidenced in the last year of the analysis when, discussing how I felt about him and the disability, I began to speak of his two different views of the disability, and mine. More than once he was stunned because my point of view was so different from his father's. "With him it was all black and white; there was no gray." It is precisely a rigidity of thought, an unwillingness to acknowledge the gray, that seems to be the source of such splitting. As noted, Alter's two views of reality were not focused on issues of sexual or gender identity, which may explain the absence of perversions in this case.

My split may have been activated when I accepted Mr. Alter for treatment and agreed to sign the insurance forms. I never thought the patient was entitled to the disability. He was earning a good living as a lawyer and thus was certainly not disabled in the standard sense of the term, although both the first analyst and I agreed that he was ill equipped to perform the particular functions of his previous job. Yet in my willingness to sign the form each month indicating that he was so disabled, I may well have conveyed to him what one of my colleagues called my "mushiness" about how I felt about the disability. His nonverbal communication was, "If you want to work with me these are my conditions." Although I thought I was saying, "Okay but I don't like them and I hope you won't need me to sign the disability forms forever," what he may have responded to was simply the "Okay." Nothing beyond that mattered so long as the disability forms were signed.

In parallel to the patient's experience, and perhaps what enabled this treatment ultimately to work, was my nonverbal attitude of "I don't like being told what I can and cannot do any more than you do, even if it's against the rules. Let's see if I can't help you work this out." In retrospect, it may have been better to arrange to have someone else sign off on the disability each month, so as to diminish the contamination of the treatment. (Such an arrangement, to be sure, would have had to be a focus of analytic inquiry to avoid a continuing split.) This never occurred to me, nor was it suggested by the consultant at the time, and had it occurred to me I might have feared lest such a condition cause John to flee. Was my need for more patients so great that it caused me to forego the accepted clinical wisdom that disability considerations are major roadblocks to successful treatment? Or was it rather my grandiosity in thinking that I could conduct treatment any way I wished, despite the rules, a grandiosity that may have paralleled John's in stealing from clients? Was his thievery paralleled by mine? Had I already responded to the patient's idealizing propensity, which stimulated my grandiosity in thinking that I could treat him successfully when others could not? My dynamics in relation to my father, and even to my own analyst, were sufficiently similar to those of the patient in some important respects to predispose me to the development of a split of my own when the patient requested that I attest to his disability in return for his treatment.

Although we made headway with the diminution of the patient's grandiosity, my familiarization with Goldberg's ideas and then of my own split were needed for the healing of the split in the patient. Even late in the analysis, I wondered if the patient was ever really engaged in an analytic process. Despite less than optimal conditions, the answer, I believe, is "yes." The patient's behavior did not change merely because of his need to comply with my expectations, but because we worked through the meaning of his behavior as expressed in the transference. I was, however, by no means addressing both sides of the vertical split in any helpful way, because I then had no familiarity with Goldberg's ideas. My approach to Alter erratically swung between acceptance and moralistic judgment so that he was unclear of my stance and thus distrustful. As treatment progressed, John's idealization of me further stimulated my grandiosity and fueled my continuing split. Unwilling or unable to examine my irritation with his dubious morality, I did not look carefully at my own parallel split.

My own rigidity of thinking and behavior seemed to recapitulate that of his parents, perhaps prolonging the treatment and making healing of the split impossible. Until I understood the phenomenon of splitting and the importance of integrative interpretations, I seemed to alternate between my two views of the reality of the disability. I hated that he needed it and would not give it up, but I was persuaded by him that it was legal. I often felt torn and ashamed like my patient, and I saw no way out of the dilemma. My failure to acknowledge the reality of having to live with two views of reality was the crucial factor preventing me from helping him sooner. My own propensity for splitting, thievery, and grandiosity paralleled his.

It wasn't until literally a few days before Alter's termination that I reread parts of Goldberg's (1995) book and at last understood clearly the significance of the different views of reality with which the child and then the adult patient needs to reconcile. It is less effective to diminish or eliminate one's view, often grandiose, of reality on the unstructured side of the split, than to buttress one's ability to hold different views of reality at the same time, to be aware of both and use the resources of a more integrated personality to respond to both. Alter talked in the last several sessions of his analysis of how his greed had cost him $20,000 in legal fees. The "pull" of his grandiosity remains, albeit diminished, and requires constant vigilance.

The rationale for the additional unusual therapeutic behavior—treating two members of the same family in intensive psychotherapy and especially psychoanalysis, lay not only in my inexperience and my need for patients, but also my own continuing split. Once again, my attendant grandiosity was sufficient to overcome my misgivings and better judgment.

A parallel question arises as to whether my altered behavior was out of compliance with the expectations and pressures I felt from the casebook discussion group and its leader, or whether I too worked sufficiently through issues of my own to alter my own behavior. The criticism from my colleagues, sometimes quite withering, did contribute to a change in me, but the patient understanding and acceptance I received from the discussion leader, who seemed to have confidence that somehow I would work things out, and who conveyed an analytic attitude toward my "misbehavior" rather than a critical one (an attitude of "What can this kind of behavior possibly mean?"), was in crucial contrast, as it had been for my patient, to my experience of my father, a "my way or the highway" man, and to some lesser but still important degree, to my experience of my own analyst. By contrast, when the discussion leader, now acting as a consultant to me, told me I had to stop seeing both husband and wife and that I had to stop signing off on the disability, the result was the iatrogenic mess just described. I now believe that I experienced the consultation as having a peremptory quality rather than the "negotiated" quality of the process in the case discussion group. Actually, it was the patient, now with a much firmer self, who alerted me to the inappropriateness of my intervention by pointing out that I had overlooked his own talk of termination. Finally, many insights occurred to me while I was writing up this case and struggling to understand it, some of them after the fact.

Must the analyst's split be recognized before the patient's split may be successfully treated? Here the patient's split may have healed first and may even have contributed to my recognition of my parallel split. Alternatively, the patient's split may have begun healing regardless of the remaining split in the analyst. There were no further incidents of theft after John Alter's suspension from the bar nor for some time before. Nor did he speak of the impulse to steal except for a brief mention when moving to the couch a few years before termination. Additionally, John's wife reported that several months after termination, he was doing well and his employer had doubled his salary.

As recently as a few months prior to beginning the termination process, I would have had to report that, despite his gains, as long as the disability payments remained, his deficit had not totally healed. And I was doubtful that it ever would. In 12 years of therapy and analysis, he clung to the disability payments for support despite many gains in other areas. He no longer borrowed from clients; he no longer had fantasies of making a killing or of creating a business that would make him wildly successful. He felt better about his wife and himself much more of the time.

But something changed within the last year of the analysis. He came to feel that he could do without the disability, and felt good about doing so. He took pride in feeling more solid and functioning better. In analytic terms, we might say that this was evidence of his ability to idealize the contents of the new structures in his idealizing pole, and of its successful repair. The reasons for this successful change are not entirely clear. But my recognition of my own split may have enabled the patient to finally heal his own. By termination, there had been rehabilitation of both poles of the self, including the hallmark idealization of the contents of the idealizing pole. Giving up the disability and feeling good about doing so was the goal and it was achieved.

2

| The Case of Kool
The Psychoanalysis of a Transvestite

This chapter describes work with a patient whose fragile self-organization was effectively shored up by cross dressing. One of the "problems of perversion" Goldberg (1999) discusses is that people with perversions are often loathe to come for treatment because their symptoms produce in them a heightened sense of pleasure and aliveness, which protects them from unbearable affects. Zizek's (1992) *Enjoy Your Symptom!* (a work on Lacanian psychoanalysis and culture) might be the motto on perversion's flag. Because the path to self-transformation in such cases leads inevitably through depression, for many the cure threatens to be worse than the disease.

Goldberg (1999) writes that *perversions* are effects of a vertical split in the self. The split insures that people with perversions view their symptoms from two radically opposing perspectives: from the perspective of the reality ego they are ashamed and humiliated, but from the perspective of their split-off narcissism, they glory in their symptoms and fear to lose them. For therapy to be effective, the division in the self must be deconstructed and resolved. In this case, such an effort met with partial success before treatment broke off.

History

Kool was a 27-year-old executive. He was handsome, athletic, and ingratiating. He had two sisters, 2 and 4 years older, and two sisters, 1 and 2 years younger. He described his parents as typical upper-middle-class African Americans. His mother was a highly ambitious woman from a matriarchal family. He thought her impressionable, self-centered, and easily distracted. It was hard to keep the spotlight of her attention focused on him. His siblings were exactly like her and formed what felt to Kool like a secret sisterhood from which he was effectively barred. Father was a dour and humorless policeman organized entirely by his work. Obsessively dedicated to the needs of his union, he worked long hours and shut his study door immediately after dinner to attend to the business of his local. Kool felt his father never gave him a break. He assigned Kool twice as many chores as he demanded of the girls and thought talking to him at dinner meant lecturing him on the evils of drugs and gangs; otherwise, he ignored him. Mother took an interest in Kool only when he brought home a superior report card or was honored for his achievements on the basketball court. She wanted more than anything else for him to be successful. He remembered her asking him if he knew what Michael Jordan's teammates called him in the locker room. "Air!" Kool answered proudly. "Not Air!" his mother scoffed, "that's a TV name. His teammates call him 'Money.'" Kool felt that this is what his mother would have liked to call him. But Kool hadn't wanted to be "Money." He hadn't even want to "be like Mike." He'd just wanted to be Kool. Beneath his winning smile, he had been a sad and lonely little boy.

Psychotherapy

Kool entered twice-a-week psychotherapy with me to discuss "problems in his marriage." The subject of his transvestitism did not come up for months. He merely complained that his wife was disappointingly straitlaced and lacked imagination in bed. Eventually, however, he revealed that he had a "beautiful woman fantasy" about which he felt incredibly sensitive and ashamed. He'd hoped that by marrying a beautiful woman, he could suppress the impulse he felt to be such a woman, but the impulse hadn't gone away. He'd tried to introduce cross dressing into their lovemaking, which shocked his wife who told him he was a pervert and insisted he never speak of such wishes again. He'd done his best to comply with her demand, but doing so made him increasingly angry.

Kool had been ambivalent about marrying in the first place because he feared losing his freedom, but at the same time he had been afraid of moving alone to a new city for graduate school.

He and Jane had been living together and she wanted to get married, and he had agreed without really thinking about it until suddenly it seemed there was no turning back. Feeling panicky before the wedding, Kool decided to have a fling and slept with a prostitute. He confessed his infidelity to Jane and although she was appalled by what he had done, she had no intention of telling her parents they were calling off the wedding. On his wedding night, Kool had a dream that a beautiful woman tried to seduce him. He was compelled by the woman's loveliness, but he told her that he was married and unavailable. Proudly he told Jane the dream, expecting her to see it as confirmation of his claim that he was looking forward to their life together. Jane, however, was furious that even on their wedding night, he was struggling against a temptation to be unfaithful. Kool reported her reaction in a tone of injured virtue, but Jane's interpretation was to prove prophetic for the analysis.

Kool found psychotherapy highly gratifying because he felt encouraged to welcome rather than suppress his feelings, especially those about his beautiful woman fantasy, despite the limited place he insisted this fantasy held in his overall emotional life. He told Jane that he couldn't help the way he was, and that if she would just indulge his wishes to cross dress occasionally in the bedroom, things between them would greatly improve. She tried to do so but it was clear she was totally turned off. He was hurt and angry and felt that he couldn't spend the rest of his life with a woman who would have him suppress his deepest sexual wishes. After a year they divorced. Kool felt convinced he had made the right decision, and our work appeared to be over. Nonetheless, as we discussed plans to terminate treatment, he began increasingly to acknowledge that the beautiful woman side of his personality was actually much more important than he had allowed himself to recognize, and that it was a source of much anxiety and pain. He knew he couldn't suppress it but he worried any woman who knew of it would think him bizarre and disgusting. What was he to do? His wish to cross dress was a source of great and necessary excitement—even pride, because it made him feel godlike in his sexual complexity —but this wish was also a source of shame and embarrassment. He wanted to be a man, although he thought his masculine self essentially boring and nerdy; but he also wanted to be a woman because women were exciting, emotional, and rivetingly attractive. He wished he could be more at peace with himself. I suggested that analysis might provide a way for him to come to terms with himself so that he might indeed feel more integrated, more a whole person. He was very excited by the idea and we decided to begin after a 4-week holiday break.

Psychoanalysis: The First 6 Months

Kool was excited to be beginning analysis, but it was clear that he was conflicted about the prospect. He announced that he had found a girlfriend who was training to be a therapist. She lived out of town and loved listening to him talk for hours on the phone about his feelings, enthusiasms, sexual fantasies, and divorce. She seemed to have no problem with his wish to cross dress; indeed she thought a man who was in touch with his "feminine side" was exactly what had always been missing in her relationships. Though they were just getting to know one another, Kool was already thinking of moving to her city, which would probably be easy to do because his company had a division there.

I asked if he was having second thoughts about the analysis. Perhaps if he was serious about leaving town, we might delay until he was sure analysis was what he wanted to do. Kool insisted that his situation had nothing to do with second thoughts but there was a small chance he would want to leave town if the new relationship turned into something really serious. Nonetheless, he did not want to go back to being in therapy; he knew what that was like, and he knew that we wouldn't have "world enough and time" to explore his beautiful woman fantasy in depth that way. Hadn't I essentially argued as much when we'd discussed analysis? Couldn't we just give analysis a try, he asked, and let the chips fall where they might? I said it wasn't a good idea to undertake an analysis without intending to complete it. He insisted he was particularly looking forward to starting because he would be able to tell Mirra—his new girlfriend— about his sessions on the phone and, in effect, have twice the opportunity for self-exploration and understanding. This did little to reassure me. I thought that he was already feeling the need to defend against the potential intensity of our relations by dividing them between Mirra and me and keeping open the possibility that he might leave. I was reminded of his fling on the eve of his marriage.

Like Kool, I felt split. I wanted to begin the analysis and see where it might lead and I wanted to insist to myself that the frame of the analysis would be sufficient to contain his possible impulse to flee. Nonetheless, I felt uneasy about the likelihood of merely reenacting his history of running away from commitments that threatened his beautiful woman side. I didn't want merely to sweep my worries under the rug, but to insist that we resolve the question of his ambivalence before beginning the analysis seemed tantamount to insisting that he be cured of the very internal division for which he had sought treatment. I thought the only way to see if his resistance was analyzable was to attempt to analyze it, but I continued to worry that it was folly to begin an analysis with so dubious an intention of completing it. With a sense of considerable disquiet, then, I decided we might proceed.[1]

Kool immediately wanted to lay out the history of his beautiful woman side. He couldn't remember any very early experiences of wanting to be a girl, although he knew he liked to play with his sisters' dolls. That didn't seem weird to him because the house was full of dolls, and he thought it was only natural that he would want to play with whatever was available. He remembered that he kept a pair of one sister's panties as a sort of transitional object or fetish. He hid them so he was sure that his mother never knew, but now he wondered if that would have been possible; his mother must have known. Why had she permitted him to keep the panties, he wondered. He recalled that when he was 5 years old his mother left him alone in the house by accident in her rush to get to a church fashion show with his sisters. He was certain that the mistake had been a Freudian slip; his mother hadn't wanted him along because he was a boy. He thought he had been deeply scarred by this experience and remembered ever after being obsessed with a wish to be riveting and unforgettable. He became fascinated with women's clothing and avidly pored over the pages of his mother's catalogues and magazines. He imagined that if he had the clothes she cared so much about—if in effect he were a girl—his mother never would have forgotten him. He began secretly to put on his nearest older

---

1. When our group began meeting we were all surprised to discover that such decisions figured in virtually every one of our cases. Perhaps this reflects the way treating these patients organized us along the lines organizing them: we ourselves became split between a reality ego mindful of the rules of treatment, and a more grandiose and wayward self willing to venture beyond familiar limits in the name of making treatment possible.

sister's dresses and underwear in his room in front of the mirror. He found doing so incredibly exciting. As a teenager, he masturbated to the fantasy of being a spellbinding beauty, a centerfold in *Playboy*. Often during lovemaking he imagined he was a beautiful woman and the girl he was with a man, and he found that when he gave himself over to this fantasy, he was much more powerfully aroused. In college, he sometimes wore panties on dates, which made him feel wild and sexy rather than nerdy and dull, but even if he ended up having sex with his date, he kept the panties secret. Indeed he never told anyone about his cross dressing until he tried to get his ex-wife to let him wear her lingerie once when they were making love. But of course the results had been disastrous. Things were much better with Mirra, who seemed flattered with Kool's desire to wear and fetishize her intimate garments. Nonetheless he worried that despite her acceptance, the increasing centrality of his perverse wishes would result in her turning away from him as Jane had.

The initial analytic transference seemed idealizing. Kool saw me as remarkably wise, sensitive, and knowledgeable, because he thought me sympathetic to his beautiful woman side. At the same time, of course, it was clear he might at any moment break off treatment to go and live with Mirra, so the idealization seemed to carry with it an unspoken hollowness. In any case, the idealizing quality of the transference was short-lived. It was followed by an insistent mirror transference that held sway throughout the analysis. Kool constructed Mirra and me as foils. Each was played off the other to see who most delighted in his beautiful woman side.

Before our first holiday break, he brought in a picture of himself as a beautiful woman. Mirra had taken it on her last visit. He did not tell me who was in the photograph and asked me to guess. He was amazed that I was of course able immediately to see that it was he. Breathlessly he asked how I thought he looked. I felt extremely uncomfortable. It seemed to me his bringing in the treasured photograph was a valuable analytic gift, a picture of his hidden, grandiose, exhibitionistic self, and therefore something to be welcomed warmly and cherished. At the same time, the image didn't seem that of a beautiful woman to me at all. It was clearly that of man in drag with what suddenly appeared to be an overly large nose and a 5 o'clock shadow. The image seemed pathetic and made me sad. I felt like the child in "The Emperor's

New Clothes"—very much a tale of the vertical split—who announces the emperor is naked, thus shattering the spell of his suppression of the reality ego throughout the realm. I didn't want to do that, but I didn't want simply to lie either. What I said was the sort of thing the subjects of the emperor in the fairy tale said (those who were afraid that they had to join with the emperor on the fantastical side of the vertical split or lose their heads). I told Kool that I thought he looked "remarkable" in the photograph—which was certainly true—but also felt to me completely disingenuous. Nonetheless he was thrilled. I had said what he wanted to hear. He beamed with happiness. I asked if he brought me the picture so that I wouldn't forget him during our break. Yes, he said. His mother's forgetting him to get to the fashion show was one of his most enduring and painful memories. He did want me to remember him, and he was gratified to think he'd been successful.

My reaction to the photograph seemed to overstimulate him. In the next session, he reported dreams of floods and tidal waves. In one dream, his house was inundated with rising waters and almost swept into the sea. Feeling a bit manic, he had spent his lunch hour shopping compulsively for women's things. He said my reaction to his picture had left him feeling very excited. He was afraid he might want me to come on to him sexually, and thinking about that disturbed him. In speaking only to the wayward side of Kool's vertical split, I had succeeded in strengthening his internal division rather than beginning to heal it, which left us both uncomfortably poised on the wayward side of our vertical splits.

Kool's feelings of mania in response to showing me his photograph gave way to depression a session or two later, as if he could only hold at bay his doubts about my real feelings about his beautiful woman side—or his own—for so long. He worried too that Mirra too wasn't as enthusiastic about his cross dressing as he'd initially believed. Perhaps she only tolerated his acting out and didn't truly enjoy it. He was hoping that she had a fantasy that matched his, that secretly she wanted to be a man during sex as much as he wanted to be a woman. But this sadly was not the case; Mirra appeared to have no shameful fantasy that he could help her to accept as she was helping him to accept his. He'd been thrilled reading Janet Malcolm's The Impossible Profession to see that the psychoanalyst interviewed in the work had a beautiful woman fantasy like his own. He'd hoped I might have such a fantasy too, but that hope had faded. He was convinced I wasn't the type; too stern. Angry that neither I nor Mirra seemed capable of resonating with his transvestite excitement, he fantasized about finding the sort of mirror other he desired. He knew he could find gay men who would be eager to sleep with him. But the problem with that was that they would be into his penis, his manliness. He wanted someone who would want him as a woman. And a straight man would be out of the question. No straight man would see him as a beautiful woman. A straight man would see him as a freak, unless he were to become a transsexual—which would of course resolve the problem of the vertical split, although perhaps by virtue of a total denial of the reality ego—and he did not want that either. He liked being a man. He wanted to be both, so he felt despair. But I felt relieved to hear him say so. It was far more characteristic of him to insist, in effect, he could have his cake and eat it too. That he could stay with a distressing sense that he might be doomed to unhappiness suggested a willingness to experience painful affects that I hoped was a sign that he was becoming more structuralized, and that we would in time be able to resolve his split.

We spent a number of sessions discussing his wish for a perfectly complementary sexual partner, a woman who would want to play at being a man in bed even as he played at being a woman and would want to fuck him with a dildo. He was entirely caught up in the sexual mechanics of his wishes, but I thought that what he was ultimately talking about was a wish for someone who would completely accept him because she would be his twin through the looking glass. He'd hoped Mirra had precisely this wish even as he hoped I had a beautiful woman fantasy because his ultimate wish was to be totally understood and accepted. He was moved by this interpretation; he'd never thought of his wish for a perfect sexual partner in nonsexual terms, but it made sense. Certainly his parents hadn't accepted him in any unqualified way. His mother liked him only when he did things that suggested he'd be rich one day. Whenever he tried to tell her anything that didn't have to do with his grades or career opportunities, her eyes glazed over. On the other hand, she was completely into his sisters and could talk with them for hours about shoes, hair styles, make-up, and diets. As a small child, Kool had learned to imitate his older sister to gain and hold his mother's attention. And evidently it had worked. The story was that when his mother could see that he was "doing" his sister Lexey, she laughed and couldn't take her eyes off him. Kool's father seemed to think of him merely as a not to be entirely trusted man of all work. He wasn't even interested in Kool's athletic successes. During Kool's 4 years of high school, his father hadn't attended a single basketball game, despite the fact that Kool was always in the starting line-up.

Thinking of Kool's wish that a woman—cross dressed as a man—would insist on his becoming a woman to please her, I asked if he thought his mother especially encouraged him to act the part of his sister. The next session he reported a dream that led him to remember his mother occasionally giving his father her panties to wear to work when his shorts were in the laundry. Kool remembered being incensed—yet fascinated— that his father put up with this, and it made him wonder if his father didn't secretly harbor some cross-dressing issues of his own. Kool also recalled that on particularly cold mornings when he was growing up, his mother insisted he wear Lexey's panty- hose under his blue jeans to provide extra insulation. He had been initially furious, but came in time to find his mother's demand exciting. He'd never thought about it, but maybe his mother had wanted to feminize him and his father too. She certainly wore the pants in the family and treated his father like Morgan Freeman in *Driving Miss Daisy*. And she was loudly explicit about her preference for women over men. She didn't much like men, even or perhaps especially, Kool's father. Kool was tremendously angry with her. He knew that when he was born she had been disappointed; it was no secret that she'd wanted another girl. He wondered why? They already had two! Sometimes he imagined showing up at home cross dressed and saying angrily "Now you've got the girl you wanted! How do you like her?"

The Second Six Months

Kool was excited to think he was learning about his childhood and gaining insights into his beautiful woman side, but continued to worry that Mirra and I had only limited tolerance for his wish to cross dress. He joined a transvestite organization because he knew the members would be enthusiastic in their welcome of him. Mirra and I, he said, were doing our best to be empathic with him, but how could we understand his feelings? The men in the club really knew. He was gratified to see how impressed they were with his education, cultivation, and good looks. He told them, as he had told Mirra and me, that he only wanted to cross dress in the bedroom for an occasional added sexual rush, but they were skeptical. They said the wish for public display would become irresistibly intense. They said also that girlfriends and wives were never enthusiastic about their partner's wish to cross dress. At best, women were tolerant; shrinks were useful only insofar as they might help the transvestite adjust to life in a largely philistine world. Change that meant suppression could never succeed. Kool insisted the men in the club were overstating the case; his wish to cross dress was not going to escalate. Mirra was incredibly enthusiastic about his cross dressing, and I was entirely different from what the members said was typical of therapists. In addition, Kool felt he was already far more empathic with himself than he had ever been, hence more integrated. Nonetheless it sounded as if he were protesting too much. I said I knew he wanted to think what he was saying was true, but that I suspected the opinions of the transvestite club members expressed his own fears. I added that I thought he had joined the group in the hope of finding a response to his beautiful woman side he felt he couldn't get from me but that he needed desperately.

We spent much time during this period on the question of when he cross dressed and in what circumstances. Predictably, he tended to do so on occasions when he felt abandoned, forgotten, or criticized. He was surprised to see that this was so. He had thought his impulse was entirely random and usually a matter of opportunity. When I pointed out that he felt interrupted over weekends and so cross dressed to make himself feel better, he had a hard time seeing it. Weekends of course were times for cutting loose, wasn't it simply that? And he certainly didn't feel lonely or unhappy. I said that the beauty of his impulse to cross dress was that it transformed dysphoric affects that he wanted to avoid into experiences of excitement and anticipation. He wasn't being abandoned, he was looking forward to acting out his fantasy of being entirely spellbinding, even as he had cross dressed as a child when frustrated by his mother's refusal to focus the spotlight of her attention on him when he sought it. He thought this made sense, but it didn't explain his wish to cross dress with Mirra when she came into town for a visit, or he went to see her. I said visits were always double-edged swords. They were greatly exciting opportunities to feel connected and admired, but they also carried with them the prospect of being alone again soon. I felt that part of what contributed to his wish to cross dress with Mirra was his anxious worry about saying good-bye. By making his visits times of carnival-like excitement, he sought unconsciously to suppress such affects before they ever fully entered his awareness.

One Year

During this phase of our work, Kool began to feel increasingly hemmed in by the rules of the analysis. He didn't like having to free associate while I sat usually in silence, that he had to lie down and couldn't look at me although I could see him, that I might come late to sessions and make up for my lateness by keeping him an extra few minutes, whereas if he were late, we ended on schedule, that I was learning everything about him while revealing next to nothing about myself. All of this reminded him of his rage at his mother's insistence that he do everything according to her instructions. It also made him think of how unfair things were for men. As he saw it, women were entirely unconstrained; they could be moody, angry, irrational, wild. Men were always on a leash; they had to be controlled, reined in, made to behave. His father was a tough cop, but around his mother he was nothing but a "stepin fetchit." Kool hated being told what to do. Indeed his defiance of rules had gotten him into all sorts of trouble. At work he had failed to write reports he thought were meaningless, and ignored instructions about dealing with clients if he thought he had a way that might get better results. On several occasions he had come dangerously close to being fired despite the high esteem in which he was generally held by his superiors. Kool was always amazed when he was called on the carpet. He never viewed his behavior as defiant, merely rational, and he couldn't believe anyone would see things differently if they simply gave him a chance to explain. His attitude seemed to reflect a hole in the reality ego; his grandiosity was such that he imagined his way of seeing the world was the only one possible.

His tendency to disregard rules of behavior entered the transference when at one point he promised a professional organization he was hoping to join that I would write him a letter of recommendation without ever asking me if I would do so. I felt angry that he had made the promise without consulting me first, especially inasmuch as I felt writing such a letter would compromise the analytic relationship. He told me he was sure I would want to do as he promised and indeed, he felt so excited to think I would be his advocate that he had masturbated without relying on the beautiful woman fantasy. I was disarmed by this revelation, which seemed to suggest that his feeling of coherence as a man was bound up with the wish that his virtues be remembered and appreciated by an admiring selfobject. Of course, he had sexualized his excitement at the thought I would write for him but the idea that, in his sexual fantasy, he felt integral as a man suggested that his experience of himself as unified rather than as both man and beautiful woman lay in coming to terms with the frustration of his grandiose, exhibitionistic wishes. In other words, it seemed to me he was suggesting that he had come to feel himself split into both male and female when his wish to be admired and remembered as a little boy had been continuously frustrated. I hoped that by seeing his beautiful woman fantasy as an effort to repair his rage and depression over not being seen as a handsome and effective little boy, we would make progress in structuralizing and unifying his divided self. Nonetheless, this didn't seem to make sense. Many boys are not so mirrored, but few become cross dressers. Why, I wondered, had Kool fixed on so extreme a solution to so common a problem?

While struggling with the rules of analysis, Kool developed an interest in having sex with a dominatrix. He wanted the dominatrix to order him to give up his masculine self and become a woman and then tie him up and humiliate him. This fantasy seemed a sexualization of the negative side of the split, his sense of being used and degraded by the feminine role he had to play at some level for his mother's pleasure turned into a source of erotic excitement and mastery. The aspect of the fantasy that meant the most to him was the idea that even as the dominatrix controlled and degraded him, she would fall under the spell of his feminine beauty and become his adoring slave. I thought in addition to transforming an experience with his mother the fantasy represented a sexualization and reversal of his experience on the couch. He imagined that I forced him to him lie down and tell me stories of his sexual life for my erotic gratification. His unspoken hope was that I was falling ineluctably under the spell he cast as a beautiful woman.

The fantasy of hiring a dominatrix remained just that until I had to cancel one of Kool's Friday sessions. I asked if he could come in early on Saturday and he agreed to the change without much comment. The following Monday I learned that he had not wanted to come in on Saturday because he liked to sleep late that day, but he felt he needed the session too much simply to forego it. He'd also assumed wrongly and angrily that I would charge him for the Saturday time if he opted not to use it. He felt humiliated by his weakness, his need to see me despite his sense that doing so in this instance degraded him. During the Saturday appointment he told me he had scheduled an evening with the dominatrix that same night. The timing was perfect because Mirra was out of the country and not even reachable by phone. He had been angry with her for going away—but his anger was forgotten; while the cat was away the mouse would play, and he could think of nothing but his excitement.

During our Monday meeting, Kool reported that the evening with the dominatrix had been a terrible disappointment. She hadn't fallen for him and she had been tremendously expensive. Indeed, she had made it clear that she was very much a working girl out on a job and that she had another stop to make after her session with him. He had imagined they would spend most of the night together, but she watched the clock as assiduously as I did! I said it seemed his disappointment with the dominatrix reflected the disappointment he felt in me: he wanted to think I was unable to maintain a feeling of clinical detachment about him, that even as I made him lie down and free associate about being a beautiful woman, I was falling irresistibly under his spell. The dominatrix's failure to see him as anything more than a customer reflected his fear that he was no more than a customer to me; merely a john with money.

I thought his experience with the dominatrix specifically represented his effort to manage his feelings about my rescheduling his appointment. He felt angry about my rescheduling rather than honoring his time but his distress had been split off. He hadn't been able to tell me he felt angry and degraded by my demand any more than as a child he had been able to tell his mother how angry and unfair he felt her demands were. Nonetheless he had scheduled the session with the dominatrix to ward off the possibility of experiencing painful feelings by planning an elaborate, sexualized ritual in which cross dressing was prominent, even as he had cross dressed and masturbated in front of the mirror as a child when he felt ignored and forgotten by his mother.

We talked about the beginning of the experience he had choreographed, the experience of having the dominatrix order him to become a woman. He had wished to play a similar role in enactments with Mirra, so it was clearly very important. We wondered if the scene didn't reflect his sense as a child that his mother was dissatisfied with his masculinity, that he couldn't please her as a little boy, and that he had to adopt a feminine role to captivate her interest. He had spoken of the way he had aped the voice, gestures, and manner of his older sister Lexey as a device to interest his mother. Perhaps the enactment he wished repeatedly to play represented precisely such a sequence.

His experience of failure with the dominatrix left him feeling entirely devastated. For some hours he felt almost suicidal. It was as if having had his heart broken by his father's lack of interest in him and his mother's rejection of his wish to be her special little boy, he had staked everything on the hope that he might captivate the dominatrix by serving her wish that he be her girl. When she poured cold water on this fantasy, and with it inadvertently the fantasy that he might similarly captivate me as a beautiful woman, he felt he had no further means to achieve the enlivening feeling of specialness and importance that he craved to sustain him.

I said that Kool's feelings of hope and failure surrounding his experience with the dominatrix shed important light on his early and current experience. He thought the only thing that might begin to put him back together would be to visit Mirra as soon as she returned home and see whether she still accepted him as openheartedly as she always had. He really couldn't bear to be so upset. The analysis was beginning to really make him feel bad. I felt a great sense of hope around this revelation. Cross dressing was what I thought protected Kool from emotional pain and kept him split. If he could stand to experience his rage, depression, and frustration in the transference, and through this experience to recover it in his general sense of himself, he might no longer need the symptom that divided him. And this, of course, would suggest a process of inner healing and structuralization. But it was far easier for me to hold this view than for Kool. After a few days of misery, he cancelled all of his activities and left town to visit Mirra.

When Kool returned, he said that he was feeling a great deal better. Mirra was perhaps not his perfect sexual complement, but she was surely as accepting and devoted as anyone he could ever hope to be with. He was going to make every effort to see if he could find a job in her city. If this meant the premature end of the analysis, well, that would have to be that. It made no sense to stay with his analyst and endlessly talk about his beautiful woman side when he could go live with a girlfriend who would help bring this side to life. After all, the whole point in his mind about beginning the analysis in the first place had been to make it possible for him to find a girlfriend, and he had done that. He was certain that he was more integrated than he had ever been, more aware of his own feelings and those of others, and if he was still a divided soul, at least he was able to think about the beautiful woman side of himself openly with me and with Mirra and with the men who belonged to the cross dressers' organization. Prior to the analysis, his beautiful woman side had existed entirely as a split-off, mostly denied fantasy in his own head. Now he was able to say that although he was in part ashamed of the fantasy and saw it as a defect, he was also able to think of it as almost a divine power, like the sexuality of a Hindu god. So all in all, he was much happier than he had been previously and felt he owed a great deal to the analysis. Nonetheless, he was fairly certain he would be moving in the near future.

I said that I thought he had made great progress in understanding himself as a whole person and that doing so was beginning to stir all sorts of feelings that had always been too dangerous for him to confront. I thought that it was hardly surprising that he would want to go and be with Mirra who had been so kind to him and so accepting of his beautiful woman side, but I hoped he would try to continue in analysis precisely because he was beginning to encounter himself in an increasingly new light, however painful this might be for him. He said he would think about what I was saying; nothing was definite yet, but he thought the "die was cast."

Eighteen Months

After a holiday break, he brought in another picture of himself cross dressed as a keepsake for me. Having become aware of Arnold Goldberg's work on integrative interpretations, I tried to speak to both sides of his vertically split feelings and thoughts as I had failed to do when he brought in the first picture of himself cross dressed. I said he hoped I would remember him as a person of passionate feelings—as in effect a beautiful woman—because in his mind only beautiful women could be memorable and exciting. I added that I thought at the same time he feared I would think of the photograph as a sign that he was weird and perverted because part of him still experienced the beautiful woman side precisely that way. He said he felt excited and proud of his beautiful woman side and yet he also felt he would give anything to be rid of it.

I went on to say that Kool had asked Mirra to take the picture of him as they were parting so that she too would remember him as a riveting presence, just as he tried to show his parents what a great ballplayer and scholar he was as a child. His father had never been interested in Kool and when his mother turned away, Kool had tried to captivate her gaze by mimicking his sister, Lexey, and had begun privately to console and stimulate himself by playing with dolls and cross dressing. Enactments involving the beautiful woman side of him helped him to transform emotions that threatened sadness and pain into occasions that excited him. This was why he had brought me the picture; he was beginning to worry about leaving the analysis. He said he thought this might be so. I thus attempted to join both sides of the vertical split, the disavowed reality ego with its unendurable depression and rage, and the symptomatic solution, the expression of exhibitionistic pleasure, in the transference relation with me, in his life outside the office with Mirra, and in the past vis-à-vis his parents.

Interventions like this one led to a phase of increasing self-coherence in Kool. He felt he was more interesting and attractive as a man than he had ever been. Women seemed suddenly to be noticing him. He cut his hair in a hip new style and he began to dress more daringly, discarding his wing-tipped shoes, rep ties, and horn-rimmed glasses in exchange for designer shoes and neckwear and contact lenses. Kool said these changes were signs of his becoming more integrated, more a man of—feminine—feelings.

The accent still fell of course on narcissistic display, but finding himself enlivened and excited to be able to represent himself as a handsome man seemed a step in the direction of a more unified self-experience. Kool felt these external changes were nice, but he was more excited about the changes he perceived inside. He was certain he was far more able to experience his emotions and he was beginning to be able to appreciate the feelings of others in an entirely new way. He could see he had been in considerable pain as a child, and he was becoming more interested in the story of his life. On a recent trip home, he sought out his favorite aunt—a sister of his mother's—and asked her about his early childhood. He learned something startling that he'd never known. His mother had had a baby—a girl—before she met Kool's father. She had been only 16 years old at the time and the infant had died soon after birth. Kool's birthday was almost exactly the same as this dead half sister's and his mother had given him the same name. Together we wondered if Kool's mother hadn't always silently conveyed to him a wish that he might be this dead child. The aunt told Kool that his mother had dressed him in girl's baby clothes and put pink ribbons in his hair. He'd always insisted that his mother hadn't tried to feminize him when he was small but this new information proved he was wrong. Maybe his trying to be like Lexey brought his mother to life and made him feel special and cherished in a way he had never understood because the girl she recognized unconsciously in his behavior wasn't Lexey but Kool's dead half sister. We both thought that his mother might have repeatedly sent him a double message: that he was a boy, but that she needed him to be the dead girl whose name he bore. And we thought that such a message had to be near the heart of his conviction that there was a beautiful woman within him.

News of the dead infant half sister also made sense of Kool's mother's mysterious tendency toward depression. She wasn't the sort of person who seemed depressed, filled as she was with a sort of manic energy and liveliness; but now and then she fell into what she told her husband and children was a state of "chemical imbalance" which left her teary, vacant, and unreachable. Kool wondered if by unconsciously attempting to be her missing child he was able to rouse her from such a state. He also wondered if his experience of being forgotten by his mother —originally when she accidentally left him home alone to attend the church fashion show—had to do with his mother's feelings about this same lost half sister. Maybe what his mother had never gotten over—what she never forgot—was her longing for her dead daughter. But silently pining for this child made her forget the little boy she had. Kool's solution to the problem of being forgotten was to become unconsciously the missing, riveting, remembered child; his sexual excitement reflected the excitement he felt when, by acting like Lexey he could feel the gleam he longed for return to his mother's eye.

At this time Kool began to be interested in the arts, especially painting. He was fascinated with color because it seemed so bound up with emotion and was something he had never paid attention to before. He loved Picasso's Blue Period with its sad-looking acrobats and clowns and bought a print of "The Man with the Blue Guitar" for his room. He thought he had never been in touch with the part of him that was contorted with pain.

Nonetheless it was very difficult for Kool to stay with the idea of sadness. Almost as soon as his thoughts turned to the subject, he began to fixate on sexual matters or else on practical questions of living. He was forever asking me how to do this or that and became quickly enraged when I suggested that he wasn't so much interested in where he might, for example, buy a used computer as he was in escaping painful feelings that he seemed to be on the brink of fully experiencing and sharing. Often such interpretations infuriated him, and he would lie before me in sulky silence until the hour ended. But sometimes he thought it was clear that he was uncomfortable focusing on dysphoric affects. He remembered that his mother always insisted that actions spoke louder than words and that in their family wasting a lot of time "feeling things" was not going to pay any bills or get any of her daughters married. It seemed to me the split that divided Kool's beautiful woman side from his so-called reality ego was narrowing as he became increasingly able to expand the story of his life and to tolerate and reflect on painful affects. But while this was going on, his efforts to move continued in full swing. Indeed, the other side of his sense of being more integrated was a growing anxiety about what this change in him would mean with respect to the fate of his beautiful woman side and his wish to cross dress.

He had a scare in this regard following a visit from Mirra during which she joined with him enthusiastically in cross-dressing activities. Together they looked over the Victoria's Secret catalogue and ordered lingerie for him and shopped at the local department stores for jewelry, nylons, and dresses. Kool had been thrilled. But when Mirra returned home, she'd called and left a completely freaked out message. She said she was worried that Kool would want to become a transsexual and need her only as a buddy. She didn't want to suppress his innermost being, but on the other hand she hoped that they would be essentially a "normal" couple, and she wondered how a life with children and a house in the suburbs would work if Kool needed to spend a lot of time in drag.

Kool couldn't believe what he was hearing. He wanted to cry out like Shakespeare's betrayed and dying Caesar, "Et tu, Mirra?" He wondered again how I really felt about his transvestism. Given Mirra's reaction he found it impossible not to worry that when I spoke of his being integrated internally what I meant was that he would have to renounce his beautiful woman side. And of course, I did think his transvestism a symptom of self-pathology, and hoped one day he would be sufficiently structuralized not to rely on it for self regulation. I also think the split within him—his sense of being both male and female—was at some level deeply unsettling to me. Perhaps as his mother unconsciously needed him to be her lost girl—hence to be split—I similarly needed him to be unified. Certainly my sense of reality and of psychological well being was constructed out of a notion of either/or. I've no doubt his fear that I wasn't comfortable with his beautiful woman side had a basis in the reality of my countertransference.

That Kool felt this was suggested by an important dream he had at this time in which a precious jeweled Fabergé egg in his possession was nearly crushed by the art expert he brought in to assess—he actually said "to analyze"—its value. The dream seemed clearly to articulate Kool's burgeoning fear that the analysis would ultimately destroy his beautiful woman side symbolized by the beautiful egg.

He liked being a man of feeling—no longer one of the artist Magritte's men in bowler hats—but he didn't want to lose the part of him that had lifted his spirit throughout his life and made sex unimaginably exciting.

After a holiday break, he announced that his company had decided to grant his request to transfer to its division in Mirra's small city and he had decided to go. He did not want to interrupt the analysis but Mirra was unable to move because she was building a practice and all her connections were in the city in which she had trained. Kool said he thought about waiting until his analysis was over, but that might still be years away and it seemed foolish to keep the best relationship he ever had in an indefinite holding pattern. Mirra also was thinking about their future and children and did not think they had forever to see where their relationship was headed.

I acknowledged the reasonableness of his decision but argued that at heart it seemed to me a plan to protect his beautiful woman side from the analysis. He was angry and offended and insisted that his beautiful woman side needed no protection from the analysis because, in his mind, becoming more integrated meant that the beautiful woman side of him wouldn't go away; it would merely become a less driven, less anxiety ridden force. This he felt had already largely been achieved. And he insisted that if he needed more therapy or more analysis, he could find it where Mirra lived.

There was certainly no doubt that he knew and accepted himself better than he ever had in the past and that he also understood far more comprehensively how his transvestism functioned to protect him from unbearable affects. And this knowledge left him feeling more intact than he had been before we started. His relationship with Mirra seemed to meet many of his selfobject needs and appeared genuinely satisfying to both of them. Nonetheless, I couldn't forget his decision to leave his ex-wife over the question of his transvestism, and the Fabergé egg dream that seemed to express his fear that I would ultimately want him to give up his beautiful woman fantasy.

We spent several months terminating, but remained essentially stalemated on the question of whether he was leaving because a better life beckoned or because he felt the need to flee the analysis.

Conclusion

The analysis began for me with a sense of disquiet and ended with one of failure. I worried from the start that we wouldn't finish and indeed we did not. Perhaps we should never have begun, but I think the only way we can progress in coming to terms with psychological structures such as Kool's beautiful woman fantasy—and with our own countertransference reactions to these structures—is to confront them whenever the chance presents itself in analysis.

3
The Case of Bert
A Case of Infidelity

Bert has been my patient for 6 years. He was referred to me by the marital therapist treating him and his wife. Initially, I saw Bert face-to-face twice weekly for 3 months, until he was able to arrange his schedule for more intensive psychoanalysis three to four times per week. The frequency of his sessions is an ongoing issue.

Bert is a charming, short, well-built 56-year-old man who came to therapy longing for "intense passion." He had three extra-marital affairs and abused alcohol when with these women. Married, the father of three, owner of a commercial photography firm, he was referred to me having had other therapeutic experiences. Looking back, I may have felt I could do a better job than one of his previous therapists, a renowned analyst.

His job necessitated frequent travel, so our first analytic negotiation was about frequency of sessions and my fee-charging policy. He adamantly refused to pay for missed sessions, a repetition of what he had done in his previous analytic experiences. I agreed not to charge if he canceled with 24 hours' notice.

Bert's history is of a boy whose every authentic wish was stifled by his controlling mother. The patient was the only child of immigrant Jews; mother was 35 when he was born, a tiny woman who (family lore had it) single-handedly kept the Bolsheviks away from her younger siblings, and emigrated to the United States at the age of 17. Bert's father had been a widower, so Bert had a half-sister 15 years older whom he said his mother never loved. Father was a manufacturer. As a young man Bert's father had performed song and comedy on stage, but his family forbade him to seek his dream career in vaudeville. Bert was afraid of his father, who occasionally locked him in the bathroom and spanked him with a hairbrush. However, having been a semiprofessional ballplayer, he eagerly came to watch Bert excel at games. At Bert's 12th birthday, his father, age 50, had a massive fatal heart attack. Embarrassed in school at his teacher's public expression of condolence in front of his classmates, Bert later lied to his friends that his father was alive. A widowed aunt (mother's sister-in-law) moved in with Bert and his mother. The aunt, a beautiful blonde in her 30s, doted on Bert; they frequently slept in the same bed. When he was 12, the aunt told him that his mother forbade them to sleep together anymore, and citing mother's "executive decision," the aunt began criticizing his mother, thus putting Bert in painful conflict. His affection for his aunt quickly turned to hate. Soon the two women argued and the aunt abruptly left, never to resume contact. Mother told Bert, "You're the only one I love." He learned that love must be split between a lover and a controlling protector.

Shortly after college, during which he sought numerous different religious experiences, Bert converted and became a born again Christian, modeling himself after an older, admired boss who encouraged Bert to give himself to Christ. Bert gave up all religious affiliations when he married at age 26.

Bert is very short, with the muscle-bound physique of a compulsive weight-lifter. Affable, verbal, and seductive, he warned me from the start not to be taken in by his "sales-pitch bullshit." He was a superb salesman who automatically became what the customer wanted; this capacity to be a con man was not what he wanted to happen in analysis, although he knew he would try to charm me. Throughout the years of treatment, he attempted to engage me in some light banter as he walked in, seeking eye contact with me. I did not consider or interpret this as part of our analytic process until the 4th year of treatment.

In the first few months of treatment, Bert recalled dreams of squirrels attacking him, tearing him apart and of people's genitals being exposed. This was the first glimmer I had of his vulnerable fragmentation-prone self, which he was trying to conceal under the "salesman bullshit." Bert reviewed experiences with his first analyst, Dr. A. When he began that analysis, Bert was addicted to Valium in order to sleep. The analyst decided to gradually wean him off Valium, but Bert did not remember any understanding of this addiction beyond Dr. A's insistence that he stop.

He was letting me know that when his analyst took away his Valium, the cohesion of his self was at risk.

When he first consulted Dr. A, his former, now deceased, analyst, Bert was having an affair. In reviewing this treatment, Bert revealed how used he felt, like one of Dr. A's research "guinea pigs." The doctor gave him mechanical tantrics to say such as "short-term pain is needed for long-time gain," but this was not accompanied by understanding of Bert's addiction or romantic obsession. Bert recalled that even though the analysis had been helpful, "I hated, then as now, spending money for shrinks, including Dr. A, for something you cannot touch or taste." One time Bert wrote a check for $11 instead of $1100. Dr. A interpreted this as Bert's anger at him; Bert never accepted that interpretation, convinced that ultimately Dr. A was more interested in his own writing and research than in Bert. The one issue Dr. A thought had been left undone was Bert's inability to discover romantic sexual excitement with his wife.

When Dr. A died, Bert took a leave from his company in order to begin a new business. He adored the new enterprise's beginnings and the creativity involved, although he was completely naive about the intricacies of running the business. Turning away from his feelings about his analyst's death, he noted, "The challenge was like a mistress; I felt like a king." Six years later, Bert began an affair with an employee, which led to Bert's request for a referral from his former analyst's widow, whom he knew was a mental health professional. Bert saw this new male analyst for 1 year and then quit. That analyst was "too effeminate." After the new business eventually failed, Bert returned to his original firm. One year later, Bert's admired original partner died. At the same time, Bert's wife became symptomatically menopausal and depressed. With characteristic determination, seeking a new challenge (this time not a mistress), Bert decided to learn a new language (a first step toward fulfilling his retirement dream of living in Europe). Over the years, he had also devoted a great deal of time to photography as an intermittent weekend artist in a studio with a small darkroom.

During the first couch hour, Bert told me that all his affairs began in July (the current month and the month in which his father died). He complained of loneliness and emptiness. He was sick of always having to do the right thing, of feeling obligated to be a father to everyone, especially to his employees.

In Bert's first dream in this analysis, he heard a noise in his backyard, went out to investigate, and as he approached, there was an explosion. He associated to frightening dreams occurring early in his first analysis, an analysis that put an end to those nightmares. He complained about how bored he now felt. I silently wondered if his boredom was a protection from an anticipated explosion with me, and from sexualized dangers "outside."

In the first month of analysis, I participated in the first of what I now feel were four significant enactments. The first concerned my financial contract with him, our "deal," in which he agreed to come four times weekly as long as I did not charge for cancellations with 24-hour notice (unlike Dr. A's policy). Because his business necessitated travel, and I was able to schedule him four times weekly at the end of my day, I agreed not to charge him if he gave me advance notice of his business trips. Starting at the onset of his referral to me, although I did not consciously recognize it, my grandiosity was stimulated. I imagined that I could do as well, or perhaps even better, than his first analyst, whom I admired.

As Bert left an early session, facing me with gleeful defiance, he revealed he had canceled a session in order to attend a Cubs game (not for a business trip as had been our "deal"). I was as provoked as the mother of an adolescent son, but it was too early in our work to challenge his macho display, which I did not yet understand. Bert then dreamed that he had walked out of someplace into the open and put on an Indian chief's hat. He was aware of lots of struggling, watching some political scene with great disdain. He reported that recently, in his associations, he had been feeling more optimistic and not so lonely. Bert was struck again by the idea that he never had a childhood, "got married and had babies immediately. My mother even planned my destiny." I privately wondered if his connection to me provided optimism and an experience of wearing an Indian chief's grandiose costume, as does a child. This temporarily allowed him to feel that he had a new growth opportunity via my responsiveness. I did not consider that his disdain was a response to my compliance with the "financial deal."

An early indication of his use of sexualization was conveyed by a dream just prior to my first vacation: Bert was in a basement with his colleagues, who were making innuendoes and discussing rumors about his infidelities while outside, people were rollerblading. "I felt helpless or maybe guilty." The patient associated to the dream saying, "This is one time in my life that those rumors are not true. Blading is for the young. I feel old. I felt some guilt about canceling for the Cubs, but pleasure at flaunting it. I am not going to give up my pleasures to do this analysis!" I commented, "If I can cancel you (for my vacation), you can cancel me" (because I, like his mother, would require him to do it her way). On my return, Bert dreamed of killing, in a murderous rage, a woman who reminded him of the stalking lover in the movie *Fatal Attraction*. In the dream, Bert confided his crime to two colleagues. He did not think this dream was in any way a response to my vacation.

I imagined I might lose my analysand should I require Bert to schedule our sessions my way. I was not then ready to change my no-charge cancellation policy. In retrospect, I realized that Bert indicated his own readiness to reconsider the policy and expressed his anger when in the 4th month of analysis he asked, "Are you afraid of me?" I was astounded by the question and asked him about it. He replied, "If we were to disagree, it would be fun, not unpleasant. If I feel comfortable, as I do now, I can be a jerk." I silently wondered if he was picking up some wariness in me about his anger, and my uncertainty about his commitment to the analysis.

Bert's dreams repeatedly evinced his rage and its displacement onto his wife, as well as his use of sexualization and disavowal. In a dream similar to those of desperation with Dr. A, Bert's wife and he were in their bedroom. He saw raccoon paw indentations on their crisp white sheet. His wife left, unconcerned. "Then I saw the animal, so I decided to trap it in my bedroom, but I realized the space under the door had grown larger. As it crawled out into the dining room, I poked it with a chair. It got furious as it leapt at me with nails and teeth."

Bert realized he had not dreamed of such an animal attack for years:

I fear I'm being attacked by my own uncomfortable desires and guilt. I've an image from when I was 10 to 13. There was a gorgeous girl with the longest nails. She flirted with me. Her flirting kept me alive, as I was enthralled by her sexy long fingernails. I remember a movie about a rapist who was scratched and scarred by a woman with long nails. In reality, when I was a kid, I was attacked by a squirrel as a friend and I threw stones at it. Then I reacted like a coward just like the time I saw my daughter pulled in by the lake's waves: I froze with fear.

When I said, "These old dangers and feeling of being trapped are coming alive again as you feel more involved with me in the analysis," Bert could not consciously relate to feeling trapped. Instead he complained about loneliness over the weekend:

It feels like when I came home after father died and mother was working. During the weekends of my first affair, when my married lover wasn't available, I was so lonely that I felt paralyzed. How can I be honest with you if I care about what you think of me? I thought of you this weekend in as positive a manner as I ever did of my previous analysts. It struck me that maybe for 45 minutes you are all mine, as you want me to be all yours, spiritually. It feels like a unique intimacy. That's why I wanted to see a woman. After the birth of our first child, I developed a "Madonna" syndrome: You don't make love to a mother. I remember an episode from when I was about 7. I was lying on top of my mother. I was intrigued with her big breasts on a tiny woman and touched them. She was awkward, embarrassed. With Dr. A, I was uncomfortable talking of sexual problems. The more I drink, the more I am able to be passionate, and able to maintain an erection.

I explored Bert's use of alcohol. He drank one to two glasses of wine on social occasions. However, when involved in his affairs, his drinking increased and enabled him to become more passionate. When on vacations with his wife, they both drank more wine than usual, which enabled them to make love successfully. They had no sexual life at home. Bert had no wish to alter this.

Soon after discussing alcohol, he complained, "My wife and I are at each other. She hates my language teacher. I am having romantic fantasies about being with someone who adores me, energizes me. In fantasy I am 23 years old." I suggested that he hoped to feel energized by the analysis and me.

As Bert struggled with his empty and angry state over weekends, he mused about resuming work in his darkroom, but could not get himself to go there. When I wondered why, he explained he was hesitant to mobilize himself to "do art" because

> it will take over like my French lessons have. But I am angry at my French teacher. She is giving me short shrift. When working in the darkroom, I am not empty although I can feel frustrated. I first recall this empty feeling when I heard my mother screaming from the other room. I knew my father was dead and I crawled under the covers. Soon my emptiness was replaced by embarrassment at school. Then I developed a crush on my aunt.

I understood but did not interpret the progression he described: an emptiness leading to death. The resulting psychological paralysis led to his sexualization of his aunt and a temporary feeling of aliveness.

In our second mutual enactment, I did just what his mother did. I planned for him. Expressing my countertransference concerns about Bert starting another affair with the language tutor, I suggested that he try going into his studio to see what got stirred up. (Bert referred to my cue as "our contract" and from then on regularly reported his studio accomplishments to me while I wondered if his working in the studio was for me.) Bert then obtained an astrological reading: "The woman astrologer understood I want to be known, famous. She said I must take time to do photography, enjoy, and do not worry about money." Bert reported, "I did honor our contract and went to the studio this weekend. I said to myself, 'I don't need to excel. I will just do it for pleasure.' I felt calm, not empty." Soon Bert made a photograph of himself. "I don't want to care what anyone thinks. The picture has energy, vitality, and explosiveness in it, but my wife won't like it. I don't want to be as rigidly realistic as I have been. Flow is the thing."

The next month, Bert had to cancel twice because of work. "I worry when I cancel that you won't believe me. That you'll get angry. I don't want to have to worry about you or any others. Doing photography is about me alone." Sexualized fantasies about me at times of interruption became an established pattern, which I interpreted. For example, in the first session after my vacation, Bert reported a dream of being in an office with a girl:

"The scene was very romantic and flirtatious. Then we were in a back seat of a limo kissing, wonderfully. One time I had to move her hair away, but my mother's presence somehow kept interfering." Associations led to a memory of necking in college in the back of a car, when his girl's fake ponytail fell off. "That was such a tremendous, repulsive shock! To my knowledge we haven't necked here in analysis."

I wondered if I had some unrecognized pleasure in his erotized attachment to me, and if the fake ponytail was some clue to his ideas about a disavowed part in me. I asked: "Are you flirting with me?"

Bert replied:

It's not like I hadn't seen you in so long. My thoughts about you are not sexual but very erotic from the neck up. You are so pristine, untouchable. I am curious about you in a social situation. I am very uncomfortable socially. At home I am petty, angry, dull. I carry a black cloud reminder that I am not good enough. That's been true all my life, not just because of my father's death.

From then on, issues of his macho salespitch phoniness and a beginning awareness of his depression emerged. I was still unaware of colluding with the phoniness.

During this first year of analysis, Bert and his wife continued in marital therapy. At the start of the second year, Bert reported:

My wife wants to see the marital therapist alone. She says I am her jailer. Do I really control her spending money? On the weekend I felt no one appreciates me. My anger is probably more a depression. I am in a terrible mood. I am a phony, a coward, not real. I feel not smart, not well educated, unlike brilliant Ed (his original partner, now dead). I am a chameleon, superficial.

As Bert and his wife left for a planned trip to France, he worried:

I am nervous that this week I blew you off for a second time because of work. I had a terrible fight with my son. It was so painful that I feared I lost him. You can't imagine how I behave when I lose my temper. The next day, I hugged him and told him that I loved him. Had I been at my father's side when he had his heart attack, could I have saved him?

I interpreted that this time away from me was especially difficult because Bert was now dealing with his painful, sad, and angry feelings. Would he once again lose someone so important: his son, his analyst? His trip to France turned out to be wonderful because he practiced fluency in his new language and received local admiration beyond his expectations. As was typical on vacations with his wife, they had satisfactory sex, so unlike at home, where they had virtually no sexual contact. The couple's increased consumption of alcohol was marked on these vacations.

Two months later, Bert's daughter invited him to attend the delivery of her second child, a watershed for Bert. In the following session, he was more alive and ecstatic than ever: "The birth was the most exciting thing I ever saw! It all had a calming influence over me. I felt an intimacy of being at one with my daughter, my son-in-law and the baby." Bert returned to the experience often, seeking to recapture it when creating his photographic montages. Although we then spoke of it as breaking through a wall (of inhibition), I now consider it a new experience of unfettered affect, and of his hope for a psychological rebirth.

Bert's excitement did not last. He grew more and more aware of his depression. His firm hired a new production assistant, a young woman, O, who had just moved to the city. The next week Bert complained, "Over the weekend, loneliness came over me, hit like a wave. My romantic fantasies about being in love prevails. I watched my new employee, O. I want her to like me, think I'm wonderful. I took her to lunch and acted like a benevolent millionaire."

The next week, Bert said:

My heart is breaking for brave O, whose mother is dying. I had an argument with my wife regarding my son's irresponsibility. I had a dream in which I was talking to a car service manager, but could not understand him even though I heard the words; they were not gibberish. I felt no anger but worried if he was taking advantage of me. I have some doubts about that flimflam business.

I asked, "Is this about me and psychoanalysis?" Bert denied the possibility, claiming, "You are more creative than a mechanic, but, like paying for car maintenance, I am your annuity. There is no end. I felt pangs of loneliness today. Just empty." Despite Bert's denial, my analytic attempts were gibberish-like to him. They did not diminish his pain.

At the end of Bert's second year in analysis, as my vacation approached, he reported two dreams each, in retrospect, demonstrating that he was feeling flooded beyond his capacity to contain his feelings without his acting out again. In the first,

> I was in a room flooded with water, which was approaching the first of two bunk beds. Others were there; I was in the lower bunk. I saw an enormous rat, the size of a cat, swimming to get to a dry place. I watched with curiosity and anxiety. Then in the second dream, the room was now dry. An old hag came, took the rat, and wrung its neck; I could hear the neck click. Then my wife returned angry, not hysterical, feeling I cheated on her. No matter what I explained—this part is fuzzy—I felt terribly lonely. She did not love me anymore.

I asked, "Am I correct that you called me Sunday, the night of the dream?" Bert agreed. "Yes, the dream came after my call to cancel my analytic session for my thallium stress test. Some ischemia was found. I will not live forever! I am afraid I'll die before I can become a major art photographer." Quickly changing the subject, he pointed at an envelope, "I brought slides of my art for you to see. Only for you! I told my wife that I'm going to die, so it's important to do what we want: Europe and art. I always felt not good enough to become 'the artist' so I became the con-artist."

Anticipating our interruption and feeling empty, Bert described driving past an actual suicide scene; a man had hanged himself on a tree. Bert considered this

> the epitome of loneliness. It looked surreal in the snow. I wanted the freedom to stop right there and photograph it. I had a fantasy a few days ago of a middle-aged man on the beach with a young boy on his shoulders. They walked into the water and the kid held on. I told my friend, who said it

is my story with my father. I would rather be dead with him than alive without. I want to bawl. I know it is about not wanting to grow up.

I said, "It's about what you lost when he died, and how you fear it could happen again if someone lifts your spirits and becomes too important."
On my return, Bert lamented,

I kept thinking, where the hell are you! I was feeling angry, depressed, and lonely. So I got real involved in developing a romantic fantasy. When my business is successful, every-thing feels empty. Even though I seem the extroverted coach, a cheerleader on the job, on the inside I feel introverted. When I am like this, I am afraid to answer the phone. I'm just back to that little runty kid with big dreams. I could convince you that my success in business had nothing to do with me. I just happened to be in the right place at the right time.

The next month, Bert reported that

things are heating up with O [his new employee]. I feel lousy. I feed myself on the idea of intrigue with her. I am upset with you that you are not being more heavy-handed about this. You are a chicken shit. Yes, I know you say a new woman is a symbol of feeling vital and alive when I feel depressed (especially after that last thallium stress test). Like the infatuation with French, I am searching for some-thing to embellish my intelligence, that would make me feel better about myself. Like when I started the new company where I lost half a million of my own money.

Bert canceled the next session for a business meeting; I did not charge for the missed hour. I realized my cancellation policy was my way of not being heavy-handed, and recognized that I, like Bert, was avoiding his anger and depression. I had to deal assertively with his cancellations.
Bert, temporarily buoyed by being featured on a television program about entrepreneurs, observed:

I feel I am getting stronger. My empty hole does seem to be filling. There was a turning point yesterday at the marital session. I told them a story that previously I had told only you. It was my fantasy of my wife dying when I had an 'out of body experience'; when I felt destitute and frozen; that I would die too. It's about how much I need her.

At the same time, he talked more and more about O. They began an affair. Imagining that the affair was a response to Bert's increased intolerance of his empty depression, I recognized my countertransference act of allying myself with one side of Bert. I wanted to preserve his marriage (my friendship with the marital therapist was also a factor in my countertransference). But I wanted to handle the analysis in a way different from the temporary repair of his first analysis. I arranged a consultation with Arnold Goldberg. Goldberg strongly recommended I change "the deal" about not charging for missed sessions. The deal enhanced Bert's use of disavowal and permitted the negative maternal transference to be acted out, rather than reexperienced and interpreted in the analytic here and now. I agreed, and decided to try to renegotiate our deal.

Goldberg further suggested that I interpret to Bert his wish that I give him advice as would a father. Goldberg thought that Bert looked for my sincerity and smiling approval, but as he tried to read my face, like a child, he wondered whether my smile was genuine or the smile of the preoccupied transference mother. Noting the two aspects of Bert, the complaining, resentful self and the excited, grandiose, megalomaniac self, Goldberg predicted that Bert's grandiose self might modify if it was part of an integrated, realized whole.

At the next session, Bert reported a dream:

O was in bed with me, but we were not having an illicit affair, it was not sexual, she was just with me. I was trying to convince her of something. She did not believe me; she was cool, uncomfortable, then nasty. I got up to go to the toilet but shat all over. It was not buried, just ugly. It's easy to understand. This affair with O is like crapping all over, a mess.

I agreed that both Bert and I were concerned that he was in a mess again, and angry at me for it: he wanted me to be stronger, not a chicken shit. Therefore, I recommended that there would be a more effective exploration of this if he paid for four sessions, whether he canceled or not. As Bert considered this idea and the session ended, he reiterated that the change would be impossible. Facing me, he correctly perceived my raised eyebrow: "Why are you giving me a skeptical look regarding how impossible it would be?"

Over the next few weeks, we continued to discuss changing our deal. Bert revealed more of his analysis with Dr. A: "I became couch meat. All he cared about was money." "When did you begin to feel that?" I asked. "I think it was sometime in the second of the 4 years." "Did you tell him?"

No. I cannot express feelings to men the way I can to women. I was paying for every session. After 3 years back with my wife, I missed a few. Dr. A got angry and bawled me out. I would get angry at him when I couldn't make four sessions. It was drudgery to go with nothing to say, especially when I was feeling fine. He would mention over and over 'the out-of-town patient' who could use my time if I did not show. The idea that you want to change our deal makes me queasy, like you are trying to get out of it. It makes me untrusting.

I asked, "Why would I want to?" Bert replied, "I'm just a patient. Yet on the other side, you explained, initially, that you do not need to fill the hour."

Reluctantly, Bert accepted the plan to pay for four sessions whether he attended or not. The consultation with Goldberg allowed me to confront my own disavowal. My own grandiosity had convinced me that I could do an unorthodox analysis and not play by the rules. I began to understand the two sides of myself: grandiose and avoiding Bert's anger on one, more realistic on the other. Only then could I more actively interpret the split selves of Bert and the shifts between them without a countertransference investment in either side. One side was the more realistic, depressed, angry Bert, and the other was the "turned on," inebriated Bert in his relations with O. Now I could better monitor my judgments about Bert's alcohol use and extramarital involvement. The study group on narcissistic behaviors helped me understand that empathy, not judgment, about both sides might result in Bert's eventual integration, a success unlike his previous analysis.

Meanwhile, O also pressured Bert for more time, and he was growing concerned about her emotional state. He told her that he would pay for her psychotherapy if she got into treatment, but he did not want any record that his wife might discover of his checks to O's therapist. He asked if he could write checks to me, an acceptable payee for his wife, so I could then pay O's therapy bill. In other words, Bert pleaded with me to 'launder' these bills for him. I pushed him to explore the meanings of this request as well as other payment options. Only if I became his accomplice would he be convinced that I really understood his dilemma. Eventually I complied with his wish. This laundering enactment once again reflected my own grandiosity: I could break the usual rules. I felt in a bind with my very own split: On the one hand, I would be participating in lying to his wife; on the other, I hoped that if O were in treatment, she could face her own symptoms, and Bert would either join her, as a healthier woman, or leave her. He fantasied that she, like he, might attempt suicide if he stopped their affair.

Thus began Bert's 2-year struggle to end either his affair or his marriage; his vacillations were intense. I attempted to stay neutral and interpret each constellation's transferences and fantasies; but, I too, oscillated. He lied to both women in a manner I sometimes adjudged ludicrous, approaching psychotic or sociopathic behavior.

For example, Bert described being on a business trip with O: "We had drinks, and I patted her cheek, and told her, ' I love you.' That made me distraught all weekend at home, so I was catatonic. Unlike my previous lovers, O is a very fragile woman. I want to get hold of myself about my continuing this. You'll be mad, disappointed. This lonely, wonderful patient of yours has not done right."

This was the opportunity for me to wonder about the function of Bert's use of alcohol. Although he was able to be aroused by O, this was not the case with his wife except when drinking on vacations. He explained that drinking also allowed him to overcome his fears of impotence. Furthermore, both O and Bert drank so they usually finished a bottle of wine before making love.

As Bert explored his "lovesickness" I suggested, "The most significant thing about O is how much she admires you and makes you feel young." Bert added, "Additionally significant is how I called O's mother before her death, and complimented her on her daughter. O said her mother cried with joy that I was in her daughter's life and would take care of her. Then her mother died." Bert tearfully continued, "I feel so choked up." I wondered, "What moved you just now?" "Just the idea that I could help . . . like O, when she is in all this pain. There are lots of happenings at work but it's all meaningless to me. O comes into my office and does-n't leave. I want her company when I'm lonely but I know she's a bitch. O is constantly flirting with me. Is she devious? I am a willing victim."

After the next weekend, he said:

My wife is depressed. I was angry, even more so after drink-ing wine. I told her all she talks about is clothes and shop-ping. When she is down, everything is black. I know I am afraid of dying. I think of making love a lot. I did not think about it so much before with my other affairs. My first affair with R, she seemed like O, a beauty, tough, smart, one of the boys, a jock. She seduced me. I was in my early forties. I was naive. When I was with her nothing else mattered. Once my wife became a mother, had our kids, she seemed like a saint. When I feel depressed, O is a shot of vitality. I have a new idea. Sex is not to fill a hole or build my ego but more about making love in a free way. I can only do it when drunk. My second long affair of many months was with a woman whom I did not like, but sex was terrific. She wrote my wife, which got me to my second analyst. I don't think I really like O as she is so self-centered. My wife is soft, peachy, a gentle nurse.

Unlike O, my wife's eyes glaze over when I talk business. She calls it my mistress. As my company gets busier, on one level I feel scared, although on another level it calms me. It'll pull me away from analytic sessions and away from my wife. I've been working harder here in psychoanalysis. You were a stranger to me before. [Jokingly] Now you are just strange! Thinking about my wife, she had a breakdown when 9 years old, somewhat analogous to losing my father. She was my counterpart, my alter-ego, like when my father died, although I never thought about it until now. On the outside she had a survival adaptation, but inside she was weak. Then I think of the blonde Aunt Alice. She was tough, drove like a man, sexy. [I silently wondered whether if I, since my consultation with Goldberg, was tougher, and these days dyed blonde, more like Aunt Alice.]

I know I have cold feet about ending with O. When I am
with her I feel exhilarated, hooked. I have this insane drive
to win her over and capture her love, then it turns into guilt
and I cannot leave until I prove the relationship is honest,
that I'm not evil but loyal.

I interpreted this drive to win and sexually capture as just one
side of his split. On the other, he wanted to be honorable about
his commitments. The bind he now felt was he had committed
himself to both women.

I remember long ago when I was involved with another
lover, R. Dr. A asked: "What do you want? I will help you
choose which woman the best I can." I told O I'm leaving
my wife in two months, as if I set a date [a blatant lie]. I don't
know who I am. I have no self-respect, as I'm worse than a
drug addict. I feel panicky. Do I have to go cold turkey ?
How will I bear the loss? My wife is so depressed. I feel
guilty. (O is also down so she joined a grief group to help
with mourning her mother.) I try to tell myself, as Dr. A did,
"short-term pain, long-term gain." Back then, I left R because
I couldn't stand the loss of my wife. I weaned myself from
R. I'm never with O without wine or champagne. How I long
for the old days when your [analyst's] biggest problem was
how to get me to go to the studio.
    Everything is crashing down. I think I have made the first
step toward separating from O. As if sensing my shift, my
wife is in a better mood. I had a French assignment to write
a story. I wrote about a child, my daughter, at a lake, drowning; the clouds so mesmerize her that she doesn't see how
deep the water is; she is paralyzed, but shouts for help. It's
so sad. A part of me did die with my father.

I added, "That is how you now feel about losing either part of
your split self." Bert lamented, "I am living two lives as I sink
into quicksand. I am the scum of the earth, a liar, cheater to everyone but you."
    I responded, "That I know both parts, all of you, and still find
your struggle painful and understandable, is important in putting
them together."
    Bert agreed he had two selves but was not at all sure putting
them together was possible.

All my selfishness is about trying to replace what's missing. I am panicked about losing my wife yet romance with O is my heroin. Am I trying to make O angry so she'll leave me? I want to be a man about this, yet I am so empty. If I end up walking out on my wife and kids, it would be like O's father, who walked out on her. With either decision, I am that abandoning father, just repeating my youth. Am I so unsure of my masculinity that I drink to prolong sex, and make my partner happy beyond belief? It is as if I take three steps forward, three back. The sincerity I saw in O mesmerized me. Can't you [analyst] accompany me when I tell O it is over? You could just whisper in my ear. Don't be my doctor, be my buddy, be my father, tell me what to do, to straighten up.

I interpreted that I understood his longing for me to be the father he lost. I would not, however, tell him what to do, but help him do whatever he decided was what he wanted. Little did I know that I was about to be enmeshed with both sides of his split.

The next month, Bert claimed, "I can say today what I couldn't last week: I know I cannot leave my wife. When she is not in such pain, I can move closer. My mother's pain made me very angry. When I didn't call for a couple of days, she'd cry. Then I changed, and at the end of her life, I called her daily."

Feeling that O had "connected" with her new therapist, Bert decided to call for a "hiatus" from her, explaining to her that the break was in order to sort out his feelings. He told her he was working in therapy (lying that it was not analysis) on his fears about losing his children and his family. He asked me if he could bring her into his session, so that I could meet her and help convince her of the value of his "hiatus" plan to which she was opposed. I attempted to process the meaning of this request, but he was desperate. I now wonder if I missed an opportunity here to encounter his rage had I denied his request. Would my denial have made me the tough father of his fantasy? But, I disavowed my own typical analytic stance and merged with Bert's wish in order to protect some vulnerable aspect of myself. I regressed into a reciprocally split self. Earlier I enacted by not charging for missed sessions. Then I was his financial "laundress." Now I enacted by being his coconspirator (my third enactment). I met with O and Bert. I felt guilty that on "my watch" as his analyst, I had known that my analysand was lying to this woman. I hoped that I might convince her to interrupt their sexual contact now that I thought Bert could tolerate his feelings of loss. In retrospect, even though seeing O had been Bert's idea, I was still trying to do "damage control" for Bert, his wife, and O.

The session after I met O, Bert was eager to know if I could see why he had been so taken with her. Had I noted her sincerity, intelligence, beauty, and youth? Could I understand how much he would be giving up? "As I think of my intense feeling of loss, it is almost unbearable. It scares me. I think it is like when my father died and I heard my mother screaming. I covered my head with a blanket and told myself it wasn't true."

I replied, "All your busyness and obsessions have been geared to avoid this feeling. You've used your talents as compensatory ways to avoid this pain which you've intellectually known about but only now can face."

Bert said, "I don't know how. But I'll do it. Give me some magic word that I could repeat. I need to hold onto the idea that tolerating this pain is for the better, an absolute necessity."

I suggested, "Why not that understanding?"

Bert asked, "How does one go from a coward to being strong?"

I commented, "Step by step is how. You are doing it. By sending O to therapy, telling her you need a hiatus, and bearing your grief."

The next week, Bert revealed,

I could not do it! I lied to O that I moved to my daughter's. I am in love with O. I never believed a person like O would love me. I cannot act out of pure logic and sensibility. If my wife throws me out, it will throw me into a worse panic, but it is unbearable that O will find me too old. I need the fire or I feel dead. When I'm in this pain, there's a hole in my stomach, and I need someone to fill it with adoration and love. When I'm depressed, I feel dead.

Bert then reported his experience of relief when his wife caught him in a lie about his whereabouts. He had been with O. "I feel the peace of the criminal who wants to be caught in his slime! I asked my wife not to leave. I cannot exist with or without her. Such a dramatic split."

I exclaimed, "Yes!"

Bert pondered, "But it is hard for me to believe the two parts could be pulled together—a habitual liar like me?"

I responded, "If you give it time, our four sessions weekly, we'll find out." Although I could not guarantee his integration, I naively felt more optimistic because I had both an operating theory (about narcissistic behavior disorders) and a conviction that Bert was tolerating more discomfort, was lying less easily, and had a better understanding of his transference experiences in each side of his split: the grandiose, forever young side, and the more realistic one filled with resentment. We were beginning to note that interruptions in our sessions and his resulting feelings of depression, anger, and loneliness influenced or determined which side of his split predominated. With O he was young and powerful; with his wife, he was depressed, experiencing her demands on his time or attention as similar to mine for analytic frequency.

The next week, having announced that he "definitely" decided not to travel, Bert impulsively went to Europe to meet O, who was vacationing there. He expected his wife to make a ruckus, but predicted her sticking by him no matter how "I shit on her. It makes me sad about myself." Bert asked me, "What do you think? Am I detestable? I know you're for me, but this is a personal question that is really not relevant, Do you love me?"

I insisted, "This is relevant. You have never felt you had an unconditional kind of love connection. You always felt the connection was contingent on following the other's agenda. Not having to do it my way is crucial."

Bert went to Europe to be with O. The next month, 6 months after my consultation with Goldberg, Bert decided to move out of his home into an apartment, to try living alone.

When I look at my wife, I want to die but I want to move out, be with O, give it a shot—the adventure, freedom. I could not continue lying about O, but I think you are disappointed that I haven't become a whole person. But you are honest and would tell me if I am really making a mistake. I understand that idea of splitting [disavowal] as, I want to hold both women in my arms and promise anything. Can't you just sequester me? Just like my recently infected finger; it starts as a simple beginning and each day gets worse. My antibiotic is stopping my lies. The lies are over. I am trying to fit into everyone's agenda, take care of everybody. Then I feel trapped.

For the first time, the patient (not his analyst) connected his feelings about his wife's current depressed state with his feelings about his complaining mother. He begged me to see his wife with him, to try to explain to her his struggle to integrate, so that she might have some hope. Although skeptical that my authority could ease his wife's depression, I again responded to the intensity of Bert's panic, telling myself that his alliance with me continued to rest on my agreeing to his agenda rather than mine. I agreed to his request even more impulsively than I did before meeting O without attempting to process its meaning. Despite my attempts at neutrality, I was more identified with the cuckolded wife than with his young lover. In the third enactment, I had met with Bert and O; therefore, I rationalized, I must agree to meet with Bert and his wife. I enacted with Bert's two sides. Bert felt sure his wife would respect my view of his struggles. The session went as Bert planned. I saw husband and wife together. Countertransferentially, I felt concerned about his wife's pain, but could offer her no assurance.

The following session, Bert asked, "What do you think?" I responded incredulously, "Do you want me to choose?" Bert sighed, "I wish you could." He reported a dream:

> I was on an airplane. The pilot instructed us that in order to take off, all of us had to lean forward. However, we crashed. I struggled whether to call my wife to say I was okay, or just play dead and walk off with O. I think it means I am returning to the start, with my wife, but this time without my wings. It feels like a desperate struggle. I panic when I imagine losing O and her virginal breasts. My wife's breasts are already sucked.

I wondered aloud if crashing also anticipated my upcoming 3-week vacation; his depression and his wife's depression seemed more than he imagined he could contain.

His wife insisted on moving ahead with a divorce. The following month, her lawyer subpoenaed O, who in her deposition revealed not only the amount of money Bert spent on her but also my laundering of O's therapy payments. I was complicit, identified with my patient's deceit. I quit laundering, and Bert quit giving any monies to O. Bert noted that his wife hadn't yet told her therapist, their former marital therapist, that she was seeing Bert again—her lie.

A month before my vacation, Bert complained, "Do not smile at me. I am not your hero. I cannot stand going back to my empty flat." I responded, "It is your empty depression which you cannot tolerate. It feels worse before I leave on vacation."

When I returned, Bert requested, "Let me look at you." As he struggled with his resolve to end it with O, he described some progress but felt the ending was like a slow death. "I want to stop lying [to his wife]. I can taste it." I suggested that now that I was back, Bert felt he could proceed to end with O. He recalled that Dr. A, when away for long vacations, always sent a postcard that ended: "Give my love to your wife" (I did not send a postcard). He beseeched me to help him resolve now (in analysis) what he did not do with Dr. A.

Meanwhile, his wife reported to him her attorney's prediction that "Bert will screw around for the rest of his life." While we worked on his use of disavowal, Bert noted that when subjected to his wife's angry accusations, "I can get into a fantasy that I haven't done anything wrong." Seemingly out of the blue, he reflected, "I didn't get to know and trust you until this past year." I wondered what prompted the change. He said, "I don't know. But I know you care."

A torturous struggle to break off with one or the other woman continued for another year and Bert's depression increased. He could not imagine an ending without alcohol to numb him. For a month, he considered the suggestion of a male friend's (a recovered alcoholic) that he enter an "in-patient detoxification" program for alcoholics. After obsessing about the necessity of such a program, he decided to go "cold turkey" himself. I stayed neutral about the program or his abstinence decision. In fact, during this time, his alcohol use diminished as he learned to tolerate feeling depressed in the sessions.

Bert's truth telling was abetted by his realization that his lies about his whereabouts were held in suspicion by both women; he attempted to get one of the women to stop seeing him in order to resolve his dilemma, rather than making the choice himself. As we worked on these dynamics, he reflected that he was in love, not with O, but with a fantasy. He understood more about his negative maternal transference to his now chronically angry wife: "I was my mother's whole life. I am my wife's life." Sex was never satisfactory with his wife. He recounted that alcohol initially cured his premature ejaculations in his first affair, prior to which he masturbated three times a day, yet was unable to achieve an erection with his wife. He insisted that if he did not become a full person who wanted to be with his wife, he would be alone forever.

Toward the end of the year, Bert dreamed of looking in the mirror, noticing a considerable amount of hair growing on his bald spot, and asking some other person if he liked it; he did. Bert thought the dream represented his continuing search for youth, explaining that, 15 years ago, he tried to cover his bald spot. I suggested the dream might point to new growth, not to a phony cover-up.

When I left for professional meetings the week before Christmas, Bert feared my absence, and reluctantly, he decided to follow through on his "promise" to O to take her away for a last trip. Bert lied to his wife, saying he was at his in-town flat, and traveled out of state for a long weekend with O. As usual, he sneaked away from O in order to call his wife. Despite knowing how, he "forgot" to block his location on her caller-ID device. His wife realized he was out of town and felt devastated by yet another lie. In the next session, he differentiated his panic when imagining his wife's despair from his milder feelings about losing O. He moaned that he wanted to be honest: "How do sociopaths just keep lying?" I suggested that prior to this past year, Bert had built a wall to block his own pain and that of others. He was breaking down that wall. In my increasing conviction that Bert's "forgetting" to block the caller ID was a preconscious move toward integration, I told him he wanted his wife to know he lied. Just as he wanted both women to know about both sides of him, he wanted each side of him to know the other.

Bert grew even more depressed as did both his women. We developed a language metaphorically relating the challenge of the step-wise measuring of his new psychological growth to the small muscular incremental changes in weight-lifting, which he recently needed to decrease to accommodate his painful arthritis. Now I more assiduously interpreted in the transference the waxing and waning of his depression secondary to missing sessions and weekends. Without telling O that he was attempting to reconcile with his wife—another lie by omission— Bert gradually stopped all contact with O. As I tried to understand his reluctance to tell O the truth, Bert ranged in his explanations from "It would be too painful for her" to "I need to avoid her wrath." It recurred to me why I had made the initial "deal" about not demanding four-session payment: He would have left the analysis, just as he left his "other women" when they grew too demanding.

For the second time in the analysis, Bert brought me slides of his newest photos. I was impressed by his talent and the changes in his work and I told him so. He had moved from incredibly detailed representational work to abstraction. Bert reflected that at 60, he

> pissed away so much time and money, that at my age now, I cannot afford to just retire and do photography full time. But my life was not dull. I was a good father until my kids were 9 or 10 years old. I know photography can be very lonely. My business always had people around, which helped me avoid my loneliness inside. I think I could manage that loneliness now.

Until this reflection, I had not realized that Bert had distanced himself from his children when each reached the age he had been when his father died. We discussed this dynamic.

Bert's divorce became final as his wife insisted despite his renewed commitment to her. Their financial negotiations were arranged by Bert's long-time male accountant, whom Bert and his ex-wife trusted more than either of their individual lawyers. In his accountant, I interpreted, Bert had found his longed-for, "tough, straight-talking father."

After the divorce was final, Bert felt depressed but not panicky. He had a sense of not belonging anywhere,

> floating without stability. I do want my freedom and the opportunity to be spontaneous. I am not obligated to anyone. There are no deceptions, no lies. I see how the intrigue, lies, and adventures nurtured me, but I don't feel that deep lonely feeling as I did 1 year ago. The photography is now feeding me. This is the most peaceful that I have felt in years. I'm wondering, "What do you think?"

When I told him that it was important to him that I appreciated his changes, he exclaimed:

> I have a huge photo in mind and yet am a big blank film. I had a dream that I was playing golf but had no tees. I was

the last of my foursome to tee off. All my tees were broken so I went into the clubhouse to buy more. The ones I got were huge, six to seven inches above the ground. But I took a swing anyway and completely missed the ball. It was more like a baseball swing. I was aware I should hit the tee down into the ground. It was very frustrating. Then I was like on a split screen. I could see there were definitely two parts to me. On one side, I was hitting the ball really far, like the TV tournament with Tiger Woods, a new young star, not a very big man, but wiry. I drove the ball 330 yards. This is about the unrealistic, wished-for champion part of me. The other is the me without the correct [psychological] tools [tees]. I can see myself as the big picture with my split. The photography is about my wish to express myself in a different manner. Can I be unsplit, all together, without imposing unrealistic perfection? Otherwise I am so restricted.

I did not further interpret his analogy between his artistic goals and the psychological ones.

Just prior to my departure in December, Bert dreamed that an intruder was discovered behind a door in his suburban home. His major concern was how the intruder got in, because the alarm never went off. This was particularly upsetting because the alarm was brand new. "I know this is an aspect of me. The intruder was a very tall, big man. I am wanting to know how I prevent this [affair] from happening again. I am derelict in my responsibilities. I am already flirting with a 23-year-old switchboard operator." I suggested that he was more likely to flirt and be aroused because I was canceling sessions: He felt he still needed my help in order to use a more reliable edition of his internal alarm system.

While I was away, Bert started a series of photographs of the Crucifixion. When I returned, he reported a new insight: "This is the first time I can feel inside my gut that my father's death molded me so dramatically." He photographed a scene representing his father's death.

The images of my father and me are in white. That's the part of me that died with him. In the work, my mother is screaming. I have a tremendous feeling of satisfaction. This is the closest I have come to getting my emotions depicted. I was able to override my old tight technique. I think I can mourn my loss now. When my first analyst died, I was not able to mourn his death. I can now. You are my comrade in arms.

I asked about how he understood me as a comrade in arms. "With you (unlike Dr. A), I know you are passionate about art. That feels good."

I silently wondered if in this belief about my sharing his passion, I was the idealized and mirroring father he had missed. I suggested to Bert that only now had he developed the capacity to mourn yet not feel himself dead, the result of relinquishing his affair of vitalization with O. In fact, Bert found the pain of controlling his sexual behavior with various women who approached him nearly excruciating. As he mourned the loss of his former behaviors, he complained, "I am disappointed; perhaps in you and the whole process, but more in myself. I lack strength. I am still missing some part."

In the autumn, after moving from his apartment back to his home with his (now) ex-wife, Bert dreamed of being in a hunting party looking for small animals.

I had a long small-barrel rifle. All of a sudden there was a deer. I asked for permission to shoot at point-blank range. I missed. Then all of a sudden, fifty yards ahead, was a bear! As I went to shoot I had to reload my rifle, but instead of bullets, I was putting in film. There seemed to be no way I could escape as I ran up a hill covered with snow. I finally got to a house on the left, but I couldn't close the door. Just as the bear approached, he took his head off; it was a guy in a costume! He had a silly look on his face.

Bert's association was to a sexual attempt with his ex-wife. "I am often shooting blanks. I want to work things out sexually with her, but I doubt that it is possible. At least I am not lying. There's no hoax there!" I interpreted that some of his sexual acting-out was an expression of bear-like rage at his ex-wife and at me, a rage not as threatening as it was formerly to him.

During many subsequent months, we worked on Bert's rage, his disappointment in the analysis, and in the parts he had not yet worked through. I made more active interpretations of his tendency to split his views of me by referring to these times he asked me what I really thought as he faced me off the couch. This split represented his two views of me, like the discussions of the two Berts: the split between Bert with his wife and the split between Bert with O. I interpreted that he envisioned the analyst-me when he was on the couch, and differentiated this perception from the passionate, comrade-in-arms-me he saw when face-to-face with me. By this time, he understood my interpretation that looking at me provided him with the longed-for affirmation he had sought in reality: the continuing remnant of his enacting an unrealistic, expansive aspect of himself with me. He no longer required a sexualized enactment outside the analysis.

In the next-to-last year of the analysis, Bert walked in smiling: "Just call me Steichen." He had won a juried prize and was offered a gallery show. "When will this bubble burst? Like I don't deserve this. Like my mother would say, 'When will this be taken away?' I'm just a little Jewish boy from the ghetto." In childhood, winning artistic awards threatened his insecure masculinity. Now recognition as an artist affirmed his more stable masculine self.

As if prophetic, the next month Bert faced a "taking-it-all-away" crisis in his family, one that provided an opportunity to review his analytic insights and accomplishments. His daughter decided to divorce and acknowledged her year-long falsehood about an extramarital affair. Although Bert's ex-wife was enraged, Bert could empathize and reflected, "I've been there. I almost ruined my life, so let me try to help our daughter so she does not destroy hers." He offered to pay for her individual therapy.

Bert worked on his guilt in his sessions: How much had his offspring identified with his behavior and the family's inability to deal with its children's painful feeling states? (Although I did not say so, I noted an intergenerational transmission of the parents' use of disavowal. I, too, had disavowed my enactments with him.) Bert continued, "I want to bawl my kid out, but I feel like a hypocrite. I want to be a cop and say, 'I don't believe anything you are telling me anymore.' I want to threaten to disinherit if the affair continues. Let the 'shrink' be sympathetic and work out the whys and wherefores. I want to say, 'You can control your desires. It's the behavior today that counts.'"

I thought Bert seemed conscious of his conflict about how he, as a parent, "should" behave. I viewed this as a product of the analysis and reviewed our own experience in analysis. I asked, "You often asked me to tell you what to do when you were having the affair with O. One day you dogmatically proclaimed you would not go to Europe to meet O. The next day you called to tell me you were going. Do you think if I had said, 'Don't!' you would have stopped? Or would you have started lying to me?" Bert nodded.

> I am not sure how I have come from those days to here. It seems to have happened without my knowing, by osmosis. Even so, maybe I could get my kid back in control now. If I could be the father I never had, maybe it would be different. But I know I am now in a different place than those days of running off with O. As if someone is testing me, guess who called me this week? O, as well as a woman from the gym, who said, 'Take me to lunch, get me drunk, and do with me as you will.' I haven't heard from O in two years. I was not interested in either of their offers.

As the session ended, Bert faced me and with characteristic humorous repartee, as I handed him my bill for the month, asked, "What is this? Is it a love letter?" I smiled and noted inwardly his ability to seductively tease in the session without risk of enactment.

Bert's ex-wife grew skittish about attending his photography opening. Bert understood her worry that, in all his excitement, he might "stray" again. I asked if Bert thought that was likely. "No. My unrealistic fantasies these days are more about exhibiting my work in Paris." As he said this, he turned his head on the couch to look at me. "I slap my face and say, 'Bert, stop!' Then I consider maybe Sotheby's or Christie's will award me as the Emerging Artist of the Year." He kept turning to see me smile as he jokingly revealed his expansive fantasies.

The analytic work continues. Unanswered questions include: At termination, will Bert have healed enough to tolerate the loneliness of working in his studio without a continuing source of affirmation from critics, galleries, and his business associates? Is his creativity an adequate source of narcissistic supplies at age 60 when his sexualization seems of less value? Have we worked through enough of his rage at his demanding analyst, mother, wife?

Countertransferentially, I feel more positively involved with Bert, a reflection of my response to his "new" authenticity and integration as well as to the residues of my discomfort with his relationship with O. I now experience Bert's feelings as real. The con-artist aspect is gone. I also realize that I, like Dr. A, am increasingly impressed with Bert's artistic talents. In this regard, I have to be vigilant in interpreting these maternal transference aspects of "my" agenda and judgments.

Discussion

My own grandiosity was initially stimulated by my idea that I could offer Bert a "better" analysis than the esteemed Dr. A. Fearing I would lose this opportunity, I did not risk confronting Bert's anger. This was first evident in my agreeing not to charge for missed sessions. Later, following consultation with Goldberg, I began to understand my own disavowed "greatness" and how it converged with my patient's. As Bert's affair with O developed, he began increasing his alcohol consumption. I increased my unorthodoxy by not analyzing by the rules: I laundered Bert's payments for O's psychotherapy and conducted joint sessions with Bert and both of his women.

As I struggled not to be judgmental, I understood and interpreted how O affirmed Bert's grandiosity. For a while, I believed he might make a new life with her. Had I also abandoned reality in entertaining a similar unrealistic fantasy? Then his negative maternal transference took hold with O as it had with his wife. For both of us, there was no utopian other. Until I changed our financial "deal," Bert's anger had not surfaced with me. When I saw each woman with Bert, I essentially lied, by omission, about the other woman. I was enacting each side of Bert's split with him. Exceedingly uncomfortable, I was more and more aware of my own disavowal.

Just as Bert had idealized Dr. A, so he idealized me as his muse–art critic. As I recognized how my enactments (my analytic misbehaviors) served to avoid becoming the target of his anger, Bert was increasingly able to experience anger with me and tolerate his depression. He also concretizes and expresses his painful affect states in his photography rather than avoid them by sexualization. His success with this creative endeavor vitalizes and sustains him although it falls short of the initial excitement of a new affair. Without my sustaining presence or the lost wings (grandiosity) of his dream airplane, Bert's waking life at termination will be the true test of his analytic integration. Only time and his art will tell that truth.

4
chapter

The Case of Janie
A Young Woman in Passionate Pursuit

Janie's case illustrates the dynamics of a stalking perversion in a young woman. The first half of her long analysis is described, arranged to demonstrate essential principles of technique in working with perversions. There were many other issues in her treatment that cannot be recounted in this summary. As understood within the framework of self psychology, and as described by Goldberg (1995, 1999), *perversions* and other narcissistic behavior disorders are diversions, distractions to avoid painful exposures of the underlying faulty self. When the behavior disorder or perversion recedes, posing less disruption to the patient's experience of the analytic process and the selfobject tie with the analyst, other fantasies and enactments representing deeper problems in the organization of the self come to the fore to be the focus of the analytic work. Therefore, the most concentrated work with the perversion must occur at the threshold of this deeper focus on the faulty self. Janie's underlying problems concerned beliefs about her own and the other person's destructive emptiness that made an intimate connection dangerous if not impossible.

In her mid-20s, Janie was a delicate pale blonde, pretty but with a hard perfection, every hair and seam in place. A friend's analyst had given her my name but otherwise she knew nothing about me. From her appearance it was hard to believe the terrible emotionally brutal stories of her present-day life, told with little affect. Scams, deceits of all kinds, sexual seduction, orchestrated to evoke a response from whoever filled the role of the current idealized motherwoman of the moment. Beginning in kindergarten with a neighborhood woman, her life has been organized around stalking and attempting to encounter women, nearly

73

all of an age to be her mother. My own age is exactly right. The women in this series were all remote and self-preoccupied, traits she mistakenly identifies as strength. With few exceptions, they were heterosexual and ultimately unresponsive to her homosexual approaches, although for long periods Janie had unrealistic hopes of their response. She was coming for treatment now because she was trying to disengage from a particularly narcissistic, chaotic, and painfully abusive woman, and found herself again starting a relationship with a new one, a waitress in a cheap restaurant who was both seductive and off-putting. Janie believed this to be a repetitive pattern, perhaps due to some incurable flaw in herself, some inborn defect she always knew was there; her parents gave her every advantage and in no way could be held responsible. She had tried treatment once before, stopping after a few meetings because the therapist had no understanding of how awful separations were for her; at that time, her lover, one of the few women she actually had sexual relations with, had just moved out of town.

Janie had a high-paying technical job with a small company, having a certain amount of responsibility and a great deal of autonomy. She avoided going into the office, usually working at home and contacting clients over the telephone. Most days she never got out of bed and was up all night, sleeping during the day with megadoses of various prescribed and over-the-counter drugs that anaesthetized her. She reversed day and night for years, recalling her going to bed at 3 p.m. on her return home from grammar school, then to waken at midnight. She was afraid in the night, seeing "white faces" she knew were fantasies but seemed like dangerous realities. She always lived with her parents, even throughout college, until 2 years ago when she moved into an apartment in the same neighborhood.

Mother had facilitated the pattern of daytime sleeping, bringing Janie dinner in bed when she came home from school at midafternoon so she could sleep on a full stomach and not be deprived. Mother herself was often in bed, and did nothing with her life but go to the gym, then wait for her daughter, her only child and only pleasure, to come home. Mother was sweet, depressed, vacuous, and overwhelmed. Janie felt sorry for her, but hated to be with her and experienced her as cloying. Mother was depicted as being terrified of holding her as a baby, apparently never overcoming this feeling of incompetence. Nannies were hired to care for Janie from infancy through her latency years. Janie recalled one in particular, an old infirm black woman who did not talk much and sat staring out the window. Father was more vital, a hard-working and successful merchant, emotionally coarse, with an explosive temper. He directed mother and the family life, dominating mother and daughter with depreciation and loud, insistent opinions.

A lonely child, Janie had early preoccupying fantasies of being adopted and finding her birth mother, sometimes thinking she had found her in women she met. Mother spoke of Janie as so special that she was all she wanted out of life. Janie's favorite book was about an adopted girl, a story her parents read to her night after night. Janie imagined she had been adopted as a little baby because there was something wrong with her, or that her birth mother abandoned her because she was too burdensome. She was careful be helpful to the women she pursued. There were always two, one serving as "back-up" for the other primary figure. If one disappointed, she could turn to the second who she hoped would "rescue" her from the disappointment. Janie told exaggerated tales of invasive cruelty by one to stimulate rescue by the other. In adolescence, she babysat for several families; in two of these families, the mothers had become special, playing out these fantasies with her. She had manipulated these two mothers into mutual hatred; one of them was still important in her life, enacting fantasies of rescuing her from fabricated perils.

In spite of twisted relationships with older women and marginal functioning at work, Janie had a group of caring and loyal friends, most of whom she had known since childhood. Among them were several close heterosexual women, friends of her own age, and a homosexual man who also suffered with perversions. She and this man helped each other orchestrate and carry out the scams required for their perverse activities. He alone understood her fully, especially the urgency and driven nature of her sexualized longings for older idealized women. He accompanied her to our first meetings, sitting in the waiting room while she met with me.

After three sessions I recommended we meet four times a week. She was clearly pleased with my interest, but also frightened. She doubted that anyone could help or relieve her from the desperate search for the right partner, and anyway she was about to go abroad for a 2-week vacation with a lesbian lover with whom she was breaking up. She would think about it. A few days later, she had one of her close girl friends call with the message that she was leaving the next day on her trip; she couldn't make such a big commitment to treatment, but thanked me for my efforts. I felt I had underestimated her fear and called back to speak directly to her, saying I would see her however often she wished. She was surprised and pleased by my call, asking me why I called back. I responded that I always returned calls. She readily agreed to begin twice-a-week sessions on her return.

After a considerable period of treatment, I recognized Janie's perversion was organized around homosexual stalking behavior. As such, it illustrates a subcategory of a behavior disorder in Goldberg's (1995) nomenclature, defined by the presence of a vertical split in the self, and a set of preoedipal and oedipal dynamics constructed as her own "idiosyncratic narrative" of experience and development. Additionally Janie's disorder was characterized by sexualization, thus being a perverse behavior disorder. There was a pathological organization of the self around a vertical split via disavowal and denial.

The treatment of the perversion was only the first step in what was required to address the underlying faulty self, which is most succinctly described as an early developmental arrest at the point of an idealized merger with mother. The perversion and the split in the self it rests on both prevent exposure of the frail and unformed chaotic self beneath. The perversion protects against experiences of painful fragmentation or emptiness. Janie's vulnerability was primarily due to the experience of her own frightening and intense longings, resulting from a lifelong lack of parental responsiveness and particularly insufficiencies of mothering. Janie's faulty self was more a consequence of early developmental arrest than of regression from later trauma or deprivation of empathic selfobjects. Therefore, the vertical split was "deep," that is, her split-off experiences occurred frequently and were activated by a wide range of tension states, extensively compromising her adaptive functioning in reality.

In our reconstruction of her developmental failure formed over her lengthy treatment, Janie and her mother were unable to negotiate the experience of mutual admiration and spontaneous interaction typical of the normal toddler and preschool daughter–

mother dyad. This is an idealized merger experience, pushed by the development of the daughter and usually shared less intensely by mother. The little girl may playfully wear her mother's fancy high-heeled shoes around the house, ask for nail polish like mother's, and play by pretending to be mommy at work or in the kitchen. Optimally, mother tolerates and sometimes even enjoys the intrusion, but does not become invested in its occurrence to satisfy urgent needs of her own, nor repudiate or become anxious about the little girl's desire to imitate her. In Janie's experience, mother needed her admiration and attentive interest; in return mother doted on her so much that Janie felt used up and absorbed. Mother's apparent need to fill her own emptiness turned opportunities for solidifying the child's self into anxious fantasies about absorption of self into mother's needs or of destroying frail mother with her own pressing needs. Organizing the self around the vertical split was necessary to maintain any connection to mother, since direct satisfaction of her selfobject needs was not only impossible but created intense psychic disappointment and pain. Those selfobject functions associated with idealized merger phenomena were not experienced with mother, but instead were displaced into derivative and distorted attempts to engage particular nonresponsive neighborhood women. This splitting persisted into Janie's adult perversion.

During the early months of treatment, Janie described the details of her day-to-day life, particularly her attempts to establish sexual connections with three women. One was a lesbian her own age with whom she had been sexually active; she wanted to end this relationship and replace it with a new one with the waitress. The waitress stimulated her interest by a particularly penetrating and emotionally absorbing gaze—one that always drew Janie toward certain women—but the waitress was also cold and unavailable. The third woman was her childhood neighbor from babysitting jobs, an older woman with children and a man. As it turned out, all three women had two sides to them, one signaled by the absorbing and invasive gaze and the other by remote unresponsive coldness.

The lesbian partner was uninteresting, quickly discarded, and replaced with the childhood neighbor, whom Janie lied to, constructing scenarios to manipulate her into some proximity and to elicit a response. Soon the waitress exited, and I was designated the back-up when the neighbor failed or disappointed her.

Janie had revised the casting for her characteristic configuration of two idealized women, one good and one bad, now to include me as the one to whom she complained of the neighbor's indifference. She also confided the details of scams devised to present herself as a helpless victim who needed the neighbor to save her. One such scenario was of needing rectal surgery and requiring this woman to be close by her side during recovery. The neighbor was remarkably unsuspecting of this preposterous tale, and took Janie into her home to "recover." Janie was very stimulated, convinced that she and this woman would become lovers. At these moments of hopefulness, Janie felt excited and more whole. Soon, however, she was stunned with disappointment, repeating to me the details of her suffering and the woman's insensitivity. I was amazed and impatient with Janie's recurring and naive hopes, and was angry and incredulous about the woman's gullibility and apparent denial of the sexual seduction. I realized that I, too, was being positioned to play a role, the rescuer and backup who would pull Janie out of the clutches of the other bad disappointing woman. I told Janie how I felt; she was surprised and pleased that I had any feelings at all about her and her plight.

Throughout the first months, Janie was ashamed of her behavior and concerned about my reaction to her behavior, particularly the manipulative and deceitful aspects. She was convinced she was a lesbian, but wished she were heterosexual because she wanted a more normal, mainstream life, which she felt was beyond her grasp because she was afraid of men. She had dated a few times in high school, and had vivid memories of several sexual make-out episodes with a boy; when she touched his penis she was shocked at his orgasm and ejaculation, its power and violence. She wondered what I thought about her sexual orientation; she assumed I was heterosexual because I wore a wedding ring. I let her know I had no opinion about her choice, except that I knew she had unsatisfying and painful relationships with the women she pursued sexually. I was not sure she knew what a sexual relationship really was because she seemed to want another sort of connection than a sexually pleasurable one. She was relieved I was not taking an authoritarian position about the meaning of her behavior, and she was curious about my idea that she was seeking some emotional connection. This marked the start of her exploration with me into the meaning of her behavior, the beginning of the analytic work. She could tell me her worry that the sexual longing would get attached to me, that these longings were uncontrollable and repellant. In spite of this, and because we were discussing it, she grew more comfortable with me.

Several weeks before the first vacation interruption, Janie's sexualized enactment intensified. A new woman was introduced into her life, a young aerobics instructor living a *ménage à trois* existence in the home of an older woman and her husband. Again an absorbing, doting gaze from this young woman stimulated her longing, which quickly became a full-time preoccupation. As I prepared to leave for vacation, I was being replaced. Any suggestion I offered as to her feelings about my absence was brushed aside. By the time I left, the drama had escalated into situations of real danger for Janie, the psychopathic married couple possessively threatening Janie's safety in reaction to the aerobic instructor's flirtations. Janie seemed unable to stop herself from stepping into danger situations, then appealing to me for help. I was very concerned. I realized I was being led into a reaction of rescuing her from a bad, harmful woman, a familiar scenario that I was now enacting with her. I chose to tell her firmly that she was endangering her life with this affair and that she would have to stop if she wanted me to be her doctor. I would not be in a position to fix her if she got physically hurt, nor could I do my job with her emotional troubles if her life was in such danger. She took this concern of mine seriously and promised to stop seeing the aerobics instructor. As far as I know, she stopped but continued to walk or drive past the woman's home and workplace during my vacation. She also passed by my home and office building.

The stance I took with Janie about stopping the dangerous aspects of her enactment was quite important in conveying to her my involvement and firm sense of reality in the midst of her inability to consider her own realistic safety. I expressed a caring involvement directly, not in the context of an enactment outside the bounds of the therapeutic contract. The issue of boundaries was repeatedly raised and tested throughout the treatment.

After the first vacation interruption, Janie decided she was ready to come three times a week. She could never imagine using the couch; although I had not suggested it, nor had any idea it would help the treatment, she knew patients in analysis lie down and that I was a psychoanalyst. I assured her that greater frequency of sessions was desirable, but the couch or anything about the formal characteristics of analysis was not important now. She was most concerned about the prospect of developing sexual feelings for me, with the intensity of such longings proving to be unmanageable for both of us. She nonetheless felt reassured of my ability to withstand her feelings, judging by how things had gone between us thus far. It was apparent that she nearly always left her feelings outside the room, using the sessions to report events but never having feelings. In situations of intensely sad affect, for instance in telling me of a friend's grief at a funeral, Janie struggled to suppress a smile she knew was socially inappropriate. She never wept or spoke of anxiety, but experienced affect in bodily sensations such as nausea, dizziness, stomach upset, and headache. I found my experience of this phase of the treatment similar to working with a young chaotic child in several ways: in the nature of the alliance, my limit setting, and the parameters required. Janie had virtually no self-observing perspective because everything was an enactment and not recognized as fantasy. Even my own feelings about her had a quality of fantasy enactment; there were moments I experienced her as if she actually were my child. Dreams were reported rarely, when they had a quality of a nightmare and felt as traumatic fear. She made frequent demands that I respond concretely, or demonstrate that I had feelings and reactions to her. I tried to limit this to the session time but it occasionally spilled over into evening and weekend phone calls when she turned to me for help in managing her overwhelming states of fear and excitement. I listened to her and assured her that we would continue when in session together to find out more about her states. She felt she had never been taught how to live, how to recognize and label feelings or interests, how to calm herself, how to experience time as progressing and not endless when faced with frustrations and waiting, especially the waiting before sessions. I focused on telling her what I recognized about her from the process between us, and was explicit about the details of our interaction and my own observations and emotions that informed me about her affect and inner life. She felt she was being "raised" by me, that I was her parent in a way she had never known. Early on, her awareness made her feel guilty that she was "abandoning" her parents for me, having always felt that somehow she kept them alive by her involvement with them. She was learning how inadequate her parents were, particularly how sick and empty her mother was. Janie was developing a capacity to know and observe more about herself and her feelings. At the same time, she moved away from her parents both emotionally and geographically. We understood her intense wish that I be her birth mother, and her deep sadness that this was only a fantasy and could never be real.

The details of the emotional and sexual vicissitudes in Janie's relationships with idealized older women helped to construct the transference narrative. She was anxious and confused about gender—the meaning and implications of being a man or a woman—experienced concretely in fantasies about penises and vaginas. In ever-present enactment, there were two important women at any given time, one was painfully disappointing, self-preoccupied and empty, and the other promisingly strong, although still remote, and offering the possibility of sexual penetration, an invasion in quest of perfect union. When she was with the disappointing woman, Janie felt disregarded and "cut off"; when with the positively idealized woman, she felt a longing to get the woman to respond by sexually stimulating her to pleasurable sensations and orgasm if necessary. She felt herself to be a phallus that could be masochistically and disarmingly obedient, doing the idealized woman's bidding, enlivening her with pleasure, and getting inside her body. But she would be lost by absorption into the woman's body, hence her terror alongside the excitement that would destroy both of them. When with the disappointing hurtful and disregarding woman, Janie felt herself to be castrated, or disabled, which was painful yet reassuring of limits on her destructiveness. In still another way, the homosexual scenarios were an arena for gender anxiety and confusion that covered over even deeper anxieties about emotional connection. A sexual response to another woman was safe, because the other woman's lack of a phallus meant she herself could not be entered and destroyed in the sexualized connection.

As her confidence grew in my ability to tolerate her longings and negative affect, we constructed a transference narrative around her anxiety about my being empty. I might have an empty life like her mother with nothing to fill it but her, Janie, and to see that was not the case was reassuring. She was not destroying me by having a relationship with me. The heterosexuality of my life was of great interest; she imagined my husband as reasonable and kindly, unlike her father. She elaborated on many fantasies about the interior of my house, the layout of the bedrooms, and how I shared my room with my husband. The possibility of living safely and in satisfaction with a man was amazing to her; my husband could have access to my insides in a way that she, lacking a penis, could not.

Along with the construction of this transference narrative, Janie disclosed important memories of interactions, repeated for many years with her mother. In one, she was called into mother's bedroom to chat, as mother lay under the bedcovers. During their conversation, mother made rhythmic rubbing motions, which could only have been genital masturbation. Janie felt uncomfortable and wanted to leave. In another memory, Janie was awakened in the middle of the night by her mother's loud moaning. Janie ran to her side and along with father tried to rouse her from what appeared to be a nightmare. Eventually, after some effort, mother woke up, only to say she was dreaming of a man chasing and abusing her. Mother and father slept in separate twin beds in the bedroom across the hall from Janie's room, and their door was never closed. As far as she knew, her parents rarely if ever had sexual intercourse; father was disgusting and violent, mother was frightened and overwhelmed. Perhaps that was why they had only one child. Perhaps they had adopted her as an infant rather than have their own. Janie had wanted to keep her door closed, but overcame her reluctance to close it only as an older child. We understood that she enacted these configurations with me by intrusively looking in on my life.

In the transference, gender anxiety about being male or female, a male with a violent phallus versus a female with an empty vagina, were expressed as worries and curiosity about my life away from her, how I managed and indeed survived with my husband and children. Only after more than a year in treatment did Janie reveal these preoccupations and describe her usually successful endeavors to learn about me, some of which fell just short of stalking like that of the idealized mother-age women in the past. She felt very ashamed of this behavior, which she knew was intrusive and likely to be offensive, perhaps even destructive, to me. She would drive by my house, sometimes parking in front to watch, especially at night and on weekends when she believed I was home and involved with my husband and children. She went through papers in my household garbage can in the alley, collecting items that revealed details of my life. She discovered activities I enjoyed and positioned herself to watch me. I was unaware of any of this until she "confessed" after she had ceased the behavior. She felt tense excitement while carrying out her surveillance. Most of the time she was accompanied by her perverse homosexual male friend who was himself thrilled with it all.

My countertransference response to learning that Janie watched me and had gone through my garbage was similar to my reaction as a mother of a 2- or 3-year-old daughter who insisted on regularly following me into the bathroom. As with a young child, these needs would not be denied; without feeling particularly indulgent, I tolerated them as necessary and did not feel offended or violated.

Alongside the narrative content of the treatment, we paid close attention to understanding and interpreting the timing of the waxing and waning of perverse enactment with the older idealized women, which corresponded to Janie's experiences with me in the transference. Perverse enactment always intensified with separations and ruptures in her fragile sense of connection to me. At these times, it was important to explore the specific causes for her feeling that our connection was disrupted.

Although Janie wanted to feel free to pursue her own initiatives, to choose to move away from me at times, she was afraid to break our connection unless I demonstrated my intention to go after her to bring her back. When asked, "What would you do if my plane crashed?" I answered, "Your plane won't crash, it is your worry that you can't stay in the air without me there." As part of my interpretion, I mentioned a children's book about a runaway bunny whose mother had to keep going after him, reasserting that he belonged with her. This idea and my way of communicating it by alluding to a child's story made her feel safe again, as if I was treating her like my child. My manner of speaking in response to narrative content and in making interpretations, as well as allowing the enactment in the transference, were essential for assuaging anxiety and supporting her intact self. My stance of caring interest, a concrete expression of my feeling, as well as acknowledging the specific rupture, was required. No further actions or "gratification" by me were needed to repair the selfobject tie.

In 4 years, the perverse enactment with women had decreased in frequency and intensity, and was limited almost entirely to periods of weeks just before, during, and after my vacations. Her functioning on the job had improved and she had gotten a number of promotions with considerably more responsibility and income. She was sleeping during the night and active and working in the daytime, although she would still collapse into days of sleeping and staying in bed when she felt fragmented by a transference disruption. Janie felt it was time for her now to begin to come to treatment four times a week. She had decided she wanted to learn more how to be like me, to work on her concerns about being close, and her fear of men. If she were going to be close to me, she would have to see me more often because she would need me more. She wanted to have a heterosexual life and to start dating men. We spent some time discussing whether the interest in men represented her own choice to explore a different way to live, or whether it was a compliance with my choices for myself and therefore perhaps for her also. She was able to feel certain that it originated in her own initiative, but agreed that it was a problem that she might think she was being compliant at times. She wondered if she was choosing heterosexuality because it was "mainstream." She asked if I cared whether she was homosexual, and I assured her that what mattered to me was the quality of the connections she could experience with the important people in her life and that this may have little to do with their gender. It was clearly very important to Janie that she feel the choice was up to her.

Enactments in the Transference

Janie began the first day of her first four-session week with a flourish, reversing her previous choice of seating in my office that placed her far across the room from me. She sat on the couch as close to me as possible, dramatically tossing an interfering pillow aside as if to say, "Now we will get down to business." Several significant changes in Janie had altered the emotional climate of our relationship. She was more aware of her own and my affect when with me; hers was more available, although still impaired and quite variable. Her capacity to recognize her feelings with other people outside the treatment was enormously improved, as was her self-observation. She began to experience me outside

the sessions as a person with a stable presence in her life, connected to and interested in her. But these advances were often
lost when there were disruptions, particularly vacations and
breaks longer than weekends. She became painfully depressed,
especially as treatment progressed. The depression was understood as an aspect of her feeling separate from me, not being
fused with me, as she began to make her own choices. As part of
her newly increased involvement in the treatment, Janie brought
me the bag of my household garbage she had collected several
years earlier; she now told me she had been saving it in case she
someday needed it. Now she wanted to give it back to me because
it was mine to throw out. Now she hoped to get what she needed
from me in a more direct way. This portended the end of her perverse enactments with women outside the transference, which
had already decreased dramatically.

The "more direct way" Janie found to get what she needed
from me was a new form of enactment; split off but not displaced
in relationships outside the transference. It was not sexualized,
although she occasionally worried her feelings for me might
become so. These engagements were often outside the bounds
of the conventional therapeutic contract and extended beyond
the limits of the session times. Knowing that I used a computer,
Janie brought me software she enjoyed, available free to her
through the company where her father worked. She wanted to
give me something to use that we could share in our lives beyond
session appointments. My first reaction was to refuse these gifts,
based on my professional commitment to understand meanings
rather than to enact, and to keep the emotional interchanges
inside the room and within our session times. I explained this
to Janie. Although she understood my point, she was hurt, feeling I repudiated her enthusiasm for software. She experienced
my refusal as unresponsive and the treatment came to a stand-
still. Presenting me with these gifts was not only an enactment
of a "shortcut," out-of-bounds way to have a lively connection,
but also represented her need for my admiring response to her
as a person with her own initiative and abilities. My dilemma
consisted of engaging the transference while not sacrificing the
fragile gains in her self-observing capacity. Both of us had to be
aware of and responsible for this dilemma; we agreed that I could
accept her software gifts as long as we tried to understand their
meaning and the hoped-for response from me. We did as best as

we could, but at this time could see the gifts as nothing more than an evocation of my connection to her. She thought the gifts and our discussions about my learning and using the software brought a reassuring playfulness into our relationship, which otherwise often felt uncomfortably self-consciously reflective and interpreted. Another type of concrete enactment outside the bounds of scheduled treatment times consisted of phone calls on weekends and during my vacations. I continually raised for discussion her need for these calls, but we found no particular meaning to them besides her need for reassurance of my real involvement with her. I adopted a wait-and-see policy toward them.

Janie began dating, usually feeling vulnerable, frightened, and wishing for my nearby protection. A date could be an occasion for a weekend phone call to tell me of her fear and to obtain reassurance from hearing my voice. She met a sensitive man who did not insist on having sexual relations right away. They shared interests and came from compatible family backgrounds. She gradually fell in love with him, marriage arose as a possibility, and he became her first male lover. Sometimes orgasmic although initially very frightened, by the end of the first year of their relationship she was more comfortable and able to feel more pleasure. Feeling safe with him required her to control their frequency of meeting, as well as everything they did sexually and otherwise. Over time she relaxed some control and developed a pleasurable response to his spontaneity, yet continued to feel discomfort with his longing for her company and his apparently normal need for her response and love.

Although Janie's involvement with her lover deepened, a transference theme concerned a fantasy of losing me if she included him in her life. Janie was aware of preoccupying thoughts of me outside the sessions, yet rarely experienced feelings when with me. She worried lest I withdraw my interest and investment in her because her life beyond our relationship was now enriched in ways that did not concretely include me. She also worried she might stray too far from me and my protection; she felt particularly unsafe with sexual penetration. Her continuous concern about losing me intensified with vacations and other absences, when she reverted to her search for an older idealized woman, a back-up to me, one who was inevitably empty and incapable of being responsive, again enacting the old and familiar perverse scenarios. Her enactments, however, were of shorter duration than before, in that she was fully aware that they represented longings for me, and she could usually stop them. They never included physical touch, nor went beyond telephone contact. Perverse enactment no longer made her feel better, and at her most difficult moments, Janie regretted "losing" this sexualized way of expressing and satisfying her longings for a maternal connection. Even if painful, sexual enactment had provided access to discharge and temporary relief in the false hopes it kept alive. Now she had no relief or self-soothing means to help her recover from separations from me; now she had no recourse other than to collapse into bed, sometimes for days, plunged into depression and isolation. But Janie felt better and stronger in her pleasure and success with her boyfriend, and after one and a half years, she accepted his proposal of marriage.

Her engagement precipitated more longings for me, shadows of perverse solutions recurring alongside her stronger capacity to experience, observe, and describe these feelings. When she understood that her longings for me were stimulated by excitement, sexual and otherwise, she began to feel freer with her fiancé even if absent from me and from my protection. She still needed protection from his penetration, his longing to be with her, and from her own intensity, all of which felt destructive. She was frightened if I did not respond to prove I was alive, and was frightened if I did, because then I might drain her the way she imagined she could drain me. This difficult and unstable emotional balance was disrupted every few weeks by even slight changes in our meeting schedule, whether she or I initiated them, after which she spent several days having no feelings about me.

When I informed her of my plans for a week's vacation, she freely complained. I had taken too much time off lately and now she needed me to hold still while she made wedding arrangements. She was not sure what to do about being mad at me. She announced her own plan, potentially missing a week of sessions before my vacation, to attend an out-of-town performance by an idealized blues singer of almost exactly my age and similar in physical appearance. We discussed her angry, vengeful motives for her leaving, but she insisted on going ahead anyway. If I could go away, she could also; another meaning of her behavior was being like a child shutting her bedroom door on mother to claim her own private space, a privilege she could never exercise in her childhood.

Soon after her announcement, her departure date days away, Janie began to feel overwhelmed and retired to bed, leaving it only to come to our sessions. Her trip lost its luster and excitement, turned into a dreaded nearly impossible task, and she pleaded with me for help. I suggested she not go, noting that she really wanted to be with me and was perhaps frightened by having shown her anger at me for my own plan to be absent. Although she could agree intellectually, she would not cancel her trip but shortened it to miss only two sessions. She called while away to tell me about feeling overwhelmed, understood as a reaction to having left me. She said she missed me; she was too terrified to be with me, and too terrified to be without me. In such moments, I always felt frustrated by her longing and my inability to respond helpfully. She couldn't be in the same room with me when she experienced this longing, so avoided it by splitting it off and directing it to another person, in this case the singer. Alternatively, she might withdraw from her affects to an anesthetized state, or reduce me in her mind to a robotic, well-trained professional doing a job.

Her telephone calls assumed significance in our relationship, in that they allowed her direct experience and expression of affect; she dared to speak of sadness and missing me, showing it with audible sobs. These feelings and their expression were not admissible in the office with me. Janie considered these phone conversations outside the context of the treatment setting, time she got from me "as a person, not a professional" without paying for it. Only under this condition could she believe I responded to and cared for her; removed from face-to-face confrontation, we both might be more genuinely expressive and safe. I allowed the calls to lengthen, sometimes up to half an hour, even though they were burdensome to me. At last I realized I had been drawn into an enactment with her in which we had a "real life" together outside the treatment sessions, on the phone, whereas the sessions themselves remained lifeless and devoid of emotional exchange. This dynamic paralleled her split-off, affective life in perverse relationships with other idealized women, which stood in sharp contrast to the emptiness in much of her everyday life. She and I were having a relationship outside the boundaries of the conventional analyst–patient roles, with "stolen moments" of passionate affect, a shortcut to a genuine encounter, like perverse enactment.

At the conclusion of the call just described, Janie sensed my impatience to end the conversation and asked if I minded taking this time with her. She did not want to burden me. I answered truthfully that the calls had grown longer and more frequent and seemed to substitute for regular sessions, and I was feeling burdened by this form of interaction. I would charge her for the time under these conditions, and we must address this further at our next meeting.

The following sessions were absorbed by her recovery from the separation of her trip and preparation for my week away. At the end of the month, she received my bill, which included time for a lengthy phone conversation. Enraged, Janie missed her next hour and arrived the day after still angry and berating me for my insensitivity in failing to warn her of my intention to charge for the phone call. I reminded her of our discussion during the earlier phone call, which she insisted had not constituted sufficient disclosure of my decision. As we talked over her reaction, she was very disturbed by the rupture in this avenue of connection, because she believed she could not risk feeling connected to me in face-to-face encounter. This event afforded a good opportunity to insist that my receptivity to emotional intimacy with her was available during our meetings and not outside the time and space boundaries of my office. I explained that this stricture would help her, and that her phone calls were an avoidance of the treatment's good effects. She would have to experience and understand the fear about her longings for connection with me. Our confrontation led to reviewing our previous understandings about her fears of being emotional with me. She recalled frequent moments as a child being afraid of her mother's vast emptiness and helplessness, and her parents' turning away from her emotional pain—their instructions not to cry, be afraid, or be sad. She relinquished the phone calls as session substitutes, and risked showing more affect while in my physical presence.

Several months later, the problem of integrating and expressing affect as the connection she felt with me was brought into sharper focus. This is shown in the following summary of one session and the events leading to it.

The Process of a Session: Hard to Believe It's "You"

Janie came in after having missed the last 2 days and the Friday before because she had the flu. She had called the morning of each missed session to leave word of her cancellation; the first 2 days she explicitly asked me to call her back. When I did, she told me her symptoms, how sick she felt, that she regretted not coming, and worried if her illness was due to emotional factors because she had often gotten sick as a child. What did I think? I agreed she must be feeling very upset, having to miss sessions after just recovering her balance after a summertime of disrupted analytic hours. It was hard to tell if that was the reason for her flu; sometimes people just got the flu. She requested a "reality check," as if she was not sure about the potency of feelings to cause concrete and physical problems. We talked about this concern, yet she still anxiously required reassurance. The third day her cancellation message said I could call her back if I wanted. Because there was nothing more to say than we had already covered, I did not call her back.

Janie arrived looking pale, still feeling ill and light-headed. She had been alone for 5 days, refusing contact with anyone. Mother had bothered her with incessant calls about wedding details. Yesterday she wanted help to change the sheets; she called an older woman friend who refused to come and finally obtained the services of her cleaning lady. She wondered if she was really sick or maybe just did not want to get married in 3 weeks. When she decided to get married, she had been excited and happy about it, but now all that was lost, gone for months. She had the healthy side of herself then, but now for a while her sick side dominates more than before. She wondered how that changed. She knew that her fiancé was the right person for her, but maybe she was not the kind of person who could have a normal life and be married. Maybe she was only getting married to be like me and like other normal people she envies. I offered the idea, as I had before, that she lost all excited feelings about me 4 months before, when she defiantly took a trip far away to attend a performance by the actress she idolized. She missed some sessions and then felt frightened; she had planned her trip while feeling angry about my upcoming vacation, and was unable to imagine how she would feel without me. These events marked the beginning of her reluctance about marriage. She agreed that her hesitation about marriage was influenced by our relationship, a concern she would be too far away from me if she went off to get married. On the other hand, it worried her that being married and having a heterosexual life would afford us more closeness as we would share a lifestyle. It was confusing because now the therapy was the most important thing in her life yet it made her so uncomfortable. That morning she had a fantasy of falling ill in the session today, and waiting in the hall outside my office before passing out; some other doctor would help her then. It was odd, she reflected, that she wouldn't want me to be the one to help, it would be too burdensome for me, disgusting. She asked me how I would take care of my child if she got sick, what I would do. She could not imagine what that would be like. Her own mother never knew what to do for her when she got ill; her mother was helpless and just stood there. I remarked on her two disparate ideas about my involvement with her feelings—she longed for me to be totally preoccupied with her, but wanted to be left completely alone for fear of being overwhelmed—just like she felt with her mother. Yes, she agreed, her mother had nothing in her life but her child, she was empty; mother would gaze at her, especially worried when Janie was sick. Janie hated that feeling of mother wanting to crawl into her skin.

Janie then told me a dream from the night before: "I wanted some help, but this awful man came who was very frightening and dangerous. I was skating with another little girl and compared to her I was no good at it. The feeling was awful, like piano recitals as a kid, I never practiced and couldn't play." She still feels incompetent; the other girl was like my daughter who gets my response if she is sick. I wondered if she had a reaction to my not calling her the day before, after she left the cancellation message. Yes, now it was hard for her since I limited phone calls. She still felt "real" responses and feelings occur only outside the formality of the scheduled session times; it was difficult for her to believe that I really had any feelings about her unless they were outside the boundaries of session time. If I called her back, maybe she could believe I am involved with her and that there is a connection between us. She looked pained. I was aware of feeling that there was no way I could comfort her, no response I could make that would be satisfying to either of us. I told her I could see how sad she was. I felt relieved the hour was over, and I too felt tired and sad.

I was exhausted at the prospect of having finally to be connected with and take care of Janie in her regressed and infantile state, and was especially distressed with the feeling of her being inside my skin. The theme of her somatic illness presaged a major development in the transference. Her fantasy that morning of falling ill during our meeting and leaving to have some other doctor take care of her expressed her usual ambivalence about letting me know her needs. Her dream indicated two other concerns, arising as defense against the wish for my help and caretaking: I was not definitively female and might be a dangerous male caretaker, a putative reference to her fear of her explosive and dominating father. Another concern was her incapacity to be a girl with the imagined feminine charms of my own real daughter. Her fantasy and enactment of somatic illness was simultaneously expression and avoidance of her longing to absorb and be absorbed by me, an intense wish that could destroy one or the other of us were it gratified. If she was ill, I am the doctor (mother? father?) compelled to take care of her, drained by her great need; if she was ill, she is passive and helpless, safer for me because she would be too insubstantial to resist absorption. This ambivalent fantasy had been present from earliest life, when her mother and father consistently responded to her only when they thought she was sick. Mother had no idea what to do, so father took her to the doctor, a family friend, who against Janie's protest routinely administered painful penicillin shots, calming her parents.

I gradually relaxed with Janie's intense longing to be inside my skin, and became more articulate and confident when interpreting these unconscious wishes; she generally responded to my interpretations by calming down. I bristled less at her insistent questions about myself, my experience, and my personal life, and usually found a way to tell her something about myself without violating my own need for privacy. Her calls to my home felt easier to manage: they were shorter, and I was more open and direct about her unconscious wishes and about my reactions. I allowed her more access to me in a more emotionally intimate sense without loosening boundaries about session times or my privacy. There was more humor and playfulness between us.

During this change of climate, I experienced a remarkable countertransference moment, which I openly shared with Janie, that illustrates the depth of our unconscious interplay. In a Friday session, the tension of the weekend interruption pressing, we were speaking of her ambivalence about our connection, how she often could not feel it even though she knew it must be felt somewhere inside of her. She was relieved that she would not have to come to my office for 2 days, but also worried how she would make it until Monday. She could not find any feelings inside. She wanted to be inside me, as close as possible, but I would not tolerate that. Close to the end of the session, as her tension about her leaving increased, I felt increasingly nauseous and thought I must be getting a stomach flu. It is unusual for me to have an upset stomach, even with the flu. With only 5 minutes remaining, I told Janie I was feeling sick and that we would have to stop a bit early. Janie departed with expressions of concern. I barely managed to get to my trash basket in time to vomit. However ill I felt, I quickly recovered and did not develop flu; I could understand no cause for my nausea save countertransference. I understood that I was repudiating her longing to be inside of me, and at the same time enacting her intense negative ambivalence toward me at our moment of separation for the weekend; she wanted to vomit me out of her life. My own affect was split off and organized as a somatic enactment of my previously disavowed affect. This experience called my attention to the intensity of the identification between us.

I called her that evening to tell her I was fine; she was relieved and appreciative that I thought of her enough to initiate the call. The affirmation that I held her in my mind over separations buoyed her for days, and enabled her to feel calm enough to discuss possible transference–countertransference causes for my nausea. She was most worried that something bad about her had made me ill, and was upset about my idea that I was throwing her out of my body. She was able, however, to consider this alongside the other side of the interpretation: I was feeling so close to her that I identified with her own repudiation of me. She knew I had to feel connected and close to initiate the phone call to tell her I was okay. A discussion ensued, spanning many weeks, about how people knew what other people felt, how empathy worked. Could she and I know what the other feels? Did I know what she felt if she herself had no clue? Her parents never knew her feelings but thought, when she was upset, that she was physically ill. She and her close women friends can recognize each others' feelings; and she could sometimes tell what her husband was feeling, and expected him now to sometimes pay attention to her feelings, too. But it was different with me, harder and often impossible to know what she and I each felt about each other.

It was time again for my vacation; Janie prepared herself by planning an expensive trip of her own with two women friends. One was her most recent unresponsive older woman friend around whom she constructed sexualized scenarios; the other was a childhood intimate friend with whom she had a brief sexual affair 10 years before. Each disliked and envied Janie's friendship with the other; the conditions were right for Janie's typical perverse scenario of two women, one as a backup to the other in whom she had a primary sexualized investment. Janie and I considered this enactment a reaction to my leaving, and she openly acknowledged that to calm herself she was trying to make an old alternative work for her again. She thought I might be going away to get rid of her. Knowing she could reach me by phone during my absence was helpful, but not enough to stem her intense anxiety. Days before departure time, the older woman withdrew from the planned trip. Janie was upset, but after some consideration, decided to go with only one friend. She felt a bit like a drug addict without her drug, with no "crutch" to get her through the vacation. She agreed, however, that the old perverse solution might not work like it used to, because she was now too aware of her involvement with and emotional connection to me, which could not be replaced by the old "crutch."

During the vacation interruption, Janie called me once when she became anxious and afterward felt very connected again. Immediately on returning from her trip, the day before our sessions resumed, she developed the first symptoms of herpes, known to be a psychosomatic reaction. After two sessions, her illness had so progressed that she stayed in bed, missed work, and canceled the next week of our meetings.

We spoke several times on the phone. She saw her internist, who prescribed medication and advised her that the illness was stress related. She viewed her symptoms as her reaction to our interruption; her intense feelings about me had nowhere else to go now that her perverse enactment was in abeyance. To make matters worse, as she was recovering from herpes, she developed a gastric ulcer. She was quite ill, nauseous, and unable to leave her bed for many weeks except for brief periods and to attend her analytic sessions.

I thereupon made an interpretation: Janie's bowel reacted to food just as she reacted to my importance in her emotional life, a dramatic concrete expression of ambivalence presaged by my own nausea with her months ago. Her safest course was to repudiate any close contact, because if she took me/food in, she would use me/it up and thus destroy me/it. The anxiety resulting from emotional contact with me was split off and experienced in the somatic enactment about food intake and absorption: She had to vomit everything out, at the risk of starvation, or at the risk of emotional isolation from me. Since this manifestation of anxiety seemed about our relationship and the transference, and she had lost 15 pounds and was not eating the foods her internist advised, I took charge and suggested yogurt as a good beginning food, even though she had never before eaten it, and pointed out that it was a form of milk that was good for everyone. Even infants got milk from their mothers; this was what she wanted from me. I gave her a container of yogurt to take home for dinner, instructing her to taste it and eat it slowly. I meant to give her permission to eat, to take me in, and explained the meaning of my gift. I understood her fear of destroying me, of using me up, but I knew this could not happen. I was treating her like a little girl. Janie began her "yogurt therapy," calling me at home occasionally to talk about her eating and nausea. I always responded by assuring her that this was desirable, and I was available, and all her nausea and eating difficulties were a metaphor for her worries about her connection to me. Weeks later she began returning to a normal diet.

Janie's ambivalent experience of taking in some parts of me as if they were food expressed the dynamic of "taking me in" or "me taking her in." This treatment period elaborated on the earlier one, which was characterized by enactment of a stereotypic perverse scenario that can also be understood as expressing the same underlying dynamic. Splitting of affect and a concomitant split in the self were present in both periods. But in the absence of manifest sexualization in the later phase, Janie's connection to me (as a selfobject and as an object) was not disavowed, and her ambivalence and my ambivalence were consciously felt, albeit with intense but more bearable anxiety. Her increased tolerance of anxiety allowed her to experience ambivalent feelings and permitted the cessation of sexualization.

The Perverse Countertransference

My countertransferential vomiting was in response to Janie's ambivalent longing for me, expressed in her own simultaneous psychosomatic nausea. She enacted a disavowed longing to absorb, a wish that evoked my own response of disavowal and enactment. Mutual contributions to transference enactment are typical in the treatment of behavior disorders and perversions, and the analyst may learn and understand the treatment process in greater depth by giving these transference–countertransference interactions the careful nonjudgmental regard required to embrace the patient's peculiar and sometimes offensive symptomatic behavior.

Another instance of intense countertransference enactment took place several years later. The depth of my emotional connection to Janie was revealed by an upsetting interaction in which I exposed my own unconscious complementary perverse tendency, only to stimulate her stalking and invasive scrutiny reminiscent of her earlier garbage picking.

As part of notes and drafts for a lecture about psychoanalysis to be given to a small group of professionals in another context unrelated to psychoanalysis, I included material from Janie's treatment as one illustration. I felt ambivalent about the lecture, flattered by the invitation to speak, yet dreading the exposure of my work to this naïve, expectably critical, and ultimately dismissive nonclinical audience. Afterward, my private appraisal of the lecture was that it was poorly received and misunderstood; the audience thought it was "garbage," and I had not succeeded. I felt humiliated for a few days, and then recovered a cheerier perspective: I had done the best I could with a very difficult audience, and probably few could have done better. Unfortunately for the events to come, I left my notes on my computer's hard drive undeleted, including details from a recent session with Janie.

Several weeks later, in her anxiety about my being out of town for a few days, Janie offered me some new software and asked to install it. We explored her request and concluded she wanted to do this now in preparation for my absence; it was an enactment that affirmed our connection and counteracted her fantasy that the tie between us would be broken. I questioned my motives for accepting her gift, but could see no particular gain for myself; I did not really care about the software itself, and adjudged my intentions only the purest. I turned over my computer to Janie with nary a thought of the clinical material still stored on the hard drive.

At our next session she arrived with my computer, software installed, and full of anger at me for betraying her confidence.

No shrinking violet, she; no lack of awareness or expression of affect: How could I do this to her, talking about her without asking her permission?! She explicitly wanted me to know that of course she hadn't read the case notes, but she could not avoid seeing that some of it was about her. She felt used. I was stunned. I had provoked an enactment, and she was right about me using her. I grew smaller by the second and shame swept through me. After a few attempts to rationalize my misbehavior to her, I stopped and accepted the accuracy of her accusations. I apologized and said I would have to think about why I had behaved so poorly. She was calmer, but still very angry. We would meet again tomorrow to discuss it further.

When I had time alone to think I realized I had committed two misdeeds: the first, not asking her permission, which I thought she would readily give; the second, giving her my computer without erasing those files regarding her case. The second was easier to grasp. What could I have expected? Of course she would have seen it! I felt my lecture was garbage and passed it on for her to pick through. I was angry at the audience's dismissal of me and my work, but I nevertheless retained shreds of my initial idealization of these professionals as important figures in their field. After my lecture failed to please, I split off and disavowed my now shattered and unacceptable longing for this group's admiration and appreciation of my work should we meet again. These longings then reappeared in a perverse form of exposing my garbage/work to Janie. Surely she would continue to admire and respect me, unlike the audience, with all my garbage in full view. If there was anyone I knew who appreciated my garbage, it was Janie.

My first misdeed, exposing confidential material without her permission, was more difficult for Janie to understand. There is a powerful commonly held view that it is fine to discuss cases with small groups of colleagues who agree to respect the patient's confidentiality. I had forgotten that Janie "owned" the case material, and it was really not mine to share without discussing it first with her. I had violated a boundary between us in assuming ownership. Although mine was not an act of perversion, it was an enactment of a necessary condition for perversions. At the height of a perverse action, the self–other boundaries are so blurred that it no longer matters who is doing what to whom. What was hers was mine. The question still remained as to why I was in such a state to begin with. In my urgent desire to favorably impress my unfamiliar and idealized audience, I did not believe I had all it would take to impress them, so I used some of Janie's material.

Discussion

Sexualization as a Key Component of Perversion

A key issue in the study of perversions is the developmental and dynamic function served by sexualization. In the extensive psychoanalytic literature, classical theorists (e.g., Kernberg, 1967; Chasseguet-Smirgel, 1984; Glover, 1933; Arlow, 1954; Freud, 1927) who rely on libido or drive theory argue that fantasy content expresses a psychodynamic conflict relating to the child's sexual development. Stoller's (1988) explanation for perversions, although not based on drive theory, nevertheless posits aberrations in the child's gender development as the cause. A self psychological theory of perversions, proposed by Goldberg (1995), differs in that the child's experience of its sexuality or gender is not considered a primary pathogen, but a "distraction" or displacement from the painful experience of threats to a fragile and deficient organization of the self. Sexualization occurs when the patient confuses the excitement and vitality of the intact self with excitement from sexual sensations and experiences. The confusion affords the splitting off of excited pleasure–pain affects from the arena of self-development into the arena of sexual pleasure–pain excitement in the perverse behavior. The object of the pervert's sexual behavior is to protect himself or herself from overwhelmingly painful fragmentation or emptiness. Sexual activity coincides with the failure to distinguish between action and fantasy, and is often inevitable during these states.

We cannot be sure why one person becomes perverse and another manifests a behavior disorder, such as delinquency or addictions, that does not involve sexualization. Janie had been exposed as a small child to her mother's erotically stimulating and anxious sexualized feeling states, as evidenced by Janie's anxious memories of repeated occurrences. These included the open door to the marital bedroom, mother's night terrors of being chased (sexually abused or gratified?) by a man, mother's exhibitionist "hoochey koochey" dancing at social gatherings reminiscent of her younger days as a nightclub dancer, and mother's open masturbation. Mother's own ambivalent sexual longings and anxieties were confused with ambivalent longings for emotional closeness, and unconsciously communicated to Janie as a little girl. Mother's own beliefs could not serve as a corrective for the child's confusion, but could only make it worse.

The cessation of sexualization, and the end to perversion, is effected by strengthening the self, especially with improvement in or an establishment of a relationship with the analyst wherein the missing selfobject functions are provided. As treatment progressed, and Janie felt she could rely on me to respond appropriately to her longings to be with me, her perverse behavior disappeared except for times of disruption in our relationship (vacations and empathic breaches) or a misunderstanding on my part. Both sexualization and perverse behavior were relieved when we were able to identify the cause of the disruption.

Somatic Enactments

The unconscious dynamics underlying her perverse enactment were revealed in Janie's narrative about our connection, which elaborated her ambivalence about such a tie, including confusion about love and hostility, intimacy and destruction, boundaries between self and other, and her gender and mine. As her anxiety intensified, her fantasies of finding and enlivening an ideal mother were intensified, vertically split off and reorganized as enactment of a stereotyped perverse scenario of sexualized encounters with cold inaccessible women who were the idealized responsive mother she could stimulate into liveliness. Janie's dynamics illustrate Goldberg's (1995) three essential conditions for a perversion: idiosyncratic dynamic content, splitting of the self, and manifest sexualization. The decrease of manifest sexualization did not alter Janie's dynamics, in spite of the change in the associated narrative fantasies, because splitting continued, for instance in ongoing concrete enactment with disavowed affect. With cessation of manifest sexualization, according to Goldberg's criteria, the patient had been cured of the perversion, although it would always remain active as a potential within the personality organization. Indeed, Janie even after the end of the treatment phase defined by perverse sexualization, occasionally relapsed into the old sexualized scenarios with unresponsive older women.

Beyond Perversion

After 8 years of treatment, Janie had given up stalking, and was not otherwise enacting involvement with idealized but empty mother women. Longings for me were no longer split off into perverse behavior. The treatment could be focused on the deeper pathology of the self. We slowly learned more about the nature of the love and attachment for the selfobject that so frightened her, creating the terror that propelled the splitting. Strikingly similar to the disorganized toddlers as described by Main and her colleague Hesse (Main, 1995; Hesse and Main, 1999), Janie affectively "froze" in my presence. She had no feelings "in the moment," although she chattered on with stories of her day, or even described intense emotions about me felt at another time, outside sessions. Janie's now integrated and naked longing for my presence and responsive attention was accompanied by terrifying and painful fantasies of my being emotionally dead. She switched off her feelings to avoid the pain of my annihilation. There were two sides to her fantasy about our relationship when we were intimate and connected: She believed her excitement about the reunion of each session would overwhelm me in my frail or near-dead state, and I might then collapse and be unavailable to her when she most needed me. Alternatively, in my deadness, I would attach myself to her lively self and drain her of all life in order to restore and sustain my own waning existence. In either case, it was safe to approach me only if she lost or hid her own affective liveliness. This fantasy was underlying the "freezing" or affective deadness that began almost every hour. One or the other of us would be destroyed in the reunion.

For many months, Janie rarely felt connected to me in my presence. Instead, she hid collapsed on her bed for the day, depressed and barely functioning, feeling as if she lived in a different world from mine. Or, in her bolder moments, she could maintain a new sense of connection between sessions by holding onto memories of me, only to have her confidence trickle away an hour or two before the start of our next hour, when she would be faced with my actual person. In this new state of mind, Janie was able to function between sessions quite effectively and was excited to feel "normal" for the first time.

Our work shifted to recapturing that new state of mind, and learning what was required to maintain it. I repeatedly had to restore her confidence in my being alive and in my independent existence outside of whatever existence she might emotionally provide me. She always carefully scrutinized me for signs of illness, tiredness, or disinterest. Weekend and brief vacation separations were occasions for her fantasies of my deadness. We spoke of countless versions of this theory of mind: She was overwhelmingly needy, thus toxic, while I was empty and incapable of responding to her except to suck her dry in satisfaction of my own overwhelming need. Of equal utility to this interpretive work was my willingness to find meaningful objects or gestures that could assure her of my nondead state during separations. We understood together that at these times she failed to hold me in her mind, and that memories of us together were not available to sustain her. An object on my desk, a book I read, or a planned phone call during my absence kept her from falling into a deep depression that might not abate for many weeks after our reunion. Beyond all else, my ability to be sensitive and respond in action to these special needs helped to reassure her that the reality of our connection was not her fantasy of it.

Janie could not share a world with a dead mother/analyst, but tentatively began to explore a world to be shared with a strong, lively mother/analyst. She described "freezing" with the dead mother/analyst selfobject:

When you can't really show someone or tell them how important they are to you it becomes very frustrating and difficult. In fact, it's much more than that. I can't really even just go to my sessions and be *me*. I'm anxious and uncomfortable. I want to cry and I can't. I want to laugh and I can't. I want to yell and I can't. I want to smile and I can't. I want to look at you and feel at the same time and I can't. I need to look away so I do.

Underneath her frozen emotional exterior lay her emotional turmoil, revealed now that perverse enactment and splitting had ceased.

It is likely that Janie will be vulnerable to some form of a perverse dynamic for the rest of her life. Complete cessation of perversion, or sexualized fantasies and (to a lesser extent) the enactment of these fantasies, may not always occur in the treatment. Perverse enactment and other forms of splitting may always remain as retreats from the pain of the disrupted and disorganized self beneath. Janie's longing for the sanctuary of a protective selfobject was ignited by the suffering of a repeating fantasy, in which she experienced the selfobject (me/mother/ husband) as dead and unresponsive to her terror of being unsafe and alone. This self-experience is avoided by splitting.

A patient may maintain a special vulnerability to perverse fantasy or enactment during painful ruptures and separations in relationship to the analyst or other important selfobjects in their life. Treatment affords an ability to recover, when periods of symptomatic relapse are shorter and less intense as the self is strengthened. In Janie's analysis, perverse symptoms recurred, but they became less urgent and intense and she learned to recognize and manage them better. Beyond our work on splitting and perverse enactment, Janie's analysis required still more work once her perversion was understood and dissipated. Patients with complex and entrenched perversions and behavior disorders have a self with more frailty and faults than most other patients, and require a lengthier and more personally demanding commitment from their analysts. This notwithstanding, the work is richly rewarding with deep personal satisfaction that comes of a lively and loving connection with a fellow human being in great distress.

5
chapter | # The Case of Peter Stone
A Case of Compulsive
Masturbation

This clinical report illustrates the treatment of a man with a narcissistic behavior disorder at the healthier end of the spectrum. Peter Stone used compulsive, ritualized masturbation accompanied by a preoccupation with pornography that displayed women with large breasts. Images of women on paper, on celluloid, or in his mind's eye were required to arouse him. A stable mirroring selfobject transference developed in the course of his analysis and his symptoms were experienced in the vicissitudes and working through of this transference. With increased internal structure and integration, Stone's symptoms diminished, reappearing only when the selfobject functions of the analyst or other selfobjects were unavailable to him.

Peter Stone was a 41-year-old divorced man who requested a referral for psychotherapy for impotence from his girlfriend Thea's therapist. Thea was fixed neither on his penis nor his erections, nor had any need that Stone get "fixed"; Stone was therefore more aware of feeling "not right" with himself. I credited both Thea's lack of pressure for Mr. Stone's inability to focus on his erection as *the* (or her) problem, and his nascent depression for bringing him into treatment. His chief complaint however, was his inability to achieve and/or maintain an erection for intercourse, speaking of masturbation as an occasional aid to relieve continued sexual frustration caused by impotence with his girlfriend. During our first diagnostic sessions, I thought that his sexual difficulties might be related to an inability to experience and/or tolerate sexual excitement, perhaps any excitement, in the context of a relationship. He presented with other vague complaints and seemed to have little energy (drive, I wondered) for sexual activity.

Peter Stone had been in treatment off and on from the age of 18 when, at the end of his first year of college, he began psychotherapy. After graduation, he sought an analytic consultation and was referred for a low-fee analysis. He had a 4-year analysis as a control patient, and terminated because his new job required frequent travel. Six months after termination, he returned to his analyst who told him that resumption of the analysis was impossible because he (the analyst) was leaving the city. Stone could not now recall either why he terminated the analysis or wanted to resume it. Shortly after his analyst moved, Stone married a woman he had known only briefly. He now believes this marriage was an effort to replace his analyst but he felt unseen and unheard in his marriage, which ended in divorce after 3 years. Stone agreed to my recommendation of twice-a-week therapy to understand his relationships with woman and the place of sex in these relationships.

Stone grew up in an intact, upper middle class family and community. His father, a middle manager, was busy, distant, and uninvolved in his son's life until Stone began to play sports at age 8; father, an avid athlete, was his coach and monitored every aspect of his play. Stone provoked his father/coach by play so lackadaisical that he appeared to throw games away, letting his opponents have control; but he also wore them out and ultimately won. He felt cool during his games and did not permit himself to get too excited. He experienced his mother as exciting, volatile, and given to loud rages; she criticized and denigrated the whole family. Stone felt he had to "manage his mother" and was exquisitely aware of her mood. He thought she required him to manage her affects and to "quiet her down." His mother entered treatment after Stone finished college, too late to be useful to him; he felt intruded on and annoyed as though her treatment was only an effort to be close to him.

Stone had a variety of traumatic medical procedures as a child, including one, at the age of 4, to enlarge his urethral meatus and increase his urinary flow: a likely locus for the overvaluation of his penis and his experience of women as preoccupied with his penile functioning, although he never knew the details of the operation or if it was medically necessary. He had back and leg braces for scoliosis, and orthodonture for crooked teeth. He felt as though he were not good enough for his mother and was being made over, bit by bit, in order to please her and to be perfected for her. Now he felt unable to proceed with his life until he got "better, perfect, unflawed," and he was waiting for this to happen before he could "get on with it."

Stone was an athletically built, well-dressed man, easily affable and charming. He worked at a consulting firm. The nature of his intimate relationships, including my own experience of him, was elusive and had a distant quality. I did not quite understand what he did for a living (fantasizing that he worked for the CIA), but soon understood that his secrecy veiled his psychological being, rather than the nature of his work. There was an "as if" quality to his relationships, including his early relationship with me. My response to him was, not surprisingly, split. I found him attractive, charming, and appealing, and unconsciously colluded with him in thinking that he just had problems finding and relating to the right woman with whom to build a life. At the same time, I resented feeling kept out, not permitted to know all parts of him, and distrusted the "CIA."

Face-to-Face Psychotherapy

During two and a half years of twice-weekly therapy, Stone enjoyed access to my face and to my reactions to him, in contrast to his previous analysis. He spoke appreciatively of my presence, my responsiveness, and my energy in the room. He acknowledged masturbating as an occasional activity and wanted my support for it as an understandable replacement for sex with his girlfriend. He directed at least some of my attention to his penis and thereby kept himself from feeling too depressed. He began to achieve and maintain erections, and to enjoy orgasms in nonintercourse sex. He felt increasingly comfortable in mutually satisfying erotic activities with his girlfriend. He was sensitive to anything perceived as criticism of him or the nature of his sexual activities. When Stone and Thea broke up, he began seeing Lara, a woman slightly older than he, and neither as attractive nor as obviously sexually appealing as most women he had dated. His choice of her was influenced by his fantasy that I wanted him with a more matronly Jewish woman and not with the "golden haired *shiksa*" of his dreams. He felt deprived of something he needed and wanted. Lara, after all, was a "real" woman with small breasts and not the beautiful sexy woman he desired. At first her flaws provided him with an excuse for not possibly finding her sexually arousing and maintaining an erection with her. Over time, however, their relationship grew more serious and Stone could, albeit intermittently, maintain erections for intercourse with her. She was preoccupied with his penis and his sexual performance, and wanted Stone to pursue medical intervention. Stone also became more preoccupied with his penis and less depressed.

Peter Stone joined a men's group to do psychologically oriented "growth work." He experienced himself as the group's facilitator, offering exercises and helping other people do their "work," even though he rarely "worked" or exposed himself, except during a cathartic session of screaming or weeping wherein he felt literally held by the group, no member of which seemed alive in his descriptions. He liked to "do exercises" with a woman psychologist, a past lover that evolved into eroticized play. Although I realized my own competitiveness with him when he played therapist, he seemed unaware of his identification or competitiveness with me. He was so sensitive to any perceived disapproval on my part or even a lack of sufficient appreciation and admiration for his "exercise" ideas, that I wondered what he brought to this group that he could not yet bring into his therapy. He was comfortable with "exercises" because they limited the possibility of spontaneous interaction; too much unstructured stimulation was dangerous.

Early on in therapy, Stone resumed piano lessons with his childhood piano teacher, a 70-year-old woman who, he believed, loved him. He bought a good piano commensurate with his self-perceived ability. Why now, I wondered, because as a child he stopped taking piano lessons when they interfered with athletics. Was this a revival of a less competitive exhibitionism that gave him pleasure in his abilities and provided a woman coach who cared about him as a person and did not see him as part object? Comfortable with his exhibitionism in this arena, he enjoyed both solitary practice and, with only slight self-mocking, the recitals his teacher held for all her students, 5 through 55 years of age. He very much wanted me to hear him play but could not bear the thought of my watching him at a recital because it might be too stimulating. He resolved this dilemma by bringing a tape recorder and tape of his piano playing to a session. Although I interpreted both his fear of humiliation in "showing his stuff" and his wish to be known and admired by me, I wondered whether he was playing the siren's song to distract us from his grandiose fantasies and depression, or perhaps I too was using him for his accomplishments? I gave him permission to play the tape in his therapy hour since the recording seemed as valid a communication as anything else he might tell me; it seemed to be a request to be admired without being taken over by my needs. What he did not tell me at the time was his elaborate fantasies of greatness as a pianist and, indeed, in all ways. This enactment served a variety of functions, enabling him to enjoy his accomplishment in the context of the transference and to see me enjoying him without having to deal with my entering or intruding on his "real" life. I only later saw it as a request for total acceptance for whatever he produced, including masturbation and its accompanying fantasies.

Stone was concerned that he had not been promoted as rapidly as most people at his job level. Specifically, he did not understand why he had not yet been made partner and what this boded for his career. He felt in need of mentoring and searched for someone to fill the role; he wanted to use me as his "coach." His potential paternal transference seemed to duplicate the most intimate, though complicated, interactions he had had with his father; it may also have been an early attempt at an idealizing transference. He changed jobs and was promised an early promotion to partner.

A crucial and complicated interaction (probably an enactment) occurred after 12 months of treatment. As is my custom when patients complain about sexual functioning, I suggested that Stone consult a urologist to rule out physiological reasons for his impotence (an enactment of his mother's concern with his penis that I then understood as my responsibility). I did not push him when he dragged his feet but I encouraged him to explore his reluctance to pursue a consultation for such a troubling symptom (unaware as yet of his use of masturbation). He received a letter from an ex-girlfriend who had just been diagnosed with human papilloma virus (HPV), writing not because she had caught it from him, but because she might have transmitted it to him; she thought he needed to be checked, both for his own sake and the sake of any partner. At his request, I explained the examination to him, and he realized that, although HPV was of little threat to his own health, it might be more serious for a female sexual partner; Thea was already on immunosuppressant treatment for a chronic illness.

Stone did not want to be examined by a urologist because he feared a humiliating and frightening experience. When I asked Stone about what obligations he felt to Thea to protect her from exposure to HPV, he was enraged. I had become Brunhilde, a mythical, powerful woman who defended women at the price of men; I was now a supporter and crusader for women; my sole investment in his therapy was to make him over, so he could be a better partner and lover for a woman, perhaps even for myself, but not for his own sake. He then disclosed for the first time that he also had herpes, and, although he was careful about examining himself for outbreaks, he had told neither Thea nor other partners about it. He did not like using condoms because they interfered with his precarious erections, so he did not offer partners that protection.

This announcement seemed to be his way of including me in his dilemma and an indication of his desire for two very different responses from me. He wanted me to understand that he "needed" to conceal these potential dangers to women. I understood him to say, "Support me in my denial that any other person has any kind of rights or claims on my behavior, in my belief that I can do anything I need or want to do to sustain myself, especially if my potency is endangered and I face the possibility of humiliation and shame." At the same time he was saying, "Help me deal with the kind of person I am and want to be, with my ego ideal versus how I conduct myself, because this behavior is not in keeping with my values and my sense of myself." I did not consider this justification merely an effort to please me but an expression of a deep division in himself. In retrospect, this may have been the beginning of a request for help in dealing with differently motivated parts of himself, that is with a vertical split.

I have conveniently left myself out of the aforementioned dilemma. I did not feel neutral in this complicated interaction, but empathized with Stone in his needs, fears, and struggles. I have treated women who contracted HPV and underwent medical procedures entailing a good deal of pain and fear, and I have treated immunosuppressed people who were justifiably frightened about the risks of infection. I was unambivalent about how any decent person would respond, and no dilemma, moral or otherwise, presented itself. I thought he should have a medical examination and share any pertinent information with his lover. I was horrified to learn that he had herpes and did not use condoms or inform his partners, but rather deemed his own efforts and standards of care sufficient. I wanted to confront him with his grandiosity, his self-centeredness, and his deplorable behavior. I wanted to educate him as to how decent people behaved. Needless to say, I did not, but I must have communicated my shock and disapproval.

But Peter Stone needed me on his side and he wanted me truly to understand the shame, humiliation, and terror engendered by a doctor's examination of his genitals in search of disease; he simultaneously wanted me to believe in him as someone who was capable of caring about another. I understood and empathized with this, and so developed a vertical split of my own. To complicate matters, my inability to identify with his disregard for others was matched by my identification with his wish to break rules and do what he felt he needed to do. I could not imagine myself singing the words to his song but I could hear myself whistling the tune. Only later would I struggle with my own grandiosity, my own wish to get away with something in this analysis.

Stone had learned the language of conflict psychology in his previous analysis and understood his problems in oedipal terms. His difficulty with erections and intercourse with a desired woman, he believed was the equivalent of an oedipal victory over his inadequate father. His relationship with his mother was charged with a high level of passion including rage and excitement; his aggression was too frightening to him. Thus, he engaged in a variety of conscious and unconscious maneuvers to remain impotent and thereby keep his anger contained. This made him less successful at work and inhibited with women, but did keep his aggression out of his awareness or at least under control. The theory appealed to him but did not cover all the bases and had not provided all he needed.

Stone thought that if he resolved all his conflicts, everything would be smooth sailing. On entering his first analysis, he fantasized emerging from it with no buttons left to push. He would end up with an absolutely smooth surface from which any possible disruptions had been sanded away. According to his fantasies, he would never react to anything; he would enter the analysis as a larva and emerge from his cocoon as a beautiful butterfly. In the current analysis his chrysalis metamorphosed into the "most perfect beautiful butterfly that ever existed." He was ambivalent about his goals for this therapy. Did he still want the smooth surface or a wider range of feelings and responses to safely experience?

Conversion to Analytic Treatment

After two and a half years of therapy, Stone announced his desire to lie on the couch for his sessions. After lengthy exploration of the idea, we agreed that the treatment had to that point been productive, with beneficial changes in his life and, seemingly, in how he felt about himself. In spite of the benefits, however, he wanted to do more, to reveal more of himself and to develop a new relationship with me by using the couch. Having just begun analytic training, I was not yet ready for another control patient; nor, in point of fact, was I ready to analyze him. I felt seduced and pushed, seductive and eager, hardly an ideal way to begin an analysis. I hoped my request to start a private analytic patient would be approved; I did not want to act without permission, but I did not want to turn away an appropriate analytic patient or to say no to Stone. Hesitant and excited, I agreed to begin and he, in turn, fantasized both his seducing me and my seducing him into the analysis, and hoped it would make him really special to me. (It did!) He wondered how he would compare to my other patients. He assumed, by placement of a chair, pillows on the couch, that I was analyzing other people, and he wanted to compete with them for my attention and admiration. He was not sure how many analytic sessions per week he wanted. I countered that I had no experience using the couch twice a week and thought it made more sense if he came at least three times a week, yielding sufficient time to deal with whatever had motivated the shift and emerged in the analysis. We started at three sessions per week with the shared expectation that we would soon move to four.

Almost at once, Stone accepted a new job necessitating frequent overnight travel a few days every other week. This schedule threatened to play havoc with the predictability, reliability, and orderliness of the analysis almost before we began. I did not yet know how crucial these three qualities would be to Stone, but wondered if an analysis could be conducted under these cir-

cumstances. I did not know if and how he was using his schedule as an escape valve or to titrate contact, or as a conscious or
unconscious test of my commitment to him, of how special he
was to me and how willing I was to show it. The change in his
schedule reminded me of his first analysis and its never understood premature termination. It seemed that this analysis might
be aborted before it ever really started.

Without a firm grasp on the specific transference meanings of
these transactions, I believed it an enactment of his seduction with
women: "Here I am, I want an intense experience with you, but
now that you want it too, I cannot, will not perform," and said,

> How did you imagine that you could simultaneously com-
> mit yourself to an analysis and travel frequently? Part of you
> wants to be here to do the work you wish to do, and at the
> same time you are fearful that, as we begin this work, it will
> stimulate feelings in you that will be difficult to manage with-
> out needing to flee.

My question grounded a reality dilemma in a complicated
metaphor, yet also made him address his split motives. He realized that he both wanted and did not want to make a major commitment to an analysis and actually contemplate changes in his
life. He wanted me to show my appreciation of what he was
attempting, of how special he was, by accommodating his schedule to make an analysis possible; it was also a request to accommodate his grandiose fantasy of being in two places at once.

I said that I would do whatever I could to make the analysis
possible. Not only could I tolerate change and disruption in my
schedule at very little personal cost, but my schedule was also
more my own than it had been for many years as my home office
afforded me easy flexibility. In addition, my own grandiosity
cheered me on! "Of course you can." We scheduled office sessions that adhered to ordinary business hours, some at very early
morning hours before he left for the airport, some evening hours
on the way back from the airport, some sessions on the phone,
and occasional sessions on the weekend. He agreed to pay for
his sessions even if he missed them, a proposal perhaps to pre-
empt a source of anger or tension between us, perhaps also to
legitimize his claims on me. Stone was pleased at my willingness
to accommodate to him.

The Analysis

As we began, he reminded me that when he was a control patient, his analyst had a supervisor. He imagined that I would not be supervised because he did not come via the clinic, and he did not want me to get consultation, which, in fact, I had already sought. My consultant understood that I experienced an exciting, illicit quality to beginning this analysis that resonated with Stone's own elusive, withholding demeanor. In spite of the complications, my consultant was supportive of my beginning this analysis. I asked Stone what my having a consultant meant to him. He wanted to be alone with me, with no one watching. When he asked me directly if I was planning to talk with someone about him, I chose not to lie or hide behind analytic silence, and cited my clinical and ethical comfort for my decision, wondering aloud why he would want to keep me from having what I needed to provide him with the best possible treatment. My having a consultant may have muted his fantasy of the perfection of our venture and the intensity of our mutative impacts on each other. The existence of a consultant reminded both of us that our grandiosity had some bounds. Stone agreed to my continuing consultation. Periodically, an image of a consultant arose in the analysis, usually as a benign presence in a dream.

In response to his explicit and implicit requests, I became quieter in the room and he became clearer about what he wanted from me. All his previous wishes that I react to, interact with, and enliven him were gradually replaced by his wish for my total and perfect responsiveness. He wanted me to listen, see, value, admire, and acknowledge him for who he was; he didn't want me to interpret, comment, question, or disrupt him. He experienced almost any intervention, including interpretation of these "orders" as a mini-rupture. He wanted me to stop wearing colorful clothing and wear only plain beige garments and white cloth shoes, wear no make-up or jewelry, have no facial expression, and make no noise of my own, responding only to him. In the clash of our grandiosities, his, of necessity, overrode my own.

At the risk of oversimplifying the treatment, I would like to give an overview of the first 2 years of the analysis and then present two events in detail. Stone now revealed his more than 20-year preoccupation with frequent compulsive masturbation, his reliance on his extensive pornography collection, and his ritualized sexual fantasies. He no longer justified his compulsive masturbation as merely a healthy outlet for a physical discharge but as an activity by part of himself wherein he frequently lost himself. He masturbated as much as three times a day, often unable to focus at work, distracted by elaborate sexual fantasies. He was careful and secretive about his behavior. When at work, he masturbated behind locked doors and had never been caught. He began masturbating when he was about 4 years old; he achieved soothing sensations that felt like orgasm, even though he could not ejaculate until 10 years later. Masturbation assuaged his loneliness when his mother yelled at him or left him. When he felt bored or out of sorts, he masturbated; when he felt lonely, depressed, or "dead," he masturbated. He found himself disengaged from situations without even realizing what prompted him to disengage and masturbate.

Having exposed his heretofore secret paraphilias, his desire to stop, and his feelings of "keep your hands off my perversion, it is what I need to function," we still did not know if he was more interested in ridding himself of his symptom and its accompanying shame and loneliness, or in getting me to give it a kosher stamp of approval. Different parts of him seemed to have different goals for the outcome of his analysis. He wanted to understand and deal with the symptom and what it protected him from, and simultaneously feared to experience its loss. Stone wanted to marry and have children, and pursued this aim by dating, courting, and attempting to get close to a woman. But he protected both his isolating masturbatory activity and his overriding aim of shielding himself from his depression. He felt deep shame not only about his masturbation but also about his obsessive fantasies and altered self-state. Because his symptom was private and did not involve anyone else, it was somewhat easier for me to remain "neutral" about it. Different parts of me joined with him to want different things for him. At times I joined his grandiose fantasy and thought, "He is right, he is fine, perfect just the way he is; then again, he can be so much more and I want that for him." There were moments when I silently protested, "So what, what's the big deal, his symptom isn't so terrible, he isn't hurting anyone, and he has not been able to stop or alter this behavior for 20 odd years." At still other times I thought, "This is just the tip of the iceberg, and until he figures out a better way of regulating his internal tension states, his excitement and his grandiosity, he is going to be vulnerable to depressions and not feel whole, or, in his words, 'healed.'" I often had to remind myself that he came to analysis willingly and was not being forced by anybody to give up anything.

The analytic schedule began as Monday, Wednesday, and Friday. Stone experienced each separation as disruptive and a break in the connection. The weekends were even harder, for then he felt disconnected from himself as well as from me. He often masturbated after leaving appointments; he masturbated on Saturday nights about midnight, only to realize that this was the midpoint between Friday's and Monday's appointments, and described it as "just finding myself thinking about women with large breasts and then masturbating." I made repeated interpretations that focused on his need for continuity, his experience of the disruptions, and the absence of connection to himself and to me between the sessions. To repeated interpretations of

> when there is a disruption in the sessions you feel lonely and isolated, and you masturbate to avoid feeling alone and depressed because our connection is broken. You were anxious that you would not be able to manage these feelings and so turned away from the feelings to a different part of yourself and masturbated. You are relieved that you have this way of soothing yourself but you are left feeling disconnected from your own feelings of the longed-for connection to me,

he responded that he felt he wanted to stop compulsive masturbating yet felt he needed it, and did not want me to deprive him of this source of comfort and pleasure: "You want me to give this up so that you can have me the way you want me, make me perfect for you." I interpreted that he did not remember if we were doing this for him or for me, that he was not sure whom this analysis was for, him or me; at times he felt that his pornography and his masturbatory fantasies were essential for his survival, and yet he felt masturbation interfered with and obliterated his ability to feel and participate in the rest of his life.

As a stable selfobject transference evolved and as the mirror transference intensified, Mr. Stone became more symptomatic when he experienced ruptures in it. He sexualized in response to empathic lapses and breaks in the treatment, just as he masturbated when others had failed to respond. I offered several bridging interpretations:

> When you felt I didn't understand your excitement, you felt abandoned by me, and you felt depressed, so you masturbated to feel better. When you felt I didn't share in your pleasure at your accomplishment or understand your need for my response to you, you felt isolated and masturbated to feel more intact and not so alone. When there are disruptions because of the missed sessions you sometimes feel depressed, "dead" and masturbate to feel more alive.

He realized he was becoming more depressed, frightened by his depression's potential depth, and anxious about being able to tolerate it. I too, was concerned about the depth of his depression. Some years before he had an unsuccessful trial of a specific serotonin reuptake inhibitor (SSRI), which neither of us thought was indicated here, but we both wished he did not have to bear these feelings. Even as I understood that his depression was a necessary part of the analysis, I wished he did not have to feel so bad and had fantasies of making him smile.

The analysis that increased his depression also made it more tolerable and less overwhelming. At the end of some hours, particularly on Fridays, he started to feel an empty depression, and then entertained erotic fantasies or masturbated right after the hour as an escape from it. He revealed his awareness of the sustaining nature of the sessions, of how removed from himself he felt outside of the analysis, of how alone he felt, and his increased commitment to the analysis, in his request for a fourth hour. He felt he was holding out on me the way he did with other women in his life, that he was not making a full commitment, that he was "getting away with something." He felt as though not making a full commitment to his analysis was equivalent to not giving his girlfriend his sexual passion or his erect penis. I, too, felt that I was "getting away with something" because I was conducting an unapproved analysis. My sense of wrongdoing, and the fear and pleasure that accompanied it, were greater than the deed warranted but they increased my capacity to identify and empathize with Stone's need to get away with something. He added, "When I get away with things, I feel I deserve to get special treatment because I am special but then I don't feel seen or known." I interpreted this to mean that if I accepted him exactly as he was, he would not feel seen or cared about, but if I expected anything else from him, he would feel I had intruded on him. He feared that the fourth hour would reduce his maneuverability and leave him less room to hide, and wondered again if I were seeing a consultant. I ventured that he was afraid that his needs were becoming unmanageable for me on my own, just as he felt his needs were unmanageable for him on his own.

Peter Stone reported that when he experienced me as holding onto an image of him or when he felt that I could sustain a sense of his feelings and see him as a whole person, who not only needed to lose himself in erotic fantasy but also wanted to focus on other aspects of his life and accomplish other things, then he could also maintain this experience of himself. If I could see him the way he wished to be, then he would also be able to maintain this sense of himself. He said, "I come to analysis to experience myself, I don't come to establish a connection to you, that just happens." When disruptions caused by travel or weekend separations or a break in the selfobject transference prevented him from experiencing himself, he felt lonely, lifeless, and dead, and bought pornography, masturbating to obliterate painful feelings of being alone. In the perverse enactment of masturbation with pornographic images of large-breasted women, Stone was redirecting and sexualizing his longings for my maternal responsiveness to his potent specialness in the form of his erect penis. I interpreted this as: "When you feel disruptions in our sessions, you feel less connected to me and to your self, and feel the need to masturbate so that you do not have to feel these longings." After one such experience and interpretation, he began to sing a song that just came to mind, "Ain't no sunshine when she is gone, a house just ain't a home when she's away."

One day, Stone made a presentation to a client group and was elated by their reception of his proposal. Later on, alone, after the meeting, he fantasized about taking over the company because he and his ideas were so terrific. He had a few free hours, felt antsy, and did not know what to do with himself. He went to a shopping mall to get "fresh air and a walk" but "found himself" in an adult bookstore purchasing a pornographic magazine, which he brought back to his room, where he masturbated. A few "lost hours," later, he could not understand how he moved from the pleasure of the meeting to masturbating in his hotel room, from letting himself "be out there to hiding in my hotel room." While reporting these events later in a scheduled phone session, he began to "know" how excited he had felt. I interpreted that he felt unable to sustain and manage his excitement after the meeting ended and sexualized it; he could neither safely enjoy nor sustain the fantasy of being important, and became grandiose, then depressed in its wake. Over a weekend he sat down to practice at the piano and had fantasies of being a famous concert pianist. He went for a walk, again returned home with pornography and masturbated. I interpreted that his fantasies of greatness as a pianist had been overstimulating to him and he sexualized it as a way of managing his longing for a response. He feared that a voice, internal or external, would humiliate him for these longings.

After 18 months of analysis, Stone explained his two entirely different varieties of sexual fantasies. They were perhaps another representation of his split and denoted two different senses of himself and different sets of values. In one, which always accompanied masturbation and brought him to orgasm, he is seduced by one or more beautiful women with "big tits," women who focus entirely on him and respond to his sexual potency. Using pictures of a college girlfriend, videos, and magazines for stimulation, he lacked all ability to fight the women off or pull himself away. Often, several women competed for him and the victor, the possessor of perfect breasts, was rewarded by his orgasm. We could view this seemingly active fantasy as a passive fantasy in which woman vie for him but then use him sexually. Subjugated but not humiliated by his enormous arousal and desire in this hypnotic, trance-like state, he had no will to, or interest in, stopping this behavior. When he felt that he was doing something wrong—"I should not be masturbating, I don't want to do this, I don't want to have to tell my analyst"—he grew even more excited and focused on his orgasm. He reminded me that I should never discount the pleasure of an orgasm as a powerful reinforcer!

Peter Stone had a second set of fantasies in which he seduced and/or gave pleasure to a woman. More "romantic," less ritualized, and not masturbatory, the fantasies boast a wider range of plots: A woman needy, depressed, frigid, abused, maimed, a survivor in some way, has never been able to feel sexual pleasure, love, or appreciated the way she wants to be, or to trust a man. He meets, rescues, and satisfies this woman, the only man who can bring her to orgasm. His motives are pure: altruism, not masturbation, fuels this activity; he assumes the role of the focused and responsive partner usually filled by large-breasted women in the masturbatory fantasies. As he described, "I am with this woman the exact way she wants me to be, you know, the way you are with me." These were compensatory active fantasies in which he was in control.

Stone often seemed to be saying, "Look at me, see me." When he reported an achievement and I responded to that aspect of him, I invariably made an error, because I saw only a part of him whereas he wanted me to admire a part of him and look at all of him simultaneously. When I interpreted this dissatisfaction with my responsiveness, his associations were to his family. He felt his mother had overvalued his body parts and viewed him as a part object; she had focused on his teeth or legs or spine that was not perfectly straight, and she had brought his penis into permanent focus because his urine stream was not how she wanted it to be. He felt his father was unable to see him as a whole person and saw him only as an athlete, whereas his mother was so blinded by her own narcissism that she too was unable to see him.

Stone's life changed significantly outside the analysis. He was teaching more and training more as part of his job and teaching at a local graduate school. His special interest was in teaching senior staff how to mentor younger staff (an identification with his analyst? a wish for something I failed to provide? a sign of structuralization or the transformation of narcissism?). He became active in organizations supporting young people in their musical and athletic interests, two of his own talents. He bought his first home, a studio condo in the same building as his girlfriend Lara, an elegant compromise solution for his ambivalence about living together. He was hurt and angry when I suggested that it might also function as a place where he could masturbate in private. The condo seemed to be a geographic representation of his split: they had sex in her apartment and he masturbated in his studio. He did not plan or anticipate his masturbatory visits to the studio; sometimes when there for another purpose, he found himself masturbating. After the relationship ended, he began to look for a more comfortable home for himself, one for both parts of him. He bought his first new car, drove up one day to my office, and said he had something to show me outside my office door. His tone led me to worry that he had driven into the bushes or destroyed something, but he was simply very anxious that I look

out and admire his beautiful new car. I was reminded of his bringing his piano recital tape into the treatment, and interpreted that
he wanted me to know how successful he was and how pleased
he felt with himself.

During the first 2 years of his analysis, Stone's masturbation
and reliance on pornography decreased as the regularity of the
sessions and the reliability of the selfobject transference stead-
ied him. He grew increasingly depressed, however, and experienced this depression largely through the vicissitudes and
working through of the transference. We had a private joke, a bit
of dark humor, utilized when he felt awful. He would say, "When
I came into analysis and I told you I was doing it because I wanted
to know and feel my feelings, these were not the feelings I was
talking about; could we please move on to the good feelings I
had in mind."

Ruptures in the Selfobject Transference

I offer here two examples of failures in the selfobject transference
and Stone's responses to them. The first event occurred in the 15th
month of the analysis. Stone requested a weekend appointment
because he was out of town and had missed his Friday hour. I
scheduled a Sunday morning session. Early Sunday morning, he
left a message on my answering machine reminding me that I
should have moved my clocks forward an hour for daylight savings time; he announced he was calling to preclude my greeting
him in my robe and slippers. On arrival he remarked that I was
more dressed up than usual, to which I replied, perhaps defensively, "Not in my robe and slippers." He expressed his fear of
surprising me by coming "early" because of daylight savings time,
his pleasure that I could accommodate him, and his anxiety about
his request. He felt I had made the time available because, "You
appreciate my overcoming incredible internal and external obsta-
cles to accomplish an analytic program." He had felt special, an
exception, the first and only person I would see on a Sunday, but
he had seen another patient leave my office and realized he need
not have worried about my figuring out the time change.

He observed that I was dressed up, yet felt I had done so not
for him but for a "real event" that would follow our session. This
was an association to both his mother and to an early hour in the
first year of psychotherapy, a quintessential summer's day. He

had noted then that I was more dressed up than usual, not in my customary sandals but in hose and high-heeled spectator pumps. He had a powerful memory of his mother, dressed in similar shoes, kissing him good-bye and leaving him for the day with a "summer girl." He felt he could almost smell the day and his mother's perfume, and he cried. His present reference to a painful memory suggested that he was reexperiencing a painful sense of abandonment and isolation, but we did not understand why it had appeared at this moment. He said he felt good that he had declared himself about his desire for a make-up hour on Sunday; he was not going to let daylight savings get in his way, even if he was afraid I might change my mind and take the appointment away. I asked why he would think I did not realize it was day-light savings time. He spoke of being angry with others, and I wondered if he was angry with me. He agreed. I did not realize and appreciate what a good, smart boy he was. As he talked of his energy "floating away" and feeling as if he were going down two roads, his liveliness diminished. (Was this the split before our eyes?) He described himself as a small, helpless, abandoned little boy and a furiously angry man who wanted to sink his teeth into something, and wondered if he should be more "in the swamps" with me, if the treatment should be more about anger and sex, wet and dirty, and not so nice. It was the end of the hour and I was confused. I commented on the emotional shift at the end of the hour but I did not understand what happened.

Monday (the next day), he called to say he would be a few minutes late and announced that a part of him was trying not to be there. On Sunday afternoon, after his session, he had felt exhausted and taken a long nap. He then stayed up late and thought of masturbating but could not because he "couldn't get any juice going," perhaps because he had seen me that morning. He felt relieved that he did not masturbate but also felt a loss. Had I taken something from him? I interpreted that he was of two minds: Part of him felt I was taking away something that he felt he needed to regulate himself, and part of him was relieved not to feel compelled to masturbate in order to sooth himself. He felt that if he was excited, I would want his excitement and would try to take it away from him. He would have to enliven me just as he felt he had to enliven his mother, just as he now hoped I would enliven him. At this very moment, he started to have a sexual fantasy of two large-breasted women attempting to excite him. I interpreted that because he felt unable to maintain or moderate his own excitement, he feared that I would either steal the excitement from him or humiliate him for feeling it. To my response, Stone enumerated the list of his childhood passions, of which his parents had made fun. He was humiliated, his excitement gone, and he felt like "a dope" for thinking his thoughts and feeling his feelings. I remarked that he felt his excitement was deflated by others, and wondered with him whether he also squelched his own excitement to protect himself from the humiliation he feared was around the corner. He referred again to his parents: "I felt like they were saying to me, 'Stupid, how could you be so stupid.' I would disappear with fear and panic. I felt like I got caught, like I was bad. I felt like she was saying, 'You are a fucking, stupid idiot and you are bad.'" I realized that he was probably experiencing me as humiliating him for his excitement, but I did not yet understand what had happened.

Wednesday, his piano teacher gave him a difficult piece to play.

If she gives me an easy piece she thinks I am too limp, too flawed to play a hard piece. I want to say to her, "You are not pushing me hard enough." If she gives me a hard piece, I think she is uncaring, "Do you have any idea of what you are asking of me, don't you realize how hard I work?"

Feeling down today, he reported the previous night's dream:

Someone is flying a helicopter, no, a small spaceship. I don't know if I am flying it or if it is the other person on board the spaceship. I drop out of the ship and I start flying without a parachute, moving on the air currents; I could plummet to earth at any moment, but I am finding air currents and doing wonderfully. I surprise the people on the other ship, they don't know someone else is out there. Last night I felt lonely and not as tired as I wanted to feel. So I masturbated. I feel like I have a map of my emotional terrain and need to figure out where I am. I don't know how I feel but it doesn't feel good. I feel numb and lost, but I have not really disconnected. When I am flying, I thought about the other ship, and thought of it as the mother ship, and wanted to get back to the mother ship. I'm riding the currents, I feel elated, cool, taking risks, not running away.

I wondered if he was feeling disconnected from me, whether something had interfered with his ties to the mother ship; relying on his abilities to soar on his own exposed him to danger. Could he safely experience all he needed to experience with me without crashing? He replied, "I smell something cooking, like bakery goods, either someone is cooking or I am having that association. It's as though you or my mom were to cook something special just for me, like sweet rolls. Or maybe they are for later." "Or for someone else," I noted, "like dressing up for someone else, for later." "Not for later, for me." I wondered silently if the events of the previous Sunday's hour, with me dressed for someone else and he feeling insufficiently appreciated by me prompted this.

Thursday, he wanted me to be completely silent, to just listen.

I am excited, but don't want to get too excited, because when I do I get too disappointed. I am becoming more interested in the world outside of me, and I might get my needs met in that world. The depression, isolation and sadness that I have been feeling is helpful to me and worth it.

This sounded promising, but he might have been talking about feeling disconnected from me while trying to find something tangible to hold onto outside of the analysis. He continued:

I want you to say, "I have experienced you differently this week, so I am not surprised to hear that." When something is disturbing to me, I automatically start a fantasy. I put a woman I know in front of me, and then the script unfolds like a daydream. I have a fantasy of this beautiful woman with large breasts and I am in her home playing the piano for her mother. It becomes a sexual fantasy of seduction.

I interpreted that perhaps he was feeling injured and diminished and then was trying to make himself feel better by performing for an appreciative audience, first on the piano and then sexually. He said he had to protect his excitement from any comment or question I might ask. "I want you to validate me by saying to me, 'My experience of your excitement matches your experience of yourself exactly.' You don't need to temper it, handle it, interpret it, ruin it, I do enough of that myself." I replied, "If I am not with you exactly, then nothing works or can happen for you but if I am with you only exactly as you want me to be, then we are selling you short." "I know," he said.

If you would let me get away with that I would love it. Then I would think, you let me get away with that because you don't care or think I am too flawed to do anything else. I want you to achieve a perfect balance between pushing too hard and too little. I want you to titrate it carefully and unlock both ends of me.

I added:

You put two mantles on me, two ways of responding to the two parts of you. You want me to totally accept you as you are and not ask anything—then you will feel perfectly understood but wounded—and you want me to acknowledge all of you, to help you connect to yourself—even though that means discomfort.

Monday, Stone began the session by referring to his repeated masturbation over the weekend as merely a function of physical need. He described, as though his self-reflective capacities were lost, the places where he felt the sperm backing up. He went to work, felt lonely and depressed. At his men's group meeting he felt,

They knew I needed to be honored and appreciated. They told me about my effect on them and what they learned from me. I had a million dreams over the weekend. You were in one of them. I was calling you to change an appointment and you said, "Can I put you on hold for 3 minutes? I'll check the clock." I [Stone] said "yes" but I didn't want to hang on and disconnected the phone. I thought you were mad. A black man, a go-between in our relationship came (the elusive consultant?). He said, "She thinks you are doing great," and my whole mood shifted, changed. Maybe I am concerned you will not accept me the way I want to be accepted. It goes too much against your belief in the way that you should do analysis, or how you feel about yourself.

By now I realized that my competing with him over who was smarter interfered with my understanding his anger and disappointment in me. I said, "It sounds like you think I will not be able to be what you want me to be because I will be too concerned about how I feel about myself." Attempting an interpretation of his disappointment to my response to his alerting me about daylight savings time, "You were proud of yourself, you felt clever, and I was not responsive to you the way you wished that I had been. When I didn't realize how aware and smart you were, you felt angry, disappointed and depressed, and masturbated to feel better." He retorted that he was proud of himself, so proud that he would do it again even if I did not realize it. "I felt I was spontaneous, and felt like you were saying 'What's the big deal, stupid, everyone knows its daylight savings time,'" then he added, "I feel depressed right now."

A second instance of failure in the selfobject transference occurred in the 22nd month of the analysis, and illustrates a subtler lack of attunement. On the Wednesday before Thanksgiving, we also anticipated another break shortly after the holiday.

I overslept before Stone's early morning hour. Although dressed and ready before he arrived, I began the day without much-needed coffee. Stone arrived for his hour with the remains of his coffee and a fresh one for me. It was with pleasure and gratitude that I accepted it. He had brought me coffee once before, early in his psychotherapy. This morning he was early, he explained, and decided to bring me coffee because that was the kind of giving person he was. He was glad he surprised me. If I had expected it, that would not be any good. He announced he was feeling vulnerable. I asked if he was concerned that his gift might not be well received. He took a risk, he said. When I noted his excitement and anxiety about my response, his associations were to his mother's response to his spending. He was afraid I might say, "What a stupid thing to do." He invited himself for Thanksgiving to my house, assuring me that he did not want to have dinner with my family and me but to be in my office like this. "No interruption, no disruption," I commented. He asked if I had filled out the insurance form that he gave me the day before, which I had not. He waited 2 months to give the form to me, he knew, but now was distressed about my delay and added, "I want more of your mind share." I said, "You want me to think about you even when you are not here and to do your insurance as soon as you give it to me. I think you are wondering if you are important to me, if I will think about you during the coming interruptions."

We did not meet on Thursday, Thanksgiving. I needed to change the time for his Friday session. We had already made one change for his convenience.

On Friday, Stone talked of feeling down over the holiday, relating in detail how his mother left no room for him in their conversations at Thanksgiving, and he had to push her to make space for what he wanted to talk about; she seemed good-natured about this. He talked of masturbating a few times since Wednesday and feeling sluggish. I thought about the disruptions in our schedule—Thanksgiving and the two and a half weeks to come in December—and wondered how he felt about my need to change his time. He replied that by agreeing to the new time, he gave up the opportunity to have my schedule revolve around him; he thought he was the pivotal appointment in my day, but now no longer believed this. I said that my requesting this for my needs made him feel pushed aside and no longer central in my thinking. I interpreted that he had felt angry and disconnected, then masturbated in an effort to feel better. He countered, because he could not connect with his feelings, could not get his needs met, masturbating was a consolation gift he deserved. I wondered if he felt that I was too pleased with his gift of coffee the other day, as if I had been more appreciative of the gift than the giver. He agreed and livened up. He had hoped I might notice him and say, "How thoughtful, generous, considerate, and lovely you are, but this should not be surprising because that is the kind of person you are in general, a lovely, giving person." I had said "thank you," but that was not what he really wished to hear: "I wanted to feel you appreciated me as a person whether or not I brought coffee for you," to focus only on him. He added that every thing his mother had mocked him for buying was either for him or presents for other people, but never gifts for her.

Stone then went away on a business trip to an exciting (to me) destination for two weeks. When he returned he did not tell me anything about his trip. He did not want to have to navigate through my curiosity or excitement about his travels, but wanted me to be only glad to see him and concerned only about how he felt about being away.

Termination

During the 32nd month of treatment, Stone made references to being able to manage on his own, without analysis, "to fly on my own." My supervisor considered this the beginning of the termination phase, and an inevitable, positive outgrowth of the analytic work. To me it seemed early in the analysis, even though I knew he had been in treatment for much of the last 20 years. I interpreted his reference to "fly," as his nascent wish to feel able to manage on his own; but I was surprised to hear these thoughts repeated over time.

I was of two minds about termination. I was engrossed in this analysis and equally engrossed in its supervision with a respected, idealized, supervisor. I had imagined both relationships continuing for many productive years. At the same time, I was excited by my first opportunity to see an analysis through from beginning to end. A terminated analysis was required in my training, one of several "tickets" necessary to graduate. I knew that unless I could deal with my own grandiosity, my own wish to disregard rules, I would not be able to report this analysis nor get credit for it as a completed case. I needed to do this for myself, and to help Stone deal with his grandiosity. I had now passed my training institute's requirements for permission to begin new analysis with private patients, and I felt confident enough in my work and reputation to approach the institute's dean. Anxious lest I be penalized for beginning Stone's analysis without permission, I fantasized the dean acknowledging all the reality reasons for beginning this analysis without permission, and saying, "My dear candidate, we both know this is about your grandiose character and your belief that you can do whatever you want to do."

I met with the dean. I confessed, acknowledging that my wish to better establish my analytic identity had contributed to my manipulating the rules on my own behalf. I used the mitigating circumstance of my earlier request for permission from him to begin work with another analytic patient, and of his pronouncing it a good idea. My other supervisors had also agreed, and I thought permission had been granted. When the educational committee sent a letter noting that it was not procedurally possible to pick up a case until after "progression," Stone had already been on the couch for 2 months. I talked with my own analyst, who said he had done the same thing as a candidate; my consultant thought that because the analysis was underway, it should continue. Although I knew that many colleagues, before they became candidates and during their early years of candidacy, had patients on the couch, this analysis, begun without permission, had an illicit flavor in which I felt a certain level of excitement that paralleled Stone's illicit feelings about his own symptoms. I reminded the dean that I had been supervised biweekly for the entire analysis, that my supervisor and I thought the analysis was going well, and that I thought that it would be suitable as a terminated case. The dean accepted the case as a possible control case without chastising or humiliating me, but also hoped I had an understanding of my action's meanings. I made an association to a woman who had a baby 6 months after the wedding, everyone counting off the months on their fingers. The dean generously said, "as long as the baby is healthy."

Now Stone and I could more fully attend to continuing the tasks of the analysis and its termination phase. Stone had frightened himself; having felt good enough to imagine the beginning of the end of analysis, he began to feel bad again and grew more symptomatic. He was hypochondriacal when traveling. He worried about his prostate, his stomach, and a plantar wart on his foot. He feared he would need procedures, surgery, and painful intrusions. He needed extensive dental work. He worried about his thinning hair and signs of aging.

After dating several women, Stone fell in love with Mimi and became her lover. Concerned enough about her own body and desirability to be distressed when Stone could not perform sexually, she grew preoccupied with his sexual functioning and wanted him to have a surgical procedure on his penis. A urologist again ruled out any obvious physiological reasons for Stone's transient impotence and discouraged him from pursuing medical or surgical solutions. Stone felt he could not possibly continue to think about termination while all this was going on. To my interpretation that his preoccupation with his body's functioning arose when he imagined not having the analysis, not having the connection to me, he wondered how he could leave the analysis, leave me, if he did not have a relationship with a woman. How would he bear it if he did not know someone would be there to meet his needs? He wondered at the end, as he had at the beginning, if terminating now was for him or for me. He asked, "If you really love me how could you let me go; how could you ever give me up?" He complained, "You are just holding on to me for your own reasons and pleasure, you just want to exploit me and never let me go, please don't ever let me go."

Almost exactly 1 year after our last session, Stone called to request an appointment. It had been a complicated and exciting year for him. He had married Mimi, now midway along a planned pregnancy, and he was looking at a job that offered a marked increase in responsibility and compensation. He had joked that his salary had more than doubled during his analysis. He saw his ability to contemplate taking this new job as a continuing benefit of his analysis. His pregnant wife had debilitating nausea and was confined to bed rest. Not surprisingly, she was frightened, demanding, and unavailable to Stone and his needs. He understood her situation, knew it was time limited, and was trying to be a good husband and good sport about it. He also felt abandoned, sad, lonely, out of sorts, irritable, and he knew it. He had little interest in his old masturbatory fantasies or pornography, not even when he tried. He knew he had come to see me to recreate the experience of being seen and known; he hoped to maintain his connections to himself and not have to deal with the experience of feeling abandoned by "acting as an observer of my own life." He yearned to be back in treatment with the focus on him.

Mr. Stone wished to return to a place, the physical space of my office, where he could make use of available, reliable mirroring to feel intact. I interpreted what he could not interpret for himself. We understood that in the absence of the selfobject functions provided by his wife, he was feeling irritable and out of sorts. After a few sessions, he began to have sexual fantasies about women, but only on his way to the sessions. We understood this as feeling more alive and safer with his fantasies, which were only passing fantasies. Because they occurred on his way to his sessions, we wondered what they had to do with his feelings about me. At first, he wanted only a handful of visits; then he thought he would like to come twice a week, and perhaps resume his analysis. I permitted him to manage the frequency of contact while we explored his purposes in returning to see me. During this brief, therapeutic encounter, my technical interventions were similar to those made throughout the analysis: I attempted to interpret what I understood to be happening within the context of the selfobject ambience. I was pleased to see him and followed his fantasies of coming once a week, twice a week, and back into analysis with parallel fantasies of my own. I also wondered if the analysis and termination would prove to be enough for him.

Peter Stone wanted to revisit the analytic termination. We both knew that he had returned to his first analyst 6 months after termination with thoughts of resuming treatment, and we wanted to understand why he was coming back to me now. He felt I had not permitted him to fully manage the termination schedule as he had wished. He wondered if it would have been easier for him to have tapered down from a four-times-a-week regimen instead of going from four to zero. We had explored both options at the time; he had not wanted to alter the nature of our relationship but he had wanted to dilute the loss. I had wanted my first analytic termination to be classical in form if not content, an amalgam of my wish to know the "correct" way to do it and my need to terminate the analysis by the rules of my training.

After 6 weeks, Stone felt he got what he needed from the contact with me: a combination of being understood, mirrored, and allowed to display his accomplishments to an appreciative audience. He felt better able to make a decision about his job opportunity and to lend support to his wife. He felt consolidated and more comfortable with himself. I assume I will hear from him after the birth of his baby.

Discussion of the Analysis

This clinical write-up is an effort to understand the analysis of a man with a narcissistic behavior disorder. The shift from a twice a week face-to-face psychotherapy to analysis made a profound difference, for both patient and the analyst, and brought new facets of the patient and his personality into transferential focus. My original lack of familiarity with the technical treatment of narcissistic behavior disorders, and my countertransference, which interfered with my full acknowledgment of the narcissistic quality and limitations of Stone's relationships, impeded our uncovering of his narcissistic behavior disorder in the twice-weekly therapy. My limitations prevented the full emergence of a selfobject transference, the revelation of his perversion, and my recognition of his vertical split. After we converted to analysis, I sought consultation. In addition to the changed circumstances of our sessions—increased frequency, use of the couch—my growing awareness and use of the transference as the organizing focus of the treatment made relief of his symptoms and reconstitution of his self possible. Stone's perversion was unexamined and unmodified during his first analysis. This symptom reflected a vertical split used to manage affect states, by warding off depression and a lack of cohesion.

Stone and I shared the expectation or wish that treatment with a woman therapist might offer a different experience in that we would have access to different material. I assumed (naively) that a maternal transference would emerge and provide some understanding of his inability to enjoy and "own" his excitement and of the specific dangers of an intimate relationship. He, however, wanted me to focus on his penis, how it worked, or did not work, and what he did with it, so that he would not have to experience his own depression. In my opinion, he was disappointed that a treatment oriented to his sexual dysfunction was not indicated; I did not yet understand the functions of his symptom. I had just been accepted as an analytic candidate when he came to see me and my analytic identity was insufficiently formed to wonder if analysis was the treatment of choice. He appeared to manage his life well and could take pleasure from it. I thought once-a-week treatment would provide neither continuity nor access to his well-defended feelings.

My initial assumption about Stone's ambivalence about his therapeutic goals later mutated into a view of two sets of contradictory aims—an indication of a split. He appeared to have a mixed maternal transference: I who have strong affects, would permit him to find and tolerate his own powerful affects, and safely contain them for/with him; I might, however, also control him, intrude on him, and use him for my own purposes. He thought I wanted, maybe needed, him to be hard (both his penis and all of him in metaphor) for himself and/or for me, depending on the state of the transference. I later understood our relationship as the transference of his unmet needs for mirroring from his mother to me, and his "false self" as his effort to keep parts of himself out of the treatment in order to maintain a sense of himself as an intact man who was neither flawed nor in need of fixing. Still later, I realized that his vertical split protected him from painful affects that he feared he could not safely experience or manage.

Peter Stone clearly felt better during the course of psychotherapy. His preoccupation with his sexual functioning dimin-

ished. He reinvested himself in his piano playing and appeared
to pleasurably assume more of the functions of an adult. His relations with his parents and his girlfriend were the best ever. He
took a new job and felt he permitted himself to make more of a
presence there. He felt physically healthy and anticipated the
future with optimism. Early in treatment, his evocation of my
concern about his sexual functioning relieved him of some of his
depression. When I truly understood that his sexual functioning
was not the problem, I evoked his anxiety about being involved
with me. I think there were two transferences in play: a more
obvious mirroring and a quieter idealizing transference. He felt
I could tolerate the intensity of his needs and affect without with-
drawing or making it my issue. He was not overstimulated in
treatment because, for him, our more flirtatious interchanges
were a distraction from the more dangerous arena. His intense
fear of shame and humiliation was not fully engaged in psychotherapy, but he benefited from my insights into his dealings
with his girlfriend, his parents, and me. I did not know that he
relied on his perversion to help him through the difficult times.
There were enactments in both psychotherapy and in analysis;
in the former, more went unrecognized and therefore unexamined than in the latter.

A few months after psychotherapy began, Stone learned that
I had started analytic training. When I acquired an analytic couch,
Stone talked more about his own previous experience in analysis and, silently at first, began to flirt with the idea of being in
analysis with me. Only later did I learn about his dual fantasy
that I had become a candidate specifically to analyze him, that
he chose me, that he would be my first and best analytic patient
in order to influence me, "train" me, and make me the best analyst around. He thought this analysis was "meant to be." It was
vital to him that the analysis be a mutative experience for both
of us.

Our scheduling arrangement conditioned Stone's entry into
psychoanalysis. My acceptance of his terms constituted an enactment I believed necessary to "seduce" Stone into analysis and to
prove that he was special to me. Over time, I made many accommodations and treated him as special. Why did I permit him,
myself, and us to lure me into an unusual way of working?
Without this accommodation, the analysis would have been neither possible nor realistic for him: our arrangement facilitated

frequency of sessions, and helped Stone experience me as profoundly available to him. I felt neither exploited nor used, nor experienced his multiple requests for schedule changes as a sign that he was trying to control me or make my life difficult. In turn, this facilitated a selfobject ambiance and his capacity to use me as a selfobject. (It is of course interesting to wonder how his analysis would have fared had I not been able, for reasons of personal style or life commitments, or willing to accommodate to his schedule.) He had the grandiose fantasy that he was probably the only consultant in America, if not the whole world, who could manage both professional travel and an analytic schedule. He wanted me to appreciate this incredible feat and to admire him for his courage and perseverance. I had a parallel fantasy that I was the only analyst who would agree to this; Stone experienced my acquiescence as a mirror to his grandiosity.

When we shifted to analysis with different goals, the treatment took a dramatic turn. I had never before converted a psychotherapy patient to an analytic patient and could not have predicted the change from twice-weekly treatment. It was as though we opened a door and entered a new room in his internal world. Stone had a somewhat playful, bantering, double- entendre manner with me when sitting up. At times the atmosphere had a libidinized, sexually charged feel. I had participated in such seemingly object-related behavior, not only for our mutual gratification, but because I was unaware that it did not represent his level of development or what he needed from the treatment. I now had to silently acknowledge my confusion, having lost this veneer of object-relatedness as he revealed other parts of himself in the transference. I now realize that my confusion was heightened by my feelings about the mutual seduction that surrounded the beginning of the analysis and by my sense of misbehaving.

The mirroring selfobject transference and his symptomatic responses to ruptures seemed so crucial to Stone that, I recognized only after termination, the existence and at times primacy of an idealizing transference. Ruptures in his effort at idealizing were obscured by the noisier, more obvious disturbances in the mirroring transference.

Peter Stone experienced me in two very different ways: loving, and understanding, with large breasts that will nurture and soothe him, and unresponsive, hard, dry, withholding, and sadistic for taking away his comfort. In the context of separations and

empathic ruptures, he saw me as unresponsive, hence weak, helpless, and in need of his care and protection, yet also, in my weakness, as controlling and intrusive. When I interpreted this split
in the transference as a split in himself, he laughed and said, "It's
convenient that you have the same split as I do." It has only been
in the course of the work in the study group whose participants
wrote this book that I learned to consider his transference per-
ceptions as reflections of parts of me and not dismiss them as
"merely" transference.

Stone's twin transference views of me paralleled his sexual
fantasies. Who is doing what to whom? Who is this analysis for?
Who is providing what for whom? Can you really see me and not
just use me for your needs? Who is the woman he seduces? Who
is the woman seducing him? Do they represent functions, objects,
symbols, or all three? Did he believe that I seduced him into analysis by being warm and responsive in therapy; that I excited and
incited him to carry him off for my pleasure, as in his masturbatory fantasies? Was his offer of himself to me as an analytic patient
the enactment of a reversed altruistic version of his central preoccupation with my responsiveness? What did he wish to cure
me of, to save me from, imagined frigidity or depression? And
did he offer himself in the role of his "romantic" fantasies, in a
role reversal of his own loneliness when he was without me?

Stone had a number of recurring experiences, behaviors, and
attitudes. I found similar or corresponding experiences in my countertransference responses that were unique to his treatment. Stone's
requests for and my accommodation around scheduling phone
sessions and other "special" needs were enactments. We each had
the wish or need to do things in our own way and at times our
individual grandiosities butted against the rules. The struggle over
who was the cleverer, manifested most obviously around daylight
savings time, resulted in temporary ruptures in the analysis. For
both of us, these experiences often elicited painful or unacceptable affects, whereupon they were disavowed and enacted in attitudes or behaviors in our relationship. These can be best understood
as behaviors or affects, which preclude awareness of other behaviors or affects. This is the nature of the vertical split in perversions
and narcissistic behavior disorders. During the analysis, we tried
to understand the behaviors and affects on both sides of his split,
to silently understand the analyst's countertransference splits, to
bridge the space between both sides via interpretation, and to help
integrate both parts of Stone.

The Case of Alice
Perverse Indiscretions of an Inhibited Young Woman

Tall and slender, bent as if against a wind, Alice walked into my office and sat meekly in the center of my couch. She was plain and childishly disheveled, slip showing, flat black Mary Jane shoes scuffed, dark blonde hair pulled back and stringing down. She said she was not sure, but she thought she needed help, someone to tell her how to straighten out her life. She had chosen me because of a colleague's recommendation. Thirty years old, Alice was a highly trained nurse, a job she managed well but at great cost. She worked many more hours than she was paid, and in spite of doing an excellent job, felt inefficient, disorganized, often distracted by her thoughts and preoccupations, always afraid that her performance was falling short of expectations. Sometimes she had vivid fantasies of her death, from illness or suicide, to be followed by an elaborate funeral, where everyone finally spoke out about her goodness. She had a boyfriend of several years who, she believed, was not good for her. He threatened to break into her apartment if she dated other men. He frightened and humiliated her at a party where, uninvited, he violently confronted her mentor and professional partner for an imagined insult. From adolescence on, Alice had steady boyfriends, each for many years, and had lived for several years with a handsome, charming man who suffered chronic impotence. Deeply religious, sexual intercourse seemed wrong, and penetration was terrifying, so Alice specialized in men who themselves had sexual inhibitions. She was still a virgin.

She was the youngest of four children with a sister and two

brothers in a family where girls were not valued; she and her sister were continuously scrutinized for faults. She wept speaking of her father's death 7 years ago from a chronic, incapacitating illness. Although he was ill since her early childhood, her father was stern and often remote, but provided a sense of safety for her, a protector who knew how things should be done, who lived an honest and hard-working life, and gave his middle-class family material advantages. He rarely acknowledged her as a feminine girl, mostly appreciating her for the devoted care she rendered during periods of his illness when his wife anxiously withdrew and turned away from his needs. Alice's mother was now aging, deteriorating with her own chronic illness, increasingly more self-centered and emotionally irrational. She and Alice had terrible fights; Alice did not really live on her own and spent most nights and off-work hours at mother's home. Her apartment was barely furnished, slept in no more than 20 nights in 2 years of rental. Mother was cold and critical, but Alice kept trying to be good to win her love.

Her manner conveyed great sadness and pain, incongruously punctuated by dazzling sweet smiles and self-mocking jokes delivered with the timing of a skilled entertainer. We agreed to meet again. Alice was desperately depressed, and I was struck by the discrepancy between the seemingly high level of her professional competence and her terrible inner state, and was convinced that psychotherapy would not help. Analysis, with its careful inching toward intimacy, the support of its frequent meetings, and its focus on interpretation rather than a new experience with the object (analyst), was in my judgment the only option. She was emotionally sequestered and nearly impenetrable. She also could not easily experience the caring or empathy needed to balance her depression, but was very bright, sturdy, psychologically minded, and prepared for the hard work of analysis.

The patient began with an eagerness that quickly settled into a mood of timidity and superficial compliance. We met three times a week for the first 2 months because we were unable to find a mutually agreeable fourth hour, due to the demands of her job and her conviction that, as a nurse, she had to be always available, analytic sessions notwithstanding. She filled the early weeks with descriptions of her painful masochistic posture in relationship to the older married couple for whom she worked, both physicians. The husband had invited her to be the chief nurse

practitioner for their office after she finished her advanced training, a great honor. But the relationship had deteriorated so that
now neither husband nor wife spoke much to her and were cold
and critical. She was responsible for this situation in that she passively but aggressively failed to follow through on important
details of her work with them, and was cloying and needy as
well.

In the midst of describing how disappointing her employer
found her, and that her way out of such trouble was to be dam-
aged and sick, she related her earliest memory. She wondered if
this was somehow related to always having felt depressed
throughout her life. She recalled being 2 years old, just beginning to be toilet trained, when she had an accident on the living
room floor. She watched her parents on their knees cleaning it
up; she felt very powerful, and the scene was almost like a joke.[1]
She remembered she was wearing a red jumper. It was even still
a vivid, embarrassing, uncomfortable memory. Alice disagreed
with my comment that she had felt very powerful, insisting that
she really was weak. She could be sick and then they would be
sorry. She had a headache from her anger now. The next day, she
reported a dream of a gentle, kind woman who administered a
hard test in physics, a subject you have to know and where you
cannot b.s. I suggested I was the woman who was testing her
here, and she was worried that I would dismiss her for her flaws
and b.s. She responded by elaborating her concerns about my
criticism once I learned how out of control she was, exemplified
by her overeating, not studying for an important professional
exam, and being late for sessions. These concerns were intensified by my impending vacation, which made her feel "cut off."
I acknowledged her feeling that I was cold and that she deserved
punishment. Relieved that I understood, she brightened, felt
more acceptable, and began arriving on time for her sessions. We
negotiated a fourth weekly appointment time. At this juncture,
the transference experience was to feel weak and depreciated
when unacceptable angry feelings were aroused. Issues about
appointment times and money were obvious and significant ways
to express these experiences, and my accepting acknowledgment

---

1. Even in this first memory, presented with the emotional quality of a
joke, there is a feeling of distance and dissociation from the recollected experience. The dissociation is a hallmark of the vertical split.

of these feelings and some flexibility about time and money matters was sufficient to move the process along.

From a classical point of view, this material early in the analysis demonstrated the overlapping of sadomasochistic themes
concerning controlling (anal) messes by/for mother. This was
closely tied to intense longing for caring response and recognition, accompanied by fears lest these longings be burdensome
and harmful to me, evoking an intrusive, critical, or indifferent
response. Alice also feared the longings would be burdensome
and harmful to herself. She expected disapproval of her erotic
wishes toward men (the red jumper she wore in her first memory). Such interests were burdensome needs or messes, or sec-
ondarily, they represented an intent to compete destructively
with mother's claims. Needs and messes were forbidden and
repellant for her parents but nevertheless evoked their response
and involvement with her, albeit a critical one. Among the factors contributing to the erotization of messiness and neediness
was a chronic painful eczema on her inner thighs; this was most
acute during preschool years and was left untreated. From a classical view, these were the main transference issues at the core of
this analysis. The transference, apparent in the early months of
treatment, was masochistic compliance accompanied by depression and poor self-esteem.

Using this framework, the best posture I found with Alice was
a response to both sides of the experience: on one side was her
need for me to accept and be responsive to her deep sense of
neglect and deprivation, and on the other side was her tension
about my reaction to her angry, retaliatory wishes for my doing
things my way and not hers, such as setting the fee, going on
vacation, and beginning the hour on time. I learned that if I did
not address the second side, her anger and sadism toward me,
she grew more depressed and the analysis did not progress. If I
did not acknowledge the first side, her feelings of longing for my
response as powerful mother, we could not reach the anger. From
this classical view, her primary dynamic objective was to express
the rage, and the consequence was the feelings of longings for
my powerful containment of those sadistic impulses.

From a self-psychological perspective, the period of the early
analysis may be described differently as her longing for a strong
idealized parent, like older male professional mentors or like she
hoped I could be, who would rescue and protect her from

mother's (or my or other women colleagues') attacks. This idealized strong protector would also prevent her own attacks on mother from becoming too destructive. As we moved along, this idealizing transference alternated with a sharper longing for an appreciative, mirroring, responsive mother; the fulfillment of these longings seemed nearly impossible due to her angry fantasies about her messiness and destructive demands and her fears about angry retaliations. Unlike the first view, this perspective defines the primary dynamic objective as a (selfobject) response to her longings for acknowledgement by the analyst/mother. The experiences of rage and destructiveness are secondary (Kohut, 1977) to her disorganization and fragmentation when the longings are left unmet or unacknowledged.

Over the next 6 months, we focused on her experience with me as an idealized omnipotent mother, one who knew of her suffering but was neglectful and did not respond helpfully. She began one hour by relating how sick and anxious she felt at work; she was in trouble because she had followed directions from the female office manager without evaluating their effect for herself. Now she was angry because she really had known it was not the right thing to do. I pointed out that she must have been angry at getting the wrong directions, but could not face that feeling. Therefore, she complied, resulting with being punished. She said that she was too ready to "fuck up" and say she was bad. I asked her if she felt I was somehow failing her now, giving her the wrong directions. Although this was true, she said, for her female manager and her male boss, it was not for me; anger was futile, she could not do things right and had to make up for the bad stuff. She thought of herself as an unleashed attack dog; she should have figured out the right direction at work before she acted. She complained that her manager, a long time ago, stopped her from taking time off, about which "torture" she is still enraged. I noted this as an example of her worry about being too aggressive, compelling her to lay herself out for her enemy to attack. She spoke of now being afraid of her manager, who might be mentally fragile, maybe sick. When I suggested that she worried her feelings could make this woman sicker, she laughed and described herself as an "ugly attack dog."

As our work proceeded, she worried about making a mess, about being fat and ugly. Dressing nicely and exposing her body were exciting and dangerous. I must hate her, yet she needed me to be "in her corner." Because her needs could be attacks that might deplete me, she was confused about anger, assertion of needs, and being in control. As she grew more confident in my benign and even appreciative maternal interest, she began dating more appealing and available men with whom she could enjoy herself sexually yet she still did not permit sexual intercourse. Her experience of me as an idealized protective parent gradually yielded to one of a powerful, mirroring, but uncertainly responsive mother. Her capacity for direct discussion of transference feelings increased, and she changed her work to a new medical partnership, showing better business acumen and less ambivalence about money. She felt shame and depression less often and thoughts of suicide were infrequent.

She elaborated on her small child versus giant memory: not only did she bring the "giant parents" to their knees in defeat with her powerful feces, she thought she really was capable of controlling her bowels. She was too old for that accident, but in choosing not to control her own body she could control her parents. In reaction to this more grandiose experience of herself, she felt like an omnipotent pile of feces, uncontrolled impulses, and chaos, while her parents—and the analyst—struggled to reassert control. An internal battle with fears about her exaggerated sense of power was expressed in an interpersonal struggle: she was the potentially dangerous, sadistic, attacking one, with the parents/analyst her victims.

Over the next 3 years, her mother's health declined rapidly and she died. The complexities of Alice's mourning and so on, although obviously important, are not taken up in this report. Not specifically only related to her mother's health, significant themes were a passive compliance in reaction to anger, and uncertainty about identifying her own needs and desires. Her reactive compliance was expressed in many ways, such as feeling compelled to take care of her patients for little or no compensation, or her insistence that her desires for ordinary sexual satisfaction, food, and even basic creature comforts were excessive and must be renounced. If she did not comply, she feared she could be out of control. The struggle about compliance versus assertion (which seemed like defiance) was fought in the transference, concerning her arrival at sessions late and not paying her bill. As these issues arose, I helped her to identify what she desired from me that was not forthcoming. These issues would come up most often when I cancelled sessions for vacations or was otherwise unavailable, and when she felt guilty for having taken steps to improve her circumstances in life or to enjoy herself. We came to understand that at these times, she wanted acceptance and reassurance from me that she was not a bad person, and needed my recognition that hers were normal interests; she expected instead my criticism and even anger. I felt it vital to understand and interpret this longing for my acknowledgment, and not to distance myself in reaction to the provocation implicit in her ambivalent struggle to stay connected to me through masochistic surrender.

One area of her experience that she usually kept hidden from me was the intensity and compelling urgency of her sexual encounters with her boyfriends. Although she now occasionally allowed intercourse and even had orgasms with these men, there was scant intimacy or caring in their relationships, and there was not much shared with these partners except a driven desire to have sex that most often did not include intercourse. She could expose her messy ugly body to these men who were sexually responsive yet not emotionally intimate. This current experience of sex as messy, submissive, and intense was linked to the early childhood preoccupation with her messes and fears of her power. She was appalled and sometimes frightened by these episodic encounters, which were accompanied in their onset by a struggle with anxiety, and seemed unreal as they unfolded. During the sexual contact, she felt both powerful and submissive, and most importantly the center of the man's interest and response. I recognized these experiences as perversions, but was kept ignorant of any details until much later in the analysis. She felt ashamed and awkward about discussing them, and expected me to somehow punish her for her misbehavior. I expressed interest but did not press for the details, taking the attitude that she would tell me when she was ready.

When she began to trust that I was not harsh and condemning and that she could hope for my interest in her difficulties, her professional work grew more productive. Alice was now able to enjoy a less sexually frightening, more pleasurable and satisfying romance with Len, an unhappily married man. For the first year of their relationship, he had no intention of leaving his wife, and it was quite clear to me that his unavailability was essential to her freedom to enjoy their intimacy, sexual and emotional. The forbidden nature of their romance made it exciting and distant, hence tolerable. Eventually, he separated and divorced, and her anxiety about commitment and openness regarding their relationship and romance diminished. They started living together and talked of eventual marriage. As the following material illustrates, however, she still had great difficulty feeling comfortable in the relationship and being confident about her womanliness and assertive about her own needs.

One of the most important aspects of our work was our focus on a sexualized enactment, or perversion, which she experienced as troublesome and painfully shameful: recurrent secret sexual liaisons she arranged with Joe, Len's best friend. Secret trysting had been a longstanding behavior, occurring during her relationships with the abusive boyfriends long prior to the analysis. Joe's being Len's friend made their sexual relationship all the more forbidden. Meetings with Joe had been arranged perhaps six or seven times over the last several years, all colored with compelling, driving intensity. On these occasions, she uncharacteristically indulged herself in unrestrained, passionate, sexual encounters, often with intense orgasms. He had a wonderfully big penis but they had no intercourse because he was impotent; he was thrilling with his hands, but he was indifferent to her feelings between these sexual encounters and behaved like a "disgusting creep." Her sense of unreality and danger of discovery added to the excitement. She usually initiated their secret meetings, feeling somehow compelled; unlike her inhibited self, she was indifferent to the risks of being caught. She rarely discussed her plans with me beforehand, sometimes met him impulsively, and felt great shame afterward.

The 4 weeks of material summarized in the following paragraphs, during the period of Alice's affair with Joe, illustrate the three defining features of a perversion (Goldberg, 1995): (1) the vertical split (sense of unreality), (2) sexualization related to a defect in idealization (e.g., her shame about being a woman), and (3) an overall narcissistic vulnerability with idiosyncratic dynamics heightened by disruption in the transference/selfobject tie to the analyst. One episode of perverse behavior was stimulated by a transference disruption, when she had an anxious reaction to a break in our meeting schedule.

Alice was upset all weekend because she had no room of her own in the house she shared with Len, and she could not just "make a mess" with her paints from a hobby she enjoyed, but instead must endure Len's complaints about her things spread out in disorder. I acknowledged her wish to have an undisturbed space, and expressed some surprise that she still had not arranged a place for her desk, even though we had already discussed this matter several times in our sessions. The next day, she spoke of her anger at Len for her compliance with his requirements for neatness. She recalled having felt out of place and unwelcome on her return from a college year abroad; no one seemed interested in her experience, and she felt comfortable only in a large public room at school where there were easy chairs and a good bathroom nearby that few people used. Private and accessible bathrooms were important because she had diarrhea related to longstanding and still continuing irritable bowel syndrome. I suggested she felt relieved to come here, where she had privacy and could express her feelings, as comfortable as she had been in that private bathroom years ago.

The next day, Alice reported that she had insisted on her own space in a cabinet she shared with Len. She then had a dream about going to meet Joe, not finding him, and not finding a private room for herself in the hotel. She had to leave, then found Joe, who was indifferent to her story and wanted to have fast sex. She worried she would miss her plane back home. Associating to the dream, she mentioned having agreed the night before to go with Len and a woman friend to spend a weekend with Joe at his cottage in the woods. She hated this place, and was going only because Len wanted her to accompany him. The next hour, she related a nightmare of being attacked and raped. The dream followed her unexpected pleasure at having the afternoon off from work during which she fantasized being naughty and having quick sex with Len or some other guy. She could get carried away with sexual lust, a "Pandora's Box." I noted that her sexual desires and the opportunity to do whatever she wanted had perhaps frightened her. She thought she was excited about being close to Joe, who was unavailable and hence more arousing. She noted that when things seemed to go better, she expected punishment and became frightened.

By Monday, she had relaxed a bit, taken care of herself, and had good sex with Len. Yet she had felt increasingly anxious since we last met, perhaps in anticipation of seeing Joe at the cottage. Tuesday she reported feeling calmer after Monday's session. She has a new patient dying of cancer because he ignored his symptoms and did not take care of himself. Because he had once been in analysis, he should have been able to take better care of himself. She worried she also might get cancer because she avoided knowing things about herself. She thought of Dennis Rodman, a basketball player who she admires for exposing a female part of himself in his bizarre and confrontational cross dressing. Her femaleness came out "all strangled," the mysteries of the body emerged distorted as cancer worries or as lust for bad fucked-up guys like Joe. The next day, she was very late to the session, explaining that she had to see another patient with cancer and then speak with his surgeon. She liked coming to analysis but felt bad that she had not paid her bill from last month. Lately she had a lot of patients who have been analyzed, and was curious to know how long their treatments lasted and what the patients got out of them. I wondered aloud what she could be feeling now about her own treatment. She gave me a cashier's check for last month's late bill as she left. I was visibly surprised that it was not a personal check.

The next day, Thursday, she complained of feeling terrible and ugly, unable to find anything to wear. She had eaten out of control yesterday. She had just seen a young female patient with a brain tumor who had improved but then relapsed, a patient whose family was devoted. Alice sobbed when she thought of her own family members who might not care if she got sick, like when they teased her because she was the youngest. I asked her whether she had any feelings about my reaction to being paid yesterday with a cashier's check: Perhaps she felt I thought less of her for paying in that manner. She thought that was the case, especially because it was a late payment. She had so many problems paying me, and it was hard to get her paycheck to the bank on time. When I asked if it was like getting to the toilet on time, she laughed, but then was tearful with worry that "things wouldn't come out of her right" and that she must seem stupid to be unable to do things that ought to be so easy.

The next Monday, Alice spoke of the weekend spent with her sister and a brother and their families, revealing for the first time that her sister had, since adolescence, a disfiguring medical condition causing embarrassing, uncontrollable movements. As in so many other instances, the parents did not seek appropriate medical help, neglecting to respond to painful and humiliating conditions of need. Their neglect made Alice feel angry, even as she told me about it. Alice associated her sister's uncontrollable movements with the thought that sexuality, too, was uncontrollable, somehow mixed up with rage that could also be uncontrollable. She noticed this weekend that she had vaginal contractions when her sister had symptomatic movements, and she thought her response was linked to this rage.

The following day she dreamed of being paralyzed by a drug, which we understood to represent her rage when her needs were being neglected, even now as in her childhood. Wednesday, she felt much better for having talked about this anger and was grateful that I let her continue coming, even though she owed me money. When I asked if it was important that I allowed her to owe me, she denied it, insisting that she would rather just pay me. However, she had become better at billing her patients appropriately and negotiating for a better salary, and was relieved that she was now paying her bills and paying off her debt to me. She let Len take care of her last night, but was still worried lest he be annoyed at the mess she made with her paints. She found childhood pictures of herself looking fat and messy, and thought this morning that her hair was awful. She would like to go to a hairdresser twice a week, like mother, so she would never have to touch her own hair. My transference interpretation was that perhaps she enjoyed the feeling that I was taking care of her and giving her something. Thursday she felt bad about her hair, her eating, her body, sex with Len; she did not want to be touched. She had fantasies of sex with Joe in order to avoid noticing that she was with Len. She received phone calls from two ex-boyfriends who were sick or dying. She said, "Its crazy, but these sick awful things seem more real today than all the hopeful parts coming from the analysis." I asked if she worried about losing sight of those hopes with all the distractions from painful things. In response, she told me of two other distracting painful things, that this day was the anniversary of her father's death, and 2 days before had been the anniversary of her beloved grandmother's death.

Over the four sessions of the next week, Alice continued to vacillate between asserting her own needs and desires and reverting to her characteristic selfless caretaker role, trying to cure sick old lady patients, while dreaming of being raped and sadistically attacked. She felt that I supported getting rid of the old ladies. If Alice's mother were still alive (she had died recently), she would be critical of Alice's asserting herself in this way. Alice believed her mother also would have criticized the wedding cake she had chosen because it looked like the one she once had. Mom had been critical of self-exposure: She would have seen Alice's wedding plans as an exposure of shameless desire and would have wanted her to "cover up" with a less revealing dress. Alice thought her wedding was a rebellion. Thursday, the last day before a long weekend, she spoke of plans for a visit with Len to Joe's cottage, and she felt near to collapsing with anxiety. She could think of nothing good about herself, she had a stomachache, and felt she was getting screwed at work. When I asked her to tell me any feelings about the coming weekend and not seeing me Monday, she told me she was feeling helpless, although the long weekend break was good because I probably needed a rest.

The month of sessions just recounted highlighted the patient's longing for some contact with me as an admired and idealized mother who would love, touch, and recognize her in some essential way. She retreated from these feelings and from acknowledging them. Her idealizing transference made her feel vulnerable to disappointment for reasons that were yet to be clarified. Other themes abounded, recognizable to all psychoanalysts, that articulate the idiosyncratic dynamics filling in the narrative of her experience: fear of losing control of both angry and excited feelings, and fear of exposure. Psychoanalytic theories based on drive psychology, notably Chasseguet-Smirgel's (1984) theory of perversion, are based on the claim that *perversion* is defined by anal themes laden with aggression secondary to libidinal conflict about access to mother's providing and gratifying body. In contrast, Goldberg's (1995) view is that these dynamics represent the failure of idealization, with an accompanying experience of shame related to oneself; in Alice's case, shame in relation to a gendered female identity. Her unfulfilled longing to idealize and for being appreciated is sexualized and focused as a sense of a womanly self with a woman's body.

The dynamics apparent in Alice's case are clinically familiar from our experience in analytic work with depressed women patients. There was ambivalence about identification with mother, a feeling of being out of place and ugly. There were frequent tensions about bowel function and related matters such as money, time, and management of messes. There were worries about controlling her eating and excessive demands or intake of emotional

supplies from Len and from the analyst. Although these particular dynamics had to be extensively discussed and acknowledged
by the patient, it was my feeling that it was fundamentally more
important that I communicate to Alice my understanding and
acceptance of her longing for contact with me as the idealized
mother as expressed throughout the excursions into these dynamic
themes. Her need for contact, for idealizing me and feeling my
appreciation of her as a female, was at the base of the excited and
angry feelings that threatened her with loss of control. Fearing I
would not respond, her solution was perverse: She disavowed
these transference longings by creating a vertical split, and invested
them instead in sexualized enactment with Joe in which a drama
unfolded, wherein she idealized his potency (even though he was
actually impotent), although she felt appreciated as a sexually
desirable woman. My acknowledgment and interpretation of the
fear about her need to be appreciated by me in this way, and how
these longings for me were disavowed and redirected in her sexual behavior with Joe, were essential to moving the analysis along.
The *bridging interpretation* brings together both sides of the split
in one moment of her and my awareness.

Alice called to cancel Tuesday citing a last-minute meeting at
work. She began Wednesday's hour with upsetting stories of
patients' deaths at the end of last week, the news about the death
of an ex-boyfriend whom she had rejected years ago, and news
that the elderly mother of a friend had died. And she got a call
from another impotent ex-boyfriend she had rejected who is sad
and lonely and now wants her back. All this propelled her to
comply with Len's wish to go to Joe's cottage in the woods, even
though she had decided earlier to stay home. The first night, she
was having a private late-night talk with Joe when he started to
kiss her and she got carried away, while Len and her woman
friend slept in separate bedrooms only ten feet away. And twice
more they made out in the woods, which really excited her. Joe
was so calm and confident with his touch and kisses; he liked
her and wanted to just be with her. I wondered about whether
her sudden decision to go on this trip could relate to my leaving
for a vacation that would extend beyond the long weekend: maybe
she wanted to be captured and held by me? She became tearful,
saying she knew I accepted and took care of her; she had wanted
to call me Friday about her decision to go but was afraid to intrude
on my vacation.

Being at the cottage had an unreal quality. Even though the sexual play with Joe was very hot, when she returned home she was eager to have regular and uncomplicated sex with Len, who had a reliable erection; Len was good at fucking, and Joe was only good at foreplay. I asked, could she teach Len what she enjoyed about foreplay? No, because it is about touching her. With Joe, all either one of them had to do was make a little signal and they went off to be sexual, while the others were napping. No one knew, it was hot, there was no future, and it was not planned, and they never actually had intercourse. There was something about the forest; as a child she had fantasies of going into the woods to kiss and "do things" with a boy, where no one could see behind the trees.

> All four of us went for a hike in the woods, it was so cool, my heart raced with the possibilities. So the next morning Joe woke me up and took me back there, to where the tree had been felled by lightning. I thought, wait until I tell my shrink about this! He undressed me purposefully, made me come, standing up, with his hands. So it was a powerful weekend, with funerals and loves lost and love found, lots of weird stuff.

I asked what she thought about the funeral and the loves lost. She answered by recounting the wrenching sight of the old woman's casket being carried into the church by her five sons, who laid it at the altar. Those strong men, carrying their mom; she knew this woman would have loved that. It is a tradition, and she had been sentimental like that, whereas her husband had been a gruff German. Alice associated to her own mother's death, the family being overwhelmed by nursing her as she was dying, and the belated realization that they needed more help from hospice.

The next day, Thursday, she thanked me for "being nice" about what she had done over the weekend. My understanding gave her room to reconsider the involvement with Joe as a response to being alone and to the deaths. She realized that her relationship with Joe was completely out of context, like floating off into another world. I agreed and wondered if she put her feeling of longing for my touch aside by instead experiencing them with Joe. She added that the hot sex with good kisser Joe was undoing the death of the bad kisser boyfriend. She was cruel and rejecting when she broke up with bad kisser, painfully listing for him all that she hated in him: He was inadequate, could not drive well, was self-absorbed, could not kiss, and talked only about himself. I commented that bad kisser was the living dead, that he was not there for her, and being with him was like the "being alone" feeling she had at the end of our sessions last week. She associated to the good feeling of being held tightly, captured, an experience she never had growing up, adding that it had not mattered to anyone how she felt or where she was. I asked if she had a reaction to having to cancel the session last Tuesday, and my not having found another time that day to meet with her. She elaborated that she had not wanted me to be mad at her for canceling, and maybe I had been relieved to have a free hour, maybe I did not care. But now, as we talked, she could see that I was concerned for her. She wished she could straighten out the bad things and messes in her before the sessions, but unfortunately she was one of those people who do not know what they feel until they talk about it; she could not take care of it herself. I noted how important it was to feel okay about needing me for that. She commented on her inability to do "girl things" like cooking and cleaning the house. Her "girl things" were a mess, like her menstrual periods, and she could not fix her hair nor put on make-up. She added, "A girl chick raised by wolves could do that!" I said she did not want to touch the mess of being a girl, and perhaps that was how she thought her mother and I felt, too. Thereupon she expressed a wish to review the dead ex-boyfriend's medical chart to see what she might have missed; she wished she had saved him. But the nice thing about analysis was that it offered a more hopeful and productive way to direct her interest in fixing things. She was aware of now having to leave and face the weekend without me; she wanted a Coke after the session to help her face the long day. A thought occurred to Alice about a comment mother made at her 75th birthday party, that it was nice to be surrounded by priests and doctors; but she herself felt it was nicer to be surrounded by me, Len, and several women friends she was to have dinner with the next night.

With the bridging interpretation of Alice's split-off, excited longing for me as an idealized and responsive mother, Alice could calm down and cease her sexualized enactments with Joe. When her fantasies about the possibility of their sexual meetings recurred, they were taken up in the transference just as were the enactments. She began to feel positively identified with me and other women, and less shame about her ordinary sexual desire when with Len.

At our next meeting on Monday she was pleased—but not excited—to tell me that her girlfriends at dinner encouraged her to set a date for her wedding; she felt their love for her. The love and encouragement of her girlfriends helped her realize a wedding was not meant to trap her with bouquets, ribbons, and pastel clothes. Talking with them about their marriages, she realized she had the fantasy that her sharing and fun with Len would end with marriage; this was irrational. Later in the weekend, as she and Len made love, she tried to show him how she liked to be touched sexually. He did not "get it right" and she was mortified by those old feelings that she could not be a girl who had good experiences like everyone else, like being touched and blow-drying her own hair. Talking about this helped her feel better, to realize these were fantasies; now she could tell friends her wedding date, discuss some plans for the ceremony, and even look at wedding rings. She hoped I could come to the wedding, encouragement from women is very important. When I asked about this encouragement, she replied that for her it was the girlfriends' direct talk about sex in marriage that trades the excitement with new and unfamiliar guys for the intimacy and security of sex with a husband. She felt so much encouragement that she had experimented with Len, explaining to him how to touch her during sex. Since our last session and the dinner with her girlfriends, there had been a "frame shift" so that she could now plan to get married. She had a revelation that "the good things with Len *won't* go away with marriage, and that we *wouldn't* be like my parents who were only task-oriented, ate mother's terrible meals, and had no fun." It was very important that last week I did not give her a hard time about missing Tuesday, and was so understanding about her upset with those deaths and her running off with Joe. And it made sense that it was all related to her feeling lost without me.

These 5 weeks of sessions illustrate how Alice's sexualization diminished with her increased understanding of the connections in the transference between her split-off, intensely erotic, "floating off" experience with Joe and her longing that I recognize, touch and capture her, a special person. Because this interpretation made sense of her experience, Alice could make a realistic commitment to marry the man with whom she shared both meaningful intimacy and sexual pleasure. The interpretation relieved her confusion of erotic feelings with insatiable need, with sexualization after narcissistic injury, and with ordinary desire. This confusion is also at the base of her gendered sense of herself as a girl with potentially insatiable, burdensome, and destructive needs, best exposed, in a split-off context, to a depreciated and unavailable man like Joe, whom she idealized.

Over the next 6 weeks, we spoke of her experience of herself as a messy, shameful pig who ate uncontrollably, and who was like a slut in her sexual desire. Being a pig and a slut are womanly qualities requiring her to hide needs like one of her friends, a male homosexual, who seeks anonymous sex in gay bars. She wanted me to reassure her, to tell her it's okay to have her wedding reception in a fancy hotel. She needed my help; she wanted to cough up stuff that is like awful green slime. She reported a dream of lying about passing a test, faking the part about psychiatry and how to talk to patients. She could be fake with me, not telling me about her hostility. Joe liked her nastiness. Sometimes she felt left alone and neglected by me, making her feel nasty; one thing good about Joe was that he liked that part of her, "doing it" behind the trees or outside Len's bedroom door. She needed to feel that I liked that part of her, too.[2]

Following a 2-week interruption due to my illness, the fantasy of her needs being destructive toward me came into sharper focus. Monday, on my return, she cried and spoke of feeling frightened and lost while I was gone, afraid for my well-being. She could not call to ask how I was because it would have been intrusive. She felt bad, had lots of fights with Len. She was better, stronger when I was around. On Tuesday, she began:

> I feel much better since I saw you yesterday, you *name* things and life seems *possible*. I bottle things up. You *know* me and I am okay with that, like you understood how paralyzed I felt with wanting to do something for you when you were sick. It was important you called, reassuring me that things were okay with you. An older woman, the mother of a good friend,

---

2. This is her acknowledgment of the importance to her of my nonjudgmental and matter-of-fact acceptance of the disavowed side of the split.

is excited and wants to shop with me for my wedding dress; she adores me, and gives me permission to want to look like a bride and to be the center of attention. She is not like Mom at all. Sorry I cried so much here yesterday, I came in here a mess, and that may be burdensome for you.

I wondered aloud if she hoped I would feel toward her the way that encouraging woman felt. She replied, "Yes, that I might be *fun* for you. You could be in the messiness and make it through okay, it would be a very different way to think of things."

Alice had a friend in analysis with a famous analyst who talked a lot about himself. She believed I was better than that; when she asked yesterday how I was, I said "great" and that was all. I wondered that my not talking about myself allowed Alice to feel she did not have to be my nurse. She responded that not having such a responsibility was a great relief. She remembered that in grammar school days, her bedroom was above the outside stairs to the house; once she had heard mom leave, then fall down the stairs. When Alice ran out to her and offered to call an ambulance, mom was mean and vicious to her. How scared Alice was, wanting to get help so mom would be okay! Mom was rattled but not hurt badly, yet as a child Alice could not tell for sure. In Alice's family, people were either deathly ill or just fine. There was no sense of ordinary illness.

The next day, Wednesday, began with the feeling of losing connection with me, and the reappearance of her old perverse, sexualized and split-off way of managing that experience as fantasies of Joe's return. However, she quickly observed this herself, and the work of the analysis could refocus on the stimulating, unacceptable longings toward me that had to be avoided. I wondered if this was her transference reaction to my impending vacation to begin after the end of next week's sessions. Alice started her reply by mentioning the many patients in her office to see and her receptionist, who was excellent, announcing her resignation; the receptionist was too talented for this job and would be taking a better one. As usual, to make matters worse, she had called Joe; she still reached out for the bad thing. I ventured that her action could have been a safe way to reach out, with the relationship to Joe being in its own little bubble. She spoke then of a wish to isolate it more, but now the anxiety and sadness leaked out into the rest of Alice's life and no longer would be contained using that method any more. Len usually tried to comfort her but that did not help. I noted that she was quite stirred by her receptionist's departure. Alice conceded that it was because she was not good with new people, and felt like weeping; there would be a minimum of a month of hell now that the receptionist is leaving. I noted that a month is about the time left before I returned from my vacation to settle down again to our work together here; maybe she wanted to replace me with Joe, or to do something to help herself get through that month? Alice paused, associating to a wish to move out of her neighborhood for the weekend because a planned street festival might interrupt her usual weekend pace. She had a phone conversation with Joe last night in which she complained bitterly of his inattention. She knew the reaction was counterproductive because she had turned away from Len and from her home. I asked if she might be removing herself from the possibility of a helpful response because she felt she was bad, just as she was not deserving of the receptionist who was too good to work for her. She sobbed, as she protested she would love it if somebody smart wanted the job, but that was as unlikely to happen as a smart person working as a check-out girl at the Jewel, a local grocery store. My comment that she depreciated herself yet maybe saw some possibility of being appreciated like a "jewel," was met by her story of a very sick patient who needed more treatment, but was refusing that recommendation and would not acknowledge her needs. I asked if she herself was like that patient here, feeling noncompliant in calling Joe, and difficult for not wanting to be direct about her needs for me. She agreed, adding that she needed more from me now, having been so scared by my illness and with my vacation coming up soon.

The integration of her longing for the analyst's selfobject function as a mirroring mother fostered the temporary reintegration of the split-off sector of her self. My bridging interpretation permitted further work on the underlying faulty self, expressed as anxiety about being destructive and burdensome to me.

Thursday, she was very anxious, expressed symptomatically with diarrhea and arguments with a nonsupportive Len. An exam she had studied for was near and she was afraid she would not pass; but she was taking a break this weekend from studying to be helpful to a friend who was getting married. I wondered if she wanted to prevent this friend from feeling dumped the way she felt with me; she could feel good about herself by taking care of her friend's anxiety. She thought she had to do that. For the rest of the weekend, she planned to stay alone to study, and not to be around Len because she was difficult company. I reiterated my thought that she probably felt that I was ditching her at a time of great stress.

The next week of sessions was the last before my vacation, and we focused on her hostility toward me for ditching her, which was converted to her conviction she was unworthy and did not belong. She hesitantly raised the possibility of phone contact during my absence. After we discussed it, I offered to call her at a prearranged time and place. My reasoning for extending myself beyond the customary boundaries of analytic contact was as follows: Alice's profound experience of neglect, while no doubt real, was at this point best understood as primarily diversionary rather than only as rage in the context of repeating past traumatic experience. Her sense of being inevitably neglected justified and mandated her keeping a distance from me when I was seen as harsh and unresponsive. Her passivity in voicing her needs, now loosening with the expressed wish for contact, and the conviction of unworthiness, insulated me from her longings and demands that could otherwise overwhelm and destroy me, thus causing me to be lost to her forever. This perspective on her masochistic behavior called for an analytic technique quite different from the standard "watch, wait, and interpret." It obliged the analyst to respond directly to the patient's repudiated longings and demands by remaining explicitly accessible and by taking responsibility for maintaining the dyadic system, thus assigning the patient's various strategies for disengagement or repudiation clearly to the patient's own initiation and the analyst's.

Alice began the Monday hour by reporting that she worked hard over the weekend studying for her exam. She felt like "a loser" and was pessimistic about her ability to do well. She had started to study because she would not do well without careful review of the material, but had been distracted by urges to take care of other people's needs; somehow, if not being a caretaker, she was not entitled to belong. I asked if she might not feel she belonged with me, that my vacation seemed like abandonment of her. She thought this "belonging feeling" was missing when she irrationally thought she should not be a bride; as a child she felt she did not belong to mother. When I am away, she would miss her sessions because here she feels okay, connected, and is able to settle down. Her connection with me was like a fine wire, easily broken. When Len went away for a few days, she could phone him, but with me, she tearfully explained, she knew she could not call me because she was just a patient. She was too scared to call me because I did not care about her. She had to be good and not make demands. She hated her mother because she could not get anything from her, yet loved her; she could not figure that out. I pointed out the similarity to her ambivalent attitude toward me, even though I was trying to discuss the phone call as a simple procedure.

On Tuesday, she felt better, more confident and less pessimistic about the exam. It helped to see the problem as a fantasy, as feelings between her and me and between her and mom; it is not about the exam. It spooked her to feel fine after being here, only feeling fine as long as I was available; it was why she did not feel good on weekends and during vacations. I commented that this lack of access made her depressed. She compared this to having diarrhea, made worse with lack of access to a bathroom. I noted she confused emotional unavailability with geographic unavailability; this emerged when we were apart during vacations, feeling then as if I were uninterested and did not care about her. If she had to bring me shitty things, like upset feelings, she might believe it vital to keep her distance, a geographic or emotional distance that prevented her from dumping all her shit on me. She thought that could be why she was sometimes glad I was away on vacation, she felt like a mess then, and was relieved then not to be with me and have that exposed, burdening me with having to respond.

I wondered if something similar happened when she shared sexually passionate feelings with a man she was not close to; was keeping that distance a way to protect the "good" man, like Len? She said this was hard to talk about, and wanted to change the subject but was unable to avoid it. Last night she tossed and turned, her mind occupied with thoughts she could not get rid of: she did not want to tell people at work she needed time off to study. She was ashamed to have failed the exam the last time she took it and wanted to keep all that bad stuff to herself. When the new scores came in the mail, how would she talk about the results, and would she be brave enough to open the envelope? I commented on her fantasy about herself as a mess. She spoke of an anxious voice inside, and could not imagine her score might reveal success, but only failure. When I asked her to tell me what "success" made her think of, she replied it would be like her wedding someday, which she could only think of in "little pieces" at a time. If she passed her exam, she could pass by the painful recollection of an admired former boss who had dismissed her. And if she succeeded, she could be proud and would have other professional opportunities to enjoy. I said it sounded like being a bride. She agreed, adding that she would be the center of positive attention. I wondered aloud if it would feel good to cut loose of her former boss, so much like a dad with all his constrictions and rules. But without rules, would she then also feel "out of place," not belonging? Yes, she always thought that her "place" was to be downtrodden. I interpreted this to fit with her notion that she would be "out of place" to call me while I was on vacation. She tearfully replied it would be inappropriate to call me, although she hoped her not calling would not make me think she did not care about me.

The next day, Wednesday, she felt upset and had a nightmare to tell: It was after some apocalypse, in a deserted town with one intact building. There were a few women and young children left who were to go to a safe place on a bus. Alice had to remain behind, with scary, empty buildings and unexploded bombs. Everything looked intact but there was danger. She first associated to the theme familiar in her dreams, the lurking danger. I asked about unexploded bombs and being left behind. She said she was glad the others were safe. I asked about how she was left behind; she replied that there were a few men who were left behind, too. She did not deserve to leave because she was not innocent, only the innocent women and children deserved to be rescued. I asked if that reflected how she felt about my leaving her behind for my vacation, as if she were an unexploded bomb.[3] She replied that even if true, she could not do anything about that, so why talk about it? She just had to get through it.

She recalled the first vacation I took; she had tried so hard to stay calm and just sat in a chair, praying. I wondered if she had

---

3. This is an example of the faulty self that is exposed, represented by the buildings in the dream that appear to be intact but are in fact dangerous and empty. When the perversion or behavior disorder is given up as a diversion, analytic work with fantasies that articulate this self-experience can begin.

been trying not to feel so alone; would it help this time if she knew she could talk to me? She said that would be too intrusive and would ruin my vacation. I suggested she might worry she could ruin things for me with her needs. She replied that she wanted to have a happy face for me; how unfathomable it was that she and her needs could matter to me! Her parents had rarely called when they went away, sometimes for weeks; when she was in school in Europe for 6 months they called only once, on her birthday. This memory makes her angry. So the idea of talking to me when I am away terrified her; she might say something that would upset me. When I asked what, she replied that it was better to say nothing than to endure the neglect and indifference she might receive. I wondered if the effect of that notion was to make the problem her flaw. She recalled that once when a small child and her parents were away, her aunt and uncle took care of her and her sister. She was sick, so ill she could not get dressed; her aunt found her struggling and took care of her, was actually nice to her! I remarked that this was a memory of hopeful possibility, that someone guessed her need for help. She replied that it was a good memory, and it is what she wants *now*, for someone to find her.

Thursday, our last session before the 2-week break, she began by reporting a visit the night before to a friend's home to study. She planned to have dinner there with him but he misunderstood and ate before her arrival. She said nothing about being hungry because she did not want to embarrass him, and decided to wait to eat until 11:30 when she got home. But being so tired, she failed to fix dinner for herself. Len saw this and—he was so great—he fixed it for her! Why was it so hard for her to receive? I asked why she thought she would have embarrassed her friend to say she wanted to eat. She replied: because that would have made it seem that he was flawed for not having anticipated that she would be hungry. She was ashamed of her hunger because of the way she ate when hungry. She has trouble exposing her need. Even now, sleep was the enemy, she was so tired that her need for sleep was overwhelming. I noted that having almost any need taken care of seemed bad; maybe this was also true of her need to talk to me while I was away. She thought it was hard to show me all she needed, although last night she imagined talking to me during vacation, a big step. This reminded her of her aunt responding when she was sick, so perhaps it would be possible to call.

But now that we were actually arranging the call, it was too scary. Well, she guessed it would be better if I called her. I agreed to this, and we arranged a time. She began to cry, saying that she would like to ask where I am going, but could not because it was too intrusive. I told her I thought it was normal to want to know where I would be. She said she did not want me to think she was not friendly, because her reluctance was due only to her fear of asking. She wanted to be closer but was afraid to hope. I wondered if she had felt like this with her parents, a feeling of "I don't belong in the same world." Alice told me of a short story she read a few nights ago when she was very anxious, about an analyst who was ill and dying, and the patient took care of her and therefore got closer. When I suggested she felt that the only way to be close here was to be my caretaker, she visibly calmed down, confiding that she thought all the time of this stuff between her and me, and that she had been trying to be very careful.

Conclusion

Following the vacation, with the resumption of the analytic work, Alice declared her willingness to expose herself further and cautiously let more of her needs be known. In the material up to this point, there were clues to what she felt she must manage about her needy faulty self, most particularly her hidden insatiable needs that when neglected could result in explosive rage potentially so damaging to both of us. Therefore it was important for her to be very careful and superficially compliant in the analysis. She was very worried about my safety and confused about her own responsibility for putting me in danger or for fixing my problems.

This description of this analytic treatment process demonstrated the importance of addressing the perversion as a necessary prelude to further work on other more crippling underlying troubles with a needy, vulnerable self. The intense sexual excitement of the perverse behavior distracted from an impending threat of fragmentation. As the analytic process deepened, and the selfobject tie with the analyst grew more important to her, the danger of fragmentation intensified with separation and empathic ruptures. At the same time, however, as our work progressed there were increased opportunities for this transference interpretation, reassuring her of my responsive interest in her state, helping to relieve her anxiety. With the increased strength of the selfobject tie, the perverse behavior faded away and her longings were experienced as directed toward me. The complexities of these longings and the vicissitudes of their expressions became the focus of the remaining analysis.

7

chapter | # The Case of Rashid
Purloined Letters—The Psychoanalysis
of a Man Who Stole Books

This is a case in which a behavior disorder, kleptomania—(specifically the stealing of books), had a structure similar to that of a perversion: it was erotized and split off from the patient's reality ego and defended him from unbearable affects. But whereas this symptom was the patient's secret, he also had a very public neurotic symptom that lay at the heart of his social identity and that he bore like a cross: this was an inhibition against writing which threatened to destroy his academic career. Over the course of his analysis, both symptoms changed. As his personality became increasingly structuralized, he stopped stealing books and became addicted to buying and selling them; then he began to read the books he bought, and finally, he began realistically to hope of producing one himself.

Rashid was a 42-year-old graduate student in history. He had been married for five and a half years to Maya, who was a graduate student in a related program. They were devoted to one another but also intensely competitive. Both saw Rashid as the brilliant one despite the fact that he had been unable to write a word of his dissertation, whereas Maya was nearly finished with hers. Rashid was supported by his department, despite his lack of progress, because he had written an important article, although he never intended to submit the piece for publication. It was merely a draft of a seminar paper he had given up on and brought to his advisor for suggestions. His advisor was so impressed, however, that he sent the paper to a journal, which immediately published it to much acclaim. Rashid was rewarded with a variety of teaching assignments at which he excelled, and he developed a reputation around the university as a passionate and brilliant lecturer. Students fought to get into his classes, but his department was forever threatening to throw him out of the program because if he would not write he could not graduate.

Meanwhile, Maya plugged steadily toward the completion of her degree. Her prospects were bright because her department considered her work solid and strong, and she was liked by everyone. Rashid was proud that much of what was most theoretically sophisticated in her dissertation had come from him, but at the same time, he was pained that she had no difficulty using his ideas, whereas he found it impossible to commit these ideas to paper. He had a number of friends around the country who regularly sent him their manuscripts because he was versed in all that was theoretically cutting edge and had a special knack for making arcane ideas clear. Like Maya, these friends eagerly incorporated Rashid's thinking into their papers and published them. It was a triumph for him to see his thoughts in the public arena, but infuriating that they always appeared under someone else's name.

Increasingly depressed over his inability to do the one thing his professional life and sense of inner completion depended on, he sought help in therapy. He first tried working on his writer's block with a behavioral therapist, but got nowhere. He then did 7 months of once-a-week psychotherapy in an effort to reduce his overall unhappiness. He enjoyed this experience but found it quite painful. His therapist believed his problems were largely due to his refusal "to renounce his infantile oedipal objects" and browbeat him into "letting go" of these so that he might "grow up." When the therapist felt he had explained all of this sufficiently to Rashid, he told him it was time for him to "be on his own." Rashid agreed—wasn't it the shrink's job to know such things?—but now he thought doing so had been a mistake. He wasn't ready to be on his own, that much was clear. He was quite miserable; often it was difficult for him to do anything but lie around watching TV. He felt he was out of shape and hated the fact that he smoked heavily. He found great relief in sex, but Maya was often too anxious about her work to be interested in it.

Rashid spent his time lecturing, grading papers, writing recommendations, counseling students, and going to meetings, but always felt too busy to work on his own project. His research required him to read thousands of pages of historic court records, work that he found unbearably tedious. Primary sources daunted him because there was no author to organize the information into a coherent shape. This, indeed, was precisely what his project was intended to accomplish, if he could only bring himself to work on it. He spent whatever free time he had, however, reading cultural theory. He loved the work of the in-vogue intellectual superstars, and excitedly awaited their latest offerings. He felt compelled to look at everything new because he feared that it would render whatever had come before it passé. He haunted the recent acquisitions tables of the campus bookstores and poured over the jacket blurbs and introductory pages of whatever he found.

He would regularly steal these books. Doing so was tremendously risky and would have meant absolute ruin were he ever to be caught, but he couldn't help himself. Yet, ironically, once he got the books home, he never read them. He glanced at them for a few moments as he had in the store and then piled them up in the basement of his building, where before long they began to rot in the pervasive damp.

Rashid was the oldest of three children born abroad to a publisher father and a rather spoiled and indolent mother. His father was aggressive, tyrannical, and subject to fits of rage. He ran a highly successful press and was famous for throwing even his most important editors and authors out of his office when he felt they were wasting his time. Mother was coquettish and vain. She had lustrous black hair, white skin, scarlet lipstick, and large teeth. Rashid referred to her as "the Orca." He remembered feeling enraged and humiliated that she made him wear shorts to school 2 years after all of the other boys had begun wearing long pants. He thought of himself as her fetish; she doted on him in a manner that was at once cloying, overstimulating, and unbearable. She often paraded before him in various stages of undress, and cuddled with him seductively. When company came over she demanded he entertain by answering questions everyone thought impossible for a child so young, and she liked to show off his pretty curls. Mother was resourceful too—like a thief. When the family was forced to flee their homeland, she spirited her most valuable jewels past the border guards by concealing them artfully in her lacquered hairdo. The money they made from the sale of the jewels kept them solvent for months following their exile.

In their adopted land, father was reduced to a position of comparative abjection. He couldn't find work in publishing for almost 2 years and for a while scratched out a living writing obituaries in the local newspaper. Although he had always been vain about his appearance, father grew shabby and depressed and soon developed the heart condition that killed him when Rashid was twenty-five.

Rashid felt highly ambivalent about his father, hating his authoritarian manner and violent temper but admiring his intellect and love of learning. Father's most prized possession had been his library; he introduced Rashid to novels, poetry, and works of political science and philosophy. He had even written a pamphlet on certain aspects of the publishing business. Rashid was proud to think him an "author," but when father beat him or his siblings, Rashid despised him. On turning 15 Rashid warned father that if he laid a hand on him again, Rashid would kill him; the beatings stopped, but relations between father and son became increasingly strained. Following an angry scene the next year, father threw Rashid out of the house because his doctors told him his heart could not stand the stress of their constant battles. For a time Rashid lived on the streets, then found lodgings in a building that housed a Dickensian company of prostitutes, writers, petty criminals, and revolutionaries. Though frequently lonely and often terrified, he managed to flourish. He found work at an underground literary magazine, wrote poetry, and became a favorite of various women writers, artists, puppeteers, and whores. In time, he moved away, attended college, traveled, worked at various jobs, and eventually found his way to graduate school and finally to me.

He began treatment after a pronounced bout of depression, which he thought had been brought on by Maya's nearing the end of her dissertation, a situation that threw their future into doubt. She would be applying for teaching jobs but there were very few available, and there was a good chance she would not find a position at an institution with the specialized research facilities Rashid's work required. Moreover, it was extremely unlikely that the institution hiring her would give him courses to teach—especially without a completed Ph.D. But what would he do if he had no income, couldn't pursue his research, and was too neurotic to write? Maya urged him to get back into therapy, alarmed by his gloomy irritability. He thought he had nothing to lose.

I liked Rashid immediately. He was passionate, serious, thoughtful, funny, and appealingly irascible. In addition, he was suffering from writer's block—a problem I had struggled with throughout graduate school and after. My own analysis had helped me but writing was still conflicted for me. I hoped my experience would be useful for our work, but worried that it might not be, even as I wondered whether in trying to help Rashid with his writing problems, I would arrive at some happier resolution of my own.

Rashid found analysis daunting but exciting. Knowing I was there—interested and, importantly, behind him, and that we would be meeting four times a week—made him feel better almost at once. He thought he was reawakening to life, and the world around him was reawakening too. His sensations felt more intense: eating an apple seemed a new and remarkable experience. Walking to my office on a rainy day, he felt the buildings had washed their faces for him. He was a hero to his friends, who all agreed that it was practically impossible to test the soul in the modern world; no jungles were deep or dark enough any more for that, but psychoanalysis was different. It was a spiritual journey into a world of inner mystery, precisely the journey for which every forbidden journey was a metaphor! And it promised to be dangerous. He dreamed of jet liners flying through starry skies and exploding into flames. He grew dizzy on the couch and feared he would black out. He felt as though he might be levitating as he lay on the couch and recalled imagining himself in childhood floating slightly off the ground as he walked. He was joyful to think that I would be with him but anxious at the same time. What would he have to do to sustain my interest and good will? He recalled that Scheherazade confounded death for a thousand and one Arabian nights by telling stories to the Sultan. Perhaps his narration would similarly beguile me? But perhaps he would be destroyed by my wrath, or perhaps I would use his discourse for my own gratification rather than for his growth, even as his mother had used his cleverness with words. He thought of mystic nuns in 16th century France who were required to confess their visions to priests of the Inquisition, lest their erotized power overwhelm the Church. Was I such an inquisitor? Perhaps analysis was also essentially a discipline of suppression, and free association a trap. Why didn't I seem more forbidding—sterner—like his former therapist? My office seemed to him a leaden box suspended in the ocean. The sounds of cars and buses below my windows reminded him of ocean waves and his childhood and made him feel both happy and sad.

Early on he reported a dream in which he was defecating, holding the warm shit in his hand. The shit was unexpectedly light in hue. He thought the dream had to do with the idea of exchange. He'd been frequently constipated, had as he put it, "retained his feces" from the time he was 10; it was still a problem. He associated to a night from that period of his childhood when instead of doing his homework, he was reading a novel. Father came into his room and became enraged when he discovered Rashid was not studying. He grabbed the book and threw it down and beat Rashid. From then on Rashid retained his feces, especially when feeling empty or anxious. He remembered a time when he lived with acquaintances of his parents after his family had been forced to emigrate. The people had a 15-year-old son who one day followed Rashid into the bathroom and tried to fondle his penis. Rashid was terrified and told the boy's mother and father, but they refused to believe him. Afraid to return to the bathroom if the older boy was anywhere around, he waited days before defecating and soiled himself when he did so, piling his dirty underwear in the closet because he didn't know how to wash it. He was terrified that the dirty underwear would be discovered, but didn't think it ever was. He remembered there was something about needing increasingly painfully to shit, and then the rush of relief when finally he did so, that made him feel comforted. The smelly underwear in the closet mortified him, but he liked that it was there. He couldn't believe he was telling me about this. He couldn't believe he had been this way, that he could remember actually wanting to feel shit in his pants—as though he were an infant!

I said his dream of shit was about feelings he thought unspeakably offensive. That the shit was warm and lighter in hue than he'd expected and that he'd held it in his hands bore witness to his hope that his shitty feelings might not be quite so dark and disgusting as he feared, and that he might touch what seemed in him most untouchable. We discussed this dream for a long time. Rashid thought that his withholding of feces had to do with his inability to write—his withholding of words. He associated to his mother and the wheedling way she had seduced him into giving her what she wanted. He imagined she had toilet trained him this way, and that he must have felt humiliated and enraged as a result. Perhaps he had confounded her maddening desire by refusing to produce! Certainly, however paradoxical it was, withholding made him feel powerful and valued. He remembered Lacan saying that desire is constituted by a lack for which the phallus is signifier. Rashid thought he was such a signifier for his department: a fantastical prick! The more he didn't write, the more fetishized he became. The department wanted what was inside him, even as had his mother! He remembered Lacan's famous essay on Poe's "The Purloined Letter." Lacan argues that the power of the Minister in the story is a function of his possession and concealment—his retention and nonuse—of a letter he filches from the Queen. It was, Rashid thought, the same with himself. As long as he retained his eagerly anticipated manuscript, the faculty was captivated; they cajoled, pleaded with, and finally threatened him like so many frustrated suitors—even as had his mother, he imagined, when she had tried to get him to shit. His "letter"—in the manner of Lacan's "petit objet à"—had come to signify the department's lack, and thus marked the inscription of their desire. One of Rashid's professors went so far as to say that Rashid had elevated "not writing" into an art form reminiscent of the "not eating" of Kafka's "hunger artist."

Rashid further remembered Lacan saying that withholding the Queen's letter also feminizes the Minister because his power consists in inaction and the removal of the signifier—the letter—from the Symbolic Order. Rashid imagined that if he were actually to write, his power would disintegrate, a prospect more upsetting than continuing to endure the infuriating, abject—feminized—role he played in the "symbolic order" of the department. Because the faculty might at any time cancel whatever instructorship they had created to keep him employed, he had forever to suffer the fools among them gladly. After particularly trying departmental meetings he would burn with desire to murder such and such a colleague only to simper ingratiatingly before the same person the next day at the sherry hour as if he were a dog.

Rashid found analysis immensely gratifying; it was remarkably affirming to discover that from various unexpected perspectives there was method to his madness, that his craziness made sense. One day he reported two dreams. In the first, a foreign word appeared prominently that had two meanings: "happiness" and "hat." In the second, he found himself in a room frighteningly overrun with rats. The previous day Maya learned that her dissertation had been officially accepted, making Rashid worry that the analysis might break off prematurely. He thought the meaning of the dreams was clear: his happiness was an effect of the analysis, but if he had to reach for his hat—if he had to leave—he'd be plagued again by the rats—the shit of his craziness.

After my first vacation, Rashid felt angry and betrayed. Perhaps analysis was just so much shit itself. He distrusted all ideologies and my idea of psychoanalysis seemed to insist on an antiquated notion of the unity of the self. Didn't I understand that Derrida had exploded such an illusion, that we were living in a post-modern age? How could he have fallen for such nonsense? While I was away, he flirted with a secretary in the department and thought of taking her to bed. She'd made it clear she was interested, and he was annoyed that he felt guilty about the idea. His sexual daring was limited to watching pornographic videos occasionally after Maya—exhausted from copyediting her thesis—fell asleep. He was enraged because she was too tired to have sex, but of course because he loved her and couldn't bear to think of hurting her, he resisted his impulse to sleep with the secretary. He couldn't believe he was becoming *more* rather than *less* repressed! How could he have guessed that psychoanalysis was ultimately an engine for the construction of *bourgeois* subjectivity? Sex—especially forbidden sex—had been the only experience in his life that had given him a sense of complete freedom and possibility, and now that pleasure was becoming impossible because he couldn't talk about such sex without feeling guilty. I said I thought he was feeling betrayed by my abandoning him to go on vacation; he was full of enthusiasm for our work and then I left him. Maya, too, was unavailable, and so he attempted to console himself with fantasies of the secretary and then with pornography. Rashid brightened quickly, surprised that I was not simply mad at him and ready to kick him out of my office for complaining that analysis was stupid, even as his father had kicked him out of the house for arguing with his rules. Maybe I was right to think that he'd felt abandoned.

Anticipating a holiday break that would force us to cancel several sessions, Rashid disclosed his habit of stealing books. It began when he was 16 and on the streets; his cousin Khalid had taught him the ropes. His modus operandi was to enter a particular bookstore on campus and browse through the new works on cultural theory, then go about his day. Inevitably, one of the books would weave a spell over him. He'd think about it casually at first but as the hours passed, he would find himself obsessing. He imagined the book would answer all of the questions that stood in the way of his writing. He imagined stealing it. The title would glow in his head all night as if the letters were written in neon. The next morning as he showered, shaved, and dressed, pressure would build in his head until he could no longer stand it, and in a state of tremendous excitement he would return to the store. Signs on the wall warned that shoplifters would be prosecuted, but the Rashid who read these warnings did not care about laws or risks; he was a different person. It was as if there were two of him.

When he was certain he couldn't be seen, he would hide the book in his pants. He felt a rush of pleasure feeling it against his body. The whole experience had the intensity of sex; his heart pounded so violently that he nearly blacked out. Sometimes, for a moment, he actually saw stars—but he had to compose himself to avoid suspicion. He would buy something cheap; *The New York Review of Books*, a legal pad, or a few pens, anything he might pay for. He had to make small talk with the cashier even as the stolen treasure pressed against his ass. There was always a moment when he knew he was safe, even before he was fully out of the store. Then he was outside, wanting to run like mad screaming that he'd done it! Nonetheless, by the time he got home, the excitement was over, and he already felt guilty and ashamed. He almost never so much as glanced at the book he had taken. Rather, he marched down to the basement—he called it his "dungeon"— and piled the book on top of the wall of stolen books, all unread, many moldy and smelly. He realized as he told me about it that he had been turning the books into shit. It made him think of the pile of smelly underwear he had hidden in the closet. This thought had never before occurred to him, and the whole matter made him feel unimaginably ashamed.

Rashid's associations led to his father, whom he had always thought of as a man of letters. Father was a passionate and voracious reader, forever poring over newspapers, journals, and books on every imaginable topic. He frequently brought Rashid books from distant cities when he traveled. Indeed, the day father beat him for not doing his homework, Rashid was reading a novel father had given him as a gift. This was why the beating had seemed such a terrible betrayal. Rashid had never understood why his father had not chosen to settle near his own parents when the family emigrated. Recently, however, he had learned from his mother that his father had been on terrible terms with his parents, that he had been born out of wedlock and was regarded as a disgrace to his family. The news seemed to explain why his father had been so devastated after the family's exile: father needed a lofty station in the world to redeem him from his abject place in the family. Even after father found a suitable situation in the new country, he was never entirely the same. Rashid was touched to see his father in a new way, not as a tyrant and buffoon, but as someone suffering and sad. Perhaps father's rage was an effect of rejection by a world he was not nearly so good at controlling as Rashid had always imagined.

I said I thought stealing books symbolized Rashid's effort to reestablish a sense of connection with the father he had idealized as a boy but who had come to traumatize and disappoint him. The books he stole represented the father from whom he had sought enlightenment but whose wisdom turned to shit when Rashid became disillusioned with him. I added that the ritual of stealing protected him from feelings of depression: stealing compelled, organized, and enlivened him, and was something he did to save his life. He was tremendously moved by this interpretation; it brought him nearly to tears to think actions he considered unforgivable and humiliating might signify something understandably human within him.

He began to dream of young boys, often black or brown, who sought his help or protection. He associated to his growing empathy with the split-off part of himself, the part he thought of as shitty and corrupt. Sometimes a strange man hovered at the edges of these dreams in attitudes of interest and concern. "Perhaps that's you," Rashid said to me. In a series of dreams, he made descents into the underworld: in one, he was told to scrape the walls of a cave that water might flow forth; he did so, cutting his hands, and then water began to run from a fissure in the rock, turning the cave walls green with verdure. In another dream a dead tree suddenly dripped blood from a broken limb. He thought these mythlike dreams symbolized the return to life of long dead regions within himself. The bleeding tree was a sign that his roots were vital after all, that even after being kicked out of his house by a degraded father now dead many years he was still part of a family tree, a tree of life. He thought that the dream also suggested a relation between feeling alive and being able to feel pain: the tree after all was bleeding and water flowed into the cave only after he cut his hands on the rock.

Rashid began to feel increasingly hopeful. Analysis seemed to him a kind of miracle. He stopped smoking, began exercising, and started to lose weight. He and Maya often made love, and he thought she was more in love with him.

On a Monday, he reported that on the previous Wednesday he had accidentally walked off with my men's room key; he had done this several times before but never mentioned it. Now he wanted to talk about it. He couldn't imagine his motive. Taking the key hadn't been intentional, but when he noticed in the elevator that it was in his pocket, he hadn't brought it back. Nonetheless, he spent the entire weekend obsessing about whether to return to the office with it, although he knew the office would be locked. He had been in a particularly bad mood that Wednesday because I had canceled our Friday appointment, and Maya had been away giving a lecture at a university that was considering her for a job. He hated to be left alone, hated when sessions were cancelled, and hated to think he might have to leave the city. The idea of leaving the analysis prematurely reminded him of his family's forced emigration and being thrown out of the house. On Sunday he felt like stealing a book. He didn't, and he was glad he didn't, but he was distressed to think that I wanted him not to steal. Jean Genet was a thief and Foucault's creativity seemed intertwined with his reckless—and ultimately fatal—homosexual risk taking. Rashid wanted to give up stealing, but at the same time he didn't want to give it up. Maybe his creativity—like Genet's—was bound up with being a thief, and it would be suicide to quit! He confessed that he had in fact given in to the impulse and taken a book on Saturday night after trying to talk himself out of it, but the act had failed to provide the usual rush, nor had it distracted him from his bad mood. He was afraid stealing was losing its kick.

I offered an integrative interpretation of the split that divided him. I said his "theft" of my men's room key was like his theft of books. Books were magical keys that he hoped would open doors for him by freeing him to write; writing would get him into rooms of power—men's rooms. When he felt I had abandoned him, he took my key in part as an expression of his rage and in part in an effort to stay connected to me. Obsessing about whether to return the key helped him to ward off the painful and angry feelings that lay behind his theft, and the tender wish to be close to me as well. The pressure to steal books emerged while he was at home, suffering Maya's abandonment of him. Both at home and in my office, stealing represented his way of transforming his passive experience of abandonment, rage, and loss into an active experience of taking possession. He justified his act by resenting Maya and me for stealing the time that was rightfully his, thus symbolically he had been evening the score—just as he had done as a child by stealing coins from his father's dresser when father was away from home on business. Simply put, stealing protected him from feeling empty, deadened, derealized—in a word, like shit.

Again, he was tremendously moved. He knew that stealing played an important if entirely secret role in his life, but he had never discussed it. It almost seemed as if someone else—someone he knew of but didn't exactly know—had done it. Now he realized that he had been routinely putting himself at phenomenal risk for years—a risk that he'd never registered, although of course he'd always known it! And the people in the bookstore were his friends! He felt he was beginning to experience himself in a new way. He was deeply grateful to me for insisting that his symptom represented his attempt to save his life, rather than proof that at heart he was irredeemably corrupt.

He remembered a dream about some sort of brightly colored object, perhaps a computer; he and a man—me, he thought—talked and talked about what the object was for, but then another man—he didn't know who—came into the room and said, "All that you are saying is true, but you are missing something." "Missing something" became a touchstone for us; Rashid often responded to my interpretations with the phrase or applied it to his own formulations without knowing quite what he meant. He assumed that the something was something Lacanian and arcane—the relation of the *petit objet à* to *jouissance*—or God knew what. Now, he thought that what was missing in the complicated and bright machinery of the dream computer or in our mutual tendency to become overly theoretical was the centrality of his split-off emotions—all that he was unable to say and hardly knew existed. Maybe, he thought, this was what Lacan had meant by the "Real," but he didn't think the figure in the dream who had said that we were "missing something" was Lacan. It was, he thought, a lost aspect of himself.

For weeks he reported no longer feeling the impulse to steal, although in a series of dreams he warned people to protect their belongings from thieves. He was enormously relieved to be dreaming of stealing rather than actually doing it: analysis evidently worked in a remarkable way. He hadn't been able to stop stealing through strength of will: he'd been unsuccessfully willing himself to stop for years. And now it appeared he had succeeded! The symptomatic quality of his attachment to books, however, did not simply disappear. Rather, this attachment seemed to undergo something of a sea change. He began obsessively to buy and sell books, although his obsession no longer carried the erotized intensity of stealing. Rashid continued to go to the bookstore nearly every day, but to shop rather than to "case the joint" in preparation for a robbery. His heart didn't pound, he didn't sweat, he was in no danger of blacking out; his desire for books no longer obliterated every other thought in his head. He bought many books on credit, at first merely adding the new works to his old subterranean hoard, but gradually he began to read them. He mined his trove of forsaken volumes for resale, bringing bags of the old books to second-hand shops, having first scraped each volume clean of mold—even as in his dream, he had scraped the walls of the cave. He used the money he made selling books to pay for the new books he wanted. He was distressed to remain addicted to the acquisition of books but very proud to be acting responsibly. He had a sense of being a new man, a businessman in a world of commercial and intellectual exchange. He thought Lacan would say that he had left the realm of the Imaginaire and entered that of the Symbolic.

On a Monday, he reported that he had spent the sort of weekend that usually drove him crazy—because Maya was out of town—building bookshelves for the living room. He wasn't particularly handy, but he'd managed to get hold of the materials he needed and had sawed, hammered, and glued to beat the band. Then he went down to his basement "dungeon" and carried boxes of books upstairs for the new shelves. He was embarrassed at how proud of himself he felt. I said I was proud of him too. I thought his building a structure in the living room to house the forbidden books was metaphorical of his developing psychological structure and the healing of his vertical split. The idealized object and the unbearable affects associated with it—symbolized by the books he had stolen—were no longer part of a secret, other self whose behavior embarrassed and endangered him, a self that couldn't be integrated within the domain of his reality ego. The books now had a place in the center of his house. They were no longer magical—beyond all price until he stole them—and utterly valueless after he had done so. Now they were worth what he could buy and sell them for in the market-place of the reality ego. He still felt conflicted about them—reading them was still difficult—but the conflict was occurring within a self that he was increasingly experiencing as unified.

There was, however, a downside to his transformation. It was true that he was no longer stealing, but he was feeling increasingly stolen from. He grew more and more aggravated with his friends for using his ideas and failing sufficiently to cite him. It was infuriating for Rashid to see them making names for themselves publishing papers that came out of conversations they'd had with him. He could often tell that they had entirely forgotten that such and such an idea had not only been his, but reflected a school of thought they had not even known existed until he had introduced them to it! His anger frightened him because it was becoming much harder for him to suppress as he always had in the past. He also felt that his anger was largely misplaced. The problem ultimately wasn't that his friends weren't sufficiently referencing him, the problem was that he wasn't writing. He dreamed of a huge tiger in a cage and decided it represented his rage at being unable to break free of the bars he himself placed around his creativity.

He was becoming increasingly fond of me. Remembering a time when he had seen his previous therapist in the street and had taken off in the opposite direction, he wondered how he would feel were he to run into me unexpectedly. He had imagined the analysis would collapse if he saw me outside of the rit-ual space of the office; now it seemed absurd to think so. Also, he was beginning to think we might not be all that different from one another. We were close enough in age and apparently shared an interest in various writers. The best thing was that we often seemed to find the same things funny.

Rashid began to dream and to think about intimate, twinship relations. He taught Conrad's *The Secret Sharer* in one of his classes and found himself renting "buddy" films like *Butch Cassidy and The Sundance Kid,* and *The Sting.* He knew I was from Chicago, a city he had always hated, but that he now found himself liking. How could he have failed to notice the coolness of the blues scene? And he liked watching the Bulls on television. Basketball was such a remarkable, jazzlike game! Did I like blues? He thought I was a basketball fan because he had seen a Bulls schedule on my desk. But then he knew I skied. How could I do something so elitist? Maybe I was just the sort of yuppie he'd always despised. He had a dream in which he saw me wearing a red scarf and schussing down a mountain. I seemed graceful and controlled although I was going very fast. The dream made him happy. He said he'd loved his father but his father couldn't control himself and had turned out to be weak and sick. He liked to think I was athletic and strong. Maybe the red scarf was a sign that my heart was in good shape. He couldn't believe he was talking this way. He sounded to himself like someone about to burst into a chorus of that awful song, "Feelings."

His symptom took a new turn during this phase of twinship. He frequented bookstores less and less and instead bought sweaters—increasingly obsessively as time went by. This was interesting because he had a leftist intellectual's disdain for fashion, and because I normally wore sweaters to work every day, something he seemed never to have noticed. He would often begin sessions by asking how I liked the sweater he'd just bought, and telling me where he'd found it and how much he'd paid. When I finally asked if he thought his sweater buying might have something to do with his recent upsurge of warm feelings for me, he was taken entirely by surprise. He hadn't realized that wearing sweaters might express a wish to be like me, but as he looked at the sweater he had on—one nearly identical to mine—he thought such a wish simply couldn't be denied. He said it felt incredibly important to be close to someone he didn't have to bullshit every minute and defer to; then, after a pause, he added that he partly did feel he had to defer to me just in case I suddenly stopped being the nice person I seemed to be. Indeed, after discussing these feelings, he had a dream in which he came into the office and discovered that I—like Kafka's Gregor Samsa—had metamorphosed into a giant dung beetle! I said his dream reflected his father's metamorphosis from a person he had idealized into one he thought of as shit.

He began to worry increasingly that the analysis might end prematurely. Maya seemed on the verge of being offered a job in another city, and he wondered if he would have time to internalize all that the analysis meant for him. Perhaps what he gained would remain superficial, to be worn, as it were, temporarily, like a sweater. Nonetheless, he suddenly found that he was able to read his primary source material. It had always bored and intimidated him, but now he was working on it with some energy. He was worried, however, because it didn't seem all that interesting. He was planning a trip home over the next holiday and thought he would try seriously to write his dissertation proposal.

He returned from his trip glowing. His friends said he seemed entirely different, vivacious and companionable, in a way they had never seen. They thought it was because he had given up smoking; he joked that it was because he had given up smoldering—with anger. He felt that analysis had changed him, making something possible that he was eager to tell me about. He had decided to scrap his old dissertation plan and to do something entirely fresh and unexpected. He was tired of sitting in the library: he wanted to do field work, like a real historian, and he wanted a project that seemed more in consonance with the person he had become than with the person he had been. He'd decided to work on the question of national unity in his adopted country. He felt that the nation's dream of itself as a united state was inscribed symbolically in a great engineering project he wanted to study. For several sessions we discussed the new idea in terms of the integration and unification of his own divided self. He then reported that he was beginning to write. He was tremendously excited. The couch seemed to him an enchanted ship, a Flying Dutchman, that might at any moment rise into the air and sail away with him.

Following the weekend break, however, everything had changed completely. Rashid was thinking of committing suicide. He had learned on Friday that his cousin Khalid—the cousin who had taught him to steal so many years ago and whose life ever after reminded him of his own—had jumped to his death from the balcony of his apartment. Rashid, beside himself, went to the bookstore several times on Saturday and Sunday, and each time stole a book. All his plans seemed absurd. He was not like me, he was like Khalid, who had been a brilliant, passionate poet, yet utterly helpless and fragile, publishing nothing. Rashid had spo-

ken to Khalid on his recent visit home, and urged him to try psychoanalysis. Khalid said he had been to a million psychiatrists
and they were all frauds; Rashid countered that analysis was different—that it had been incredibly helpful to him. Khalid said
he would look into it, but he hadn't. Rashid felt terribly guilty,
as if his new sense of possibility had contributed to his cousin's
despair. He couldn't understand why he had gone back to stealing books. Perhaps the progress he had made was simply a sham.
I said it was hardly surprising that he found himself relying on
the old symptom to hold himself together in a time of extraordinary pain. Stealing books had always helped him to avoid experiencing unendurable affects, replacing these with feelings of
excitement and triumph. Stealing books had also symbolically
connected him to his father, as now I thought it connected him
to Khalid, even as it had when the two were boys.

For several sessions Rashid mourned. He was silent, angry,
hopeless. When he began to talk, he said Khalid's suicide was
like a prophetic dream: it showed what would happen were
Rashid to be powerful and effective. He was beginning to write
and Khalid killed himself because he could see that Rashid was
achieving something that he himself would never be capable of.
Rashid thought of his father's death; he had fought with his father
and threatened him and his father had blamed Rashid for his
heart condition, as indeed Rashid blamed himself. Rashid's words
and emotions frightened him; if he didn't suppress them, he might
endanger people he cared about and even loved. He always worried that were he to write, his professors would be devastated.
He was sure they had no idea how profoundly he disagreed with
many of their ideas, and he was afraid the violence of his attacks
on their positions would thoroughly destroy their influence in
the field. Rashid was certain that his self-suppression was oedipal:
allowing himself to write meant killing his professor fathers even
as he had in effect killed Khalid. Indeed Khalid's fall from the
window made Rashid think of the fall of Icarus. If he himself
were mad enough to attempt to fly he would soar too close to the
sun, melt his wings, and crash. He remembered blacking out and
seeing stars when he had been excited at the thought of stealing
something, or of doing something great. When I said that he was
frightened of his ambitions, he replied that he sometimes felt
dizzy when he allowed himself to fantasize about the impact his
writing would have on the world.

He knew he had fantasies that he thought amounted to delusions of grandeur. It was embarrassing to say so, but at times he imagined himself as Napoleon. Absurdly, it had recently crossed his mind to inform me that, henceforward, the analysis would be conducted in the throne room of his palace! Of course he had laughed at the thought, but had thought it nonetheless. When I asked why he had never before spoken of this Napoleon self, he replied that he feared I might be offended to think he was so much greater than I and turn against him. I said his fear of overwhelming me with his greatness recalled his fear of vanquishing his professors with his writing. I wondered further if part of what he felt he needed me for was to hold him in check, because his grandiose fantasies made his so anxious. He associated to a famous rock-and-roll lyric that screams "go ask Alice, when she's ten feet tall!" The words refer to the scene in *Alice in Wonderland* where Alice, having eaten "the pill that makes [her] larger," grows so alarmingly that she bursts through the roof of her house. Indeed, he said, it was unnerving and alarming to think there was within him a Napoleon—like the Mr. Hyde within Dr. Jekyll—who stood for everything he consciously opposed: who wanted to seize intellectual power, crush his academic rivals, and dominate his field. I said I thought the problem was not that he had such ambitions, but that they represented such a threat to his equilibrium that he had to split them off from ordinary consciousness; just to talk of them as we were doing left him feeling manicky and out of control. He said it had always angered him to think that I believed in the possibility of a unified subject, but now he wasn't so sure I meant what he thought. Maybe I was talking about an opening into what he called the "otherness" of the self, rather than of its foreclosure.

When Maya was eventually offered a teaching position at a university that arranged a research assistantship for Rashid, he was at once excited and greatly distressed. The offer exceeded anything they had thought possible, but he didn't want to leave the analysis. He felt he had made extraordinary gains, but doubted we had had time enough to guarantee their permanence. He tried hard to work out a plan for staying in town and joining Maya later, but there seemed almost no practical way of making that work. He stopped buying sweaters, but felt again his old impulse to steal books. He didn't, but spoke at length of how powerful the impulse was, and how he could now see the immense role

stealing had played in his psychic economy. He was also beginning to realize how crazy and sad he had always been; he had
known it, but at the same time he had not known it. The process
of terminating analysis and preparing to leave the city painfully
reawakened the anguish of his childhood with its sequence of
unexpected and turbulent moves. He began increasingly to feel
tenderness and pity for the suffering child he had been. He had
dreams of adolescent boys struggling to live as refugees.

His sadness became nearly unbearable following the terrible
news that his most cherished professor was dying and would be
unable to finish the monograph he was writing, one that was to
represent the culmination of his life's work in the field. He made
Rashid a gift of a number of his most treasured volumes. It was
ironic, Rashid thought, that for so long he had felt undeserving
of the books in his possession, and that now he was being honored by his teacher precisely because he saw Rashid as worthy
of receiving his books and disseminating their wisdom.

He thought increasingly of the Jews because I was Jewish. Early
in the analysis he feared I would think him anti-Semitic—
perhaps he was!—and reject him out of hand. But the Jews were
the people of the Book, and had taken their Torah into the dias-
pora and found ways to transform their dispossession, persecu-
tion, and suffering into works of poetry, philosophy, and law.
And of course his family had been exiles and his father had exiled
him from their home in the new land. He was the exiles' exile,
the dispossessed of the dispossessed. And he was a person of
books, forever hoping to transform his own sense of dispposses-
sion into the literature of his field. He wondered about my history and that of my family. Perhaps our fates were similar?

He recognized that stealing books had protected him from
depression and the emptiness of loss by providing excitement,
diversion, and possessions, both material and spiritual. He
began increasingly to dream of his childhood. One dream
reminded him of his nurse who took him on the bus to the poor
district where she lived so that he could ride on her husband's
burro. The sound of buses outside my window reminded Rashid
of the children who rode the old buses without paying by hang-
ing from the railings, and of the rabbits and chickens and pigs
the people carried in their arms. He remembered feeling safe
with his nurse, accepted and loved. He found himself blinking
back tears.

He decided to use psychoanalysis as a model for his new project. Every day he wrote what came into his mind regardless of how trivial or irrelevant it seemed. He had all but scrapped his conviction that he needed to work out a master narrative completely in his head before ever putting pen to paper. He could not believe he had been governed by such a view. He had come to love what he called the "gift of psychoanalysis"—its open-ended spirit of inquiry, its willingness not so much to know as not to know, a spirit he thought psychoanalysis shared with poetry. He wanted to commit himself to that spirit in his own efforts to write.

He thought the analysis required that he rethink his Derridean contempt for a "metaphysics of presence." It made no philosophical sense to require another to serve as a guarantor of one's own being—as had Descartes—and yet the process through which he felt he had come into being in the analysis seemed ineluctably bound to the reality of my presence to him. Perhaps presence in metaphysics hadn't a thing to do with presence in psychoanalysis or perhaps he simply didn't understand what Derrida meant, but it seemed clear to him that my being there had somehow made all the *difference*.

Conclusion

The predominant transference in this case was one of idealization, which organized and structuralized Rashid and began to resolve his vertical split. This idealizing transference provided the frame for a long phase of mirroring—which initially took the form of a twinship—and made possible the transformation of his wayward grandiose self from that of a thief into that of a creative scholar and writer. Rashid saw analysis as an heroic quest into the deepest reaches of the soul and was impressed that a number of his intellectual heroes either were psychoanalysts like Freud and Lacan, or had been powerfully influenced in their own work by psychoanalytic thought—as had been Derrida. He felt better from the first knowing we would meet regularly and often and knowing that I was—literally and figuratively—watching over him. The idea that he was welcome in what he felt was an importantly sacralized space made him feel excited and empowered. When he first lay on the couch he imagined himself to be levitating above it. On his way to my office he felt as if his feet barely touched the ground. He imagined the buildings on my street washed their faces for him, recalling Kohut's description of the gleam in the mother's eye. The great question for him early on was would I be willing to let him stay with me. He imagined me as a grand inquisitor and the Sultan in *Scheherazade*, deciding every hour whether to let him continue to speak or condemning him to death. This recalled his fate growing up; his father continually threatening to throw him out of the house and eventually doing so.

Initially Rashid was disorganized, anxious, guilty, and secretly stealing. He was divided into a public persona marked by unhappiness, longing, humility, and guilt; he couldn't write and felt terrible that he was failing himself and the department that continued to put its trust in him. He wanted desperately to conform to the ideals and values of his profession, which he held in high esteem, and he hated himself for being unable to do so. His split-off persona, however, was entirely different. He saw his teachers as fools and regarded himself as a misunderstood genius. He felt he never received enough credit for his contributions to the department and to the writings of his colleagues and friends. He could tolerate feeling chronically irritated with his life, but he could not tolerate feeling abandoned, deeply enraged, or sad. When depressive affects threatened to overwhelm him, he would steal books. Stealing was dangerous, exciting, forbidden, and he gloried in being secretly above the law.

Stealing books symbolically enacted the tragedy of his relation to his father. He had idealized his father early in life as a man of high principles and cultivation. But his father traumatically disappointed him by beating him, abandoning him to the care of people Rashid didn't know when the family emigrated, throwing down the book he himself had bought Rashid as a present, and banishing Rashid from the house. The result was that Rashid had been unable to use his relations with his father to complete his internal development. Each book Rashid planned to steal carried the promise of the idealized father; the book would allow him to merge with the powerful knowledge it contained and provide the key to completing his dissertation—or symbolically, to completing what was missing in Rashid himself. But like the father who had become shit in his son's eyes, the book became unreadable as soon as Rashid took possession of it.

The analytic task was to reanimate Rashid's relation to an

idealizable object and then to make possible a phase of non-traumatic deidealization that would allow him to contain within himself the psychic structure he required for continued self-development and for the healing of the vertical split. And indeed the relation of self to idealized selfobject immediately began to organize Rashid. He felt less and less agitated, stopped smoking, and lost weight. Before long, he began to talk about his impulse to steal, rather than secretly acting on it.

When he could talk about stealing and especially the sadness and rage that lay behind it, the split began to heal. Rather than stealing books, Rashid began to buy and sell them. He moved them up from the basement—which symbolized their inaccessibility to his reality ego—and into his living room, where they became commodities he traded. Eventually he found himself able to read them.

For some time it seemed very important for him to think of me as above him, elevated by my role as his analyst—Lacan's subject "supposée à savoir." It meant a great deal to him that I knew the work of a number of the authors who were important to him and was happy to think with him when I could in their terms.[1] He worried that he might run into me in the street, fearing that outside of the sacralized space of my office I might seem painfully ordinary to him. His need to imagine me as ideal gradually diminished, and during a long phase of twinship he came to think we were rather alike. During this time he saw me as increasingly fallible, which upset him, but he was able to process his disap-

---

1. Our talk was perhaps often especially bookish and theoretical, but I believe my pleasure in such talk provided an important and empowering empathic matrix for our work. I do not think Rashid would have been able to idealize me as he needed to for a long time had he thought me ignorant of the intellectual matters that were his passion, and I also doubt that the twinship phase of our work would have been possible if he didn't think we indeed shared intrinsically common interests—as we did. Of course, such talk at times played into Rashid's—and my own—defensive inclination to intellectualize feelings. But this idea became importantly thematized in his "missing something" dream, and in our efforts to understand it. Indeed, as our work neared its completion, our talk became less and less theoretical and increasingly about the missing intense feelings. I think this change was a direct effect of his sense that I had been happy to engage with him on the intellectualized side of his split-off grandiosity. Doing so gradually helped him to neutralize the intensity of his grandiose fantasies and to tolerate the painful affects they warded off.

pointment and to rebound from the breaks it created in our empathic connection. He also feared that analysis itself would traumatically fail him, that he would see that it was nothing more than a reductive, totalizing ideology. The thought that I could be like him and his analyst—that he might see me within the office and outside it—and that analysis could be about notknowing rather than a false "purveyor of truth"—made him feel increasingly unified.

The transference next took an increasingly oedipal turn. Buying sweaters to be like me and to feel a sense of warmth from me gave way to a phase of what he felt to be his malignant grandiosity. He began to speak increasingly of his ambitions and his fear of fulfilling them. He had been afraid he was responsible both for the collapse of his father's health and his cousin's suicide, and he worried that if he allowed himself to express himself freely, he would destroy his colleagues and me as well. This would leave him hopelessly disoriented because I would no longer be available to help him contain and neutralize his dizzying grandiose fantasies. His Napoleon self—above the law and seeking hegemony over the world of his profession—was a transformation of the self that had been a thief. Gradually this part of him too became acceptable to him, largely, I think, because he could see it was entirely acceptable to me.

Which brings us to the question of my countertransference. Goldberg (1999) argued that for the analyst to stand on either side of the vertical split makes healing it impossible. Either one is too allied with the patient's wayward behavior and in violation of the values of his reality ego, or one looks with such discomfort at the split-off behavior that the patient is never able to reach the depression and longing it conceals. I had never been a thief and yet it was not difficult for me to feel sympathetic to Rashid's wayward, illegal, and dangerous behavior. I felt it was clear that he stole to try to save himself from pain and to connect unconsciously with his lost and degraded father. There was also a part of me that resonated with his daring, excitement, obsession, and recklessness. In an unconscious effort, perhaps, to manage my reactions to the split in Rashid, I found myself obsessively reading detective novels. The pleasure of such literature is in the opportunity to merge imaginatively with both the heroes and their criminal antagonists—in other words, with attitudes that represent both sides of the vertical split. Indeed the heroes of such works themselves invariably share a great deal with the targets of their investigations. They too are generally somehow outside the law—either amateurs or rebels—in the game because of their fascination with crime and the criminal mind, and compelled by their imaginative relation to the criminals they seek to outwit. They were good models for a psychoanalyst trying to resolve the case of a thief with a vertical split.

In the termination phase of the treatment, Rashid came to see the psychoanalytic process itself as a "usable" structure. He felt he had internalized a new way of seeing the world and planned to make free association the key to his writing.

I found treating Rashid a joy because he loved the process and flourished within its frame, requiring neither special provisions nor extraordinary therapeutic dexterity to make the work go forward. He held onto me during times of separation and derailment, and despite his pain and the travails he had suffered, there was something unsinkable about him that allowed him to hold himself and his relationships together. All then seemed to end well.

But was there something missing? The message of one of his most important dreams was that we were not apprehending his deepest feelings of sadness and rage. The analysis ended when he left the city for a job he had excellent reasons to take. But if it had continued, I imagine we would have faced a deeper and extended period of Rashid's painful disillusionment with me. Such disillusionment lay at the heart of his relation to his father and analytic theory would suggest that Rashid needed more time to work through such feelings in the office than we had. Perhaps theory is simply wrong about this and such an extended working-through period is not always necessary. Kohut believed that once the self of the patient is righted, the interrupted developmental course completes itself after the analysis ends. Perhaps Rashid stayed with me until he had achieved what he came for; this is what we both hoped. But perhaps he feared he would have been unable to endure the tempest of his negative affects, that they would have been overwhelmingly and traumatically disorganizing. Or perhaps he ultimately felt he had been right to fear that I would not have been able to withstand his depression and rage—that there was indeed a split-off part of me that agreed with his assessment that I liked being idealized but did not want to be hated and despised: that he should not go there. If there was an element of flight in his decision to terminate, one imagines his sense of having made analytic thinking the solution to his writing would represent something of a forced rather than an entirely real resolution along the lines of his symptomatic hope that each stolen book might save him. We always end deconstructing our cases and finally never knowing.

8

| # The Case of Alexander
Variations on the Vertical Split—
Psychotherapy of a Delinquent

When Alexander began treatment with me, he was 42 years old, unmarried, and living alone. He was employed by a large computer consulting firm, his third job in as many years. An innovative designer of specialized data bases, he had developed a technology that was to later garner him much success in his field. He had recently relocated from the southeast, where he had been raised by Mexican-Irish parents in a midsize urban community. He dressed expensively, a dandy whose razor-cut hair, manicured nails, spotlessly shined shoes, and biracially exotic looks made him stand out in a crowd.

At our first meeting, he greeted me with a long, cool stare, stiffly shook hands, preceded me into the room, and took my chair. My request that he sit elsewhere earmarked the beginning of a series of exchanges in which actions frequently spoke not only louder, but instead of, words. He gestured; I struggled to translate. He stormed; I tried to steady him. He attacked; I fended him off. My role, as he saw it, was to actively, concretely do something for him, such as provide advice, consolation, or solutions to his dilemmas. Though quite bright, and a veteran of psychotherapy, his capacity to think about himself psychologically fluctuated wildly.

Alexander complained of debilitating anxiety and was visibly distraught as he described the loneliness he felt subsequent to his recent move to town. He said he needed someone to "support and reinforce" him until he settled down in this new environment. Although he made frequent trips home and felt comforted by his mother, with whom he was close, his sense of well-being diminished rapidly on returning to his own apartment. There he propped up his video camera and talked to it, composing a video journal of his travails, attempting to bolster a faltering sense of temporal continuity and physical cohesion as he played back and watched, time and again, his interviews with himself. (Years later he resurrected this method during separations from me. Under the guise of a documentary on leave takings, he described his experience of my absence and in this way built up a sense that what he did on his own, without me, was important.)

During the early months of our meetings, Alexander was in a chronic state of near-fragmentation, primarily due to the unavailability of previously sustaining relationships with close male friends. His recent move had interrupted his contact with one man in particular—Bruce—with whom he had developed a relationship based upon daredevil activities and shared sadistic fantasies toward women. Promiscuously heterosexual, Alexander had dozens of sexual partners whom he delighted in "reeling in and throwing back." He found women burdensome and demanding "shrills" from whom he freed himself as soon as his physical needs were met. Bruce, on the other hand, could always be counted on to fill the role of good-humored playmate. Without him, Alexander said, life seemed empty.

In an effort to counteract these lonely, untethered feelings, Alexander became a master at stimulating and distracting himself. Psychedelic drugs enhanced his senses. Sexual liaisons enlivened him. Prominent in his field, he accepted without discrimination many consulting opportunities, ultimately exhausting himself with his breakneck schedule. Although these activities provided an outlet for exhibitionistic tension, more often than not the end result was one of painful overstimulation. Unable to modulate grandiose fantasies of unlimited personal perfection and power, Alexander reacted with undiluted rage to the smallest hint of criticism. Once, on the occasion of a testimonial luncheon following extensive work for a major client, he harangued his hosts for the lack of appreciation shown him during his stint on the project, listing in aggrieved tones each and every casual slight occurring during his tenure with them. What began as an occasion honoring his accomplishments deteriorated into mutual animosity and name-calling.

Alexander proudly described his frenetic lifestyle as something he had "inherited" from his mother, a vivacious woman who flitted from one social gathering to the next. From the beginning, he said, they seemed to be kindred souls, both having an excess of energy and a special receptivity to beauty, particularly fine art. Alexander had some artistic talent, to which his mother responded effusively, flattering his smallest effort, indiscriminate in her approval. Alexander, for his part, developed an inflated evaluation of his productions. As a result, he found public scrutiny alternately enhancing and humiliating, because it contained elements of both praise and criticism. As a college art major, he took refuge in artforms that required exacting craftsmanship, his painstaking approach to the medium (weaving intricate tapestries, for example) an effort to both ward off criticism and impose structure and limits on a disorganizing exuberance. He said "I forced myself to stay within the lines, when what I really wanted to do was break free and paint with reckless abandon. That felt better, but the paintings weren't any good." (Much later, in a quiet moment, he said, "I've always needed intense feelings—otherwise I lose myself.")

Alexander was his mother's fourth of five children, and second boy. According to her, he was happily welcomed into a lively, bustling family milieu. However, the first 5 years of his life were hidden behind a cloud of repression, with the occasional exception of an isolated memory flashing into awareness through his free associations or emerging in conversations with family members. He treasured these recollections, although he had difficulty deciphering their emotional meaning. For example, he had a poignant early memory of sitting by a window, watching his father and older brother leave for a fishing trip from which he had been excluded, but was not sure what this meant to him. On another occasion, he remembered his father's face changing, flattening, the light in his eyes fading, when Alexander approached him with a sketch he had drawn. As Alexander grew older, these early impressions consolidated into a certainty that his father preferred his older brother's company; both were bluff, unemotional, action-oriented sorts, abrupt and physically aggressive. Their interests were similar—sports, betting, cars; and they looked alike—red-haired, brawny musclemen. Alex was a sensitive soul, artistic, a reader, cried easily, and was generally regarded as an alien entity by the men in his family. He was frequently left behind with his mother, who delighted in his "differences" and often told him so.

During his early childhood, the patient seems to have unsteadily straddled the line between a mutually enhancing merger with his mother and repeated idealizing forays toward his father and the masculine pursuits his father represented. However, most of these latter efforts were dismissed and Alexander's adaptation was to fall back on the mirroring relationship with his mother, albeit with needs now intensified by his father's indifference.

Alexander's most distinctive early memory was of the day his mother returned from the hospital carrying his baby brother, her fifth child, in her arms. He ran screaming from the house and for weeks refused to acknowledge his new brother's presence. Shortly thereafter, his mother discovered a lump in her breast requiring a radical mastectomy, extensive chemotherapy, and repeated hospitalizations. Alexander's behavior following this series of separations was ferociously possessive and solicitous of her welfare. What before had seemed a tender closeness now became a quasiparanoid ownership. The mirroring bond reestablished and reinforced between himself and his mother was now colored by his sense of betrayal and rage and by her depression and loss of vigor—a pale vestige of the lively enjoyment they had shared in earlier years.

Alexander developed a preoccupation with his mother's surgical scar, which came to represent for him the absence of necessary supplies in their relationship. He unsuccessfully endeavored to catch a glimpse of her incision on many occasions, and had long spells of reverie about it. His adult sexual behavior focused in a fetishistic way on his girlfriends' breasts, at which he bit and pulled so aggressively that one complained her nipples were changing shape. (Later, during one of our meetings, he imagined that I was also missing a breast, a fantasy that recurred most insistently when he experienced some deficiency in my response to him.)

He worried about his own body as well. Every blemish was subjected to careful scrutiny. He had a tic in his eyelid—was it noticeable? Did it signify an incipient neurological condition? He was bothered by the shape of his ears. He relentlessly hectored his mother with his misgivings until she finally succumbed to his entreaties and acceded to his desire for cosmetic facial surgery when he was 14 years old.

At one point during his adolescence, his mother confided that she viewed her cancer as God's punishment for her loss of faith (when her own father died) and her son's devotion as her salvation. In some ways, he came to represent his mother's missing father/breast; through him she attempted to remedy a serious defect in herself. His perfection and her merger with it aimed at repairing her own sense of deficiency as a woman.

His involvement in his mother's body led him to view his own body both as marred, in need of reconstruction, and as an object of beauty, to be displayed and celebrated. In his hours with me he was alternately hypochondriacally worried and seeking reassurance, or exhibitionistically provocative. He brought in pictures taken on beach vacations of himself wearing bikini bathing trunks and usually positioned beside a scantily clad woman, and waited eagerly for me to admire his physique and his power to attract these beauties.

Whenever Alexander failed to perform the role assigned to him by his mother, she withdrew into a remote and unresponsive depression which in turn caused him great anxiety. Had they not colluded in situating her at the center of his universe? On the other hand, when things were good between them, she glorified Alexander. He was her treasure, a status conferred by virtue of his exquisite resonance to the subtlest shifts in her mood. He remembered sharing many intimate moments with her, crawling into her bed and embracing warmly following his frequent nightmares, making her famous fried cookies together, feeding each other the raw batter as they laughed and joked with one another. He was her sweetheart, she said, contrasting her husband's oafish behavior with Alexander's beautiful manners. Thus her mirroring was selective and contingent—it required the suppression of his masculine aggressive strivings.

His mother's warm indulgence extended to supporting him in various misdemeanors: he could play hookey; he could have the toy his father forbade as long as it was their secret. In these ways, both mother and son revenged themselves on the father. Alexander's sense of himself as larger than life, above the rules, and destined for stardom was an identity constructed with his mother as part of their unique bond. He avoided the knowledge that his father had rejected him as less than a man by concentrating on his mother's elevation of him as more than a man. Thus was the split in his psyche inaugurated—on one level, the depressed, rejected, defective boy forever in search of idealizable

men with whom he could merge and shore up his own masculine identity; on another, more explicit level, a grandiose, entitled self that endorsed goals compliant both with mother's stated expectations of exemplary behavior and her unstated antisocial agenda.

He said, "I've spent my whole life trying to put my mutilated mother back together again." The Humpty-Dumpty motif, in which mother was both reviled and revered, torn apart and pasted back together again, dominated his relationships with all women. As a result, he was unable to sustain a lasting link to any woman, retreating into an injured, self-justified rage at the first sign of disappointment, which he invariably experienced as the woman's neediness. He said, "My mother used me as her emotional crutch," a role Alexander rejected with a vengeance during adolescence. "If she said, 'Be careful,' I'd do something twice as dangerous just to get even. If I wanted something and she said no, I'd steal it. I felt I deserved it." When he planned a party but his new girl-friend came down with the flu and was unable to attend, he flew into an unforgiving fury, blaming her for deliberately spoiling his good time. He ranted, "I need not only a beautiful girlfriend, but a healthy one too."

Alexander never entirely relinquished hope of establishing a tie with his father; during adolescence and young adulthood he made intermittent attempts to connect with this remote man on some basis. Despite the fact that his father had refused to accept the reality of his son's temperament, his interests, his very self-configuration as a boy, Alexander now approached his father as though the latter were capable of psychological insight and self-awareness, in parallel fashion denying his father's real personality. He once advanced on father with his ever present video camera, suggested a taped interview, then posed questions startling in their tactlessness, such as, "What was the impact of Mom's mastectomy on your sex life?" He, who under other conditions had a fairly sophisticated grasp of social nuance, seemed oblivious to the emotional mayhem he created by these queries.

Nevertheless, a nascent identification with his father did develop and was embodied in Alexander's pursuit of success in his professional life. Alexander's father, by virtue of hard work, stamina, and uncanny intuition, had amassed a large fortune and was much respected by his peers. Alex set out to make a similar success of his life, devoting himself with unstinting zeal to research and product development. His efforts met with much

acclaim. Furthermore, his research was informed by an ideal—extending the knowledge base of his field—although this ideal was initially buried beneath the commercial applications of his work. This sector of his self expanded to occupy the latter part of his treatment, solidifying into a compensatory structure designed to bypass his malignant grandiosity.

Alexander's rejection by both parents at each developmental epoch had a specific impact on the way he constructed relationships with others. As a youngster, he returned to his mother for the warmth, acceptance, and positive mirroring missing in the relationship with his father. His mother, however, was unable to respond to him in his own right, as a lovable little boy developing an independent male self; he was appealing to her only insofar as he devoted himself to her and complied with her narcissistic wishes. For example, she showered him with affection when he accompanied her social clique to cultural events, especially when he impressed them with his knowledge. If, however, he chose to shoot baskets with other boys, she pursed her lips, made snide comments, and withdrew. A feminine affiliation or trend took shape in his view of himself as being like mother and her female friends—sensitive, artistic, and emotional. His exceptional mathematical abilities and athletic talents were submerged during middle childhood, playing second fiddle to his mother's desire that he become her special version of a gentleman.

His need for mirroring shifted during adolescence from his mother to a group of rebellious, angry boys, classmates who applauded his extravagant performances and gleefully joined him in a covert rejection of conventional values. Assorted delinquent acts provided the glue holding these relationships together. Glorying in snubbing the establishment, he actively engaged the rejection he had passively experienced as a child. With his cohorts in crime, he became a thief. He took whatever he wanted whenever he wanted it—candy bars, video games, or his best friend's girlfriend. There was a cold and ravenous quality to these encounters and never any sense of real satisfaction. Whatever he took was soon spoiled and then discarded, including the girl, whom he left with a sexually transmitted disease.

As an adult, his delinquencies focused on a particular target—women—and were imbricated with sadistic sexual fantasy. With his male companions, he playacted these fantasies, constructing elaborate scenarios complete with dialogue that each participant learned by heart and tossed back and forth in an escalating frenzy of mutual stimulation. One particular movie typified by abusive verbal imagery formed the nexus of their dance—which at times resembled a strutting courtship ritual, and at others the complex nonverbal mutual cuing of young children playing an old familiar game. Psychedelic drugs often enhanced the sense of power and merger achieved through this interplay. A frightening cessation of empathy for any other object accompanied his misbehavior. He temporarily obliterated the rest of his life and anyone who was in it during these spells of antic madness.

Clinical Process

Alexander, referred by his internist after he complained of anxiety, visited me on a once-weekly basis for 5 years. Occasionally he increased his hours, usually in response to an external crisis.

His initial approach to me was distant and distrustful. After a few preliminary niceties in which his mother's model boy made a brief appearance, my role in our relationship became clear: I was to be both the audience for his exploits with his friend Bruce, and the target of them. He transmitted to me, via filmed images of his fantasies, his need and contempt for women. In contrast, the relationship with Bruce was construed as conflict free. He said, "When I'm with Bruce I'm happy in a way I never feel with a woman. All the women in my life want is to take away my happiness. Demand! Demand! Demand! You with the bill and all the others who expect flowers, romance, and sweet nothings whispered in their ears!"

The pornographic art movie that he and Bruce role-played has been described as a "coming of age movie . . . in which sex has the danger and heightened excitement of a horror picture . . . a sick joke version of the primal scene" (Kael, 1989). Alexander was especially entranced by its depiction of the sadomasochistic subjugation of women, noting: "It's important you understand the meaning this movie has for me. My relationship with Bruce revolves around it. We both really like the angry violent characters in it. We do the lines together."

Alexander insisted that I watch the movie rather than discuss it with him, inexorably pushing me toward some form of action. Either I submitted to his wishes or I opposed them; there was no middle ground. He brought me his own personal copy; I delayed,

demurred, sensing I might somehow be caught up in the mael-
strom of his sexual desire through the imagery of a film that "puts
its audience into an erotic trance." For some time, I avoided actually watching what had become in my mind "his movie," resist-
ing what I experienced as a too rapid, too early transference–
countertransference regression. Temporarily, Alexander and I
side stepped a confrontation with an essential dynamic in our
relationship.

He came to his therapy hours regularly but resentfully, feeling exploited by my demands for payment, confined by the 45-
minute time limit, dissatisfied with my "lack of warmth and
uptight conservatism." He challenged me—had I ever tried
LSD?—and wanted to know whether there was any commonal-
ity in our backgrounds or experience. Although his curiosity constituted one of his first camouflaged overtures toward me as a
potentially usable selfobject, it oscillated with a view of me as a
wounded and devouring maternal figure. He was certain that I
was jealous of his relationship with Bruce and would undermine
it if given the opportunity. He gleefully described the many ways
he could deceive me if he desired. He reminisced about his mother,
her need to come first with him, and his duplicitous evasion of
this expectation. Of his trickery (mainly lying) I said, "This is the
way you create a separate space for yourself, a place where you
can do things your way and feel free of this terrible pressure to
please me. It's difficult to feel so divided—wanting us to be alike
yet worried you'll lose yourself or be taken over by my needs."
"Sometimes," I added, "I think it feels the same way with Bruce,
but you don't dare defy him out of fear he'll leave you."

Separations from me were invariably preceded by crude sexualization of our relationship and followed by intense rage. He
returned in a manic state from vacations spent with Bruce, relating with relish the sexual scenarios they had spun in which I was
the target—dehumanized, controlled, and ultimately discarded.
He minimized the significance of the relationship with me, yet
kept me in mind all the while. He evinced no shame, remorse, or
even embarrassment as he told his pornographic tales, which
seemed to express hatred and revenge in a global, undifferenti-
ated way. Often he toyed with terminating our work, either
because he had not been helped or had gotten better on his own.
Although this pattern was repeated without variation following
every separation, and I doggedly delineated its antecedents, for

quite some time his sense of loss when we were apart and his affectionate tie to me, and mine to him, remained implicit and inaccessible.

Alexander listened to my comments about his feelings and reactions impassively, neither denying nor confirming them. Most attempts to turn his attention to his inner life, specifically to aspects of the negative transference, fell on deaf ears. His symptoms were egosyntonic; he described them as intensely pleasurable diversions. Only when his tension increased to a calamitous level, which was frequent given the fragility of his self-cohesion, did these antisocial pursuits take on an all-encompassing urgency that afterward left him depleted. At these times, his readiness to hear a word or two from me increased, though mainly he regarded me and my pain-killing properties as ineffectual. His motivation for an intense, dynamically oriented treatment relationship seemed negligible. He was not overtly distressed by his antisocial symptoms. His pattern of regulating tension via action was longstanding. He had a proclivity for rage, and with it a conviction that responsibility for his problems resided outside himself. He showed little resilience in the face of injury.

However, he made a comment in our early weeks around which I was able to organize a sense of hope and purpose for our work together. Following a particularly promiscuous weekend in which he disparaged and discarded one sexual partner after another, I grew weary of listening to his stories of sexual conquest and inquired as to why he came to see me. Quite startled, his response was immediate: "I want to get married someday. I'm not sure I'll ever be able to. I feel like this therapy is my only chance." I recognized this statement as an acknowledgment of reality, hitherto hidden behind his noisy displays, and evidence of a split in his psyche within which some therapeutic work might proceed. We continued along our rough and rocky road together, albeit with an altered purpose. I was now searching for signposts of the "side-by-side existence of disparate personality attitudes in depth" (Kohut, 1971, p. 183), that might eventually be brought into some form of meaningful relation to each other. His words awakened in me a submerged sense of tenderness that, I hoped, paralleled a similar but unexpressed capacity in Alexander.

Gradually, small fissures in Alexander's bond with Bruce began to appear. The occasional offhand remark—Bruce had not admired one of his achievements, or Bruce had been unsympathetic to him, or made mild fun of him—occurred with more regularity. I responded in the vein of, "It's surprising when someone who is usually attuned to you in such special ways has a momentary lapse," encouraging him to explore the breach and its impact on his sense of well-being. Within his overriding idealization of Bruce, Alexander permitted more of his own doubts to emerge and—to me, for now—Bruce's character took more realistic shape. Bruce abused a wide variety of drugs, appeared to have no guiding ideals in his work, lied to his wife, and permitted his child to play with weapons. He exposed himself and Alexander to dangerous situations, and taunted him if he demurred. On one occasion, my patient wondered whether Bruce's unflappable, "always cool man" stance was less self-possession than callous indifference. During a frightening, eerie, bad trip on LSD, Alexander plaintively begged Bruce for help but was rebuffed and abandoned: "Your problem, man," Bruce tossed back over his shoulder as he left, looking for a willing woman and a blow job.

Alexander's description of these disappointments was both tearful and hostile. He shifted between using me as confessor to his need for Bruce and viewing me as a competitor with Bruce for his affections. When he dared to confront Bruce, the confrontation evolved into a reintensification of their bond—with me once again the target of their disdain. Giggling hysterically, he related conversations in which I was the subject of obscene fantasy. Then, shifting forward on the couch, he glared at me. "What if I grabbed you right now? Do I scare you?"

I acknowledged my uneasiness, and wondered aloud if his wish to grab me had anything to do with his sense that I was trying to snatch away his treasured relationship with Bruce? I asked if there was an even deeper feeling—of needing something from me that would not be freely given, thus requiring the use of force. His anger dissipated and as he leaned back against the couch, he sighed, "It's just so damn hard to make an impact."

This interaction, in which the patient threatened me through his verbal and behavioral provocations, illustrates the interplay of the split transference. The misbehaving sector embodied in his alliance with Bruce served to defensively ward off his need for me to step into the applauding maternal role, a need that his mother corrupted and was thereby infused with a rage and distrust so strong that it fueled wishes to literally grab and terrorize me. His sigh was an expression of the self sequestered behind the horizontal barrier, of relief that I understood his deeper, unarticulated need for a spontaneous affirmation of his germinal masculine self, one which followed its own, not his mother's, developmental program.

This event was paralleled by shifts in my internal response to Alexander. His "objectification" of me as a sexual cipher narrowed my view of him; at these times his identity collapsed for me into his misbehaviors, and I kept him at a distance. Thus we created an intersubjective context in which I became cooler and more self-protective, and he, in a complementary way, escalated his efforts to engage me. As he began to detach himself from Bruce, his need for a vivid engagement with me deepened. His threat to grab me effectively dismantled the retreat I had unknowingly constructed and propelled me into action—as I scrambled for an interpretation of his wary distrust I, at the same time, made it for myself: I did distrust his alliance with Bruce, and, indeed, my aim had been to wrench him free of Bruce's magnetism, then pull him into my own orbit. Inadvertently standing in his mother's footsteps, I unconsciously began the process of recruiting him as a selfobject who could become lovable to me—his silent resonance with my unconscious agenda had at first prompted an intensification of his bond to Bruce, but paradoxically, enabled him to experience more directly the repressed needs of his earliest relationship with his mother.

As Alexander became more confident of my comprehension of his divided self, of my capacity to speak to both sides of it, and of the depth of my involvement in a struggle that had become my own as well, his need for Bruce began to ebb. Sporadic attempts to reinstate their relationship in its old, sexualized, sadistic glory were increasingly unsuccessful; it no longer served the self-confirming, enhancing functions on which it had originally been built. Bruce was not the devoted, mentoring, paternal object he had hoped for, but a delinquent with no real empathy; their dialogues were empty. Much later, he mused that Bruce could be a stand-in for the Rob Lowe character in *Bad Influence* who, under the charismatic guise of idealized power, actually corrupts and destroys his acolyte.

These early encounters between Alexander and me were marked by constant upheaval and chaos. Almost all affect was immediately translated into perverse, antisocial action. I was concerned about his impulse control both within and outside the office. At first he had little self-observational capacity. Descriptive insights, aimed at establishing links between actions or feelings, had limited utility. The idea that his behavior might summarize an array of complex feelings was novel to him, but as he considered its ramifications in a myriad of encounters, a small, potentially neutral space between affect and action began to grow. That his behavior was a process, not just a series of discrete events, had special meaning to him. It implied the idea of self-continuity over time, and in relationships. Breaks in continuity began to have increased salience for him and it was around these disruptions that our later work focused.

Two changes occurred in the opening phase of this psychotherapy. The first, the loosening of his tie to Bruce, was brought about in part by our joint description of the needs he directed toward Bruce, the disappointments that accrued, and the accommodations he attempted in order to preserve the relationship. Although he required me to admire his dedication to Bruce, Alexander permitted my responses to soothe him in the face of Bruce's occasional disdain. Gradually this relationship was deidealized, although this was an up and down process, interspersed with periods of increased allegiance and periods of depression and disappointment.

Second, his relationships with women began to soften. He mentioned his worry lest he never be able to sustain a relationship with a woman. On the other hand, he was proud of his commitment to me. His wildly delinquent behavior diminished, as did his promiscuity. Bruce was in the background. Alexander continued to look for powerful male companions but now his choices were more benign.

Having disentangled himself from the lockstep stranglehold of his addictive dedication to Bruce and involving himself in a more meaningful way with me, Alexander began to recognize the depth of his need for sustaining relationships. At this point, he met a young woman, Mary, and much to his surprise, fell in love with her and she with him.

A stormy courtship ensued. She was the embodiment of perfection; she was a harridan bent on destroying his peace of mind. Her beauty enhanced him; her illnesses infuriated, embarrassed, and diminished him. He was continuously separating from and reuniting with her and, in parallel fashion, with me. Preservation of the relationship with Mary, he realized, required the continuation of his therapeutic work; otherwise his hypersensitivity to the smallest variations in her understanding led to overwhelming tantrums from which he felt unable to recover. He felt trapped, he said, like a tiger pacing in its cage, snarling at the confinement imposed by his emotional ties to Mary and to me.

Our work elaborated the various ways in which his emotional stability hinged upon the responsiveness of his selfobjects. Alexander began to appreciate the enormity of his vulnerability and the extent of his need for affective attunement. These insights were accompanied by depression. He described me as an island of calm in the stormy sea that was himself (foreshadowing an idealization that would gradually take over the latter part of our work). At this time, my function was primarily to mirror him: he imagined himself my favorite patient; he simultaneously savored and feared my fantasied envy of his love for Mary; he worried lest I stop paying attention to him, as had his mother whenever he put his needs first.

Following an 8-month courtship, Mary (now his fiancée) agreed to live with him. No longer faced with recurrent separations from her, stabilized by the "dailiness" of their life together, Alexander's volcanic furies abated. He began to settle down. For her part, Mary provided a milieu that contained and calmed him. No longer distracted by external crises with Mary, Alexander turned his attention to himself and his relationship with me.

Separations from me now became occasions for spells of psychological disequilibrium. Each disruption seemed to entail a threat of self-dissolution. Alexander had terrifying fantasies that I would die and leave him alone and helpless. A poignant detail of these fantasies emerged: he suffered an accident and was left paralyzed and brain injured, unable to perform even the most rudimentary self-regulatory functions on his own. He dreamed his spinal cord was severed and he was covered with feces, screaming to be killed, images dramatically delineating his fears of regression in the absence of his sustaining objects.

He had a recurrent preoccupation that I, like mother, was missing a breast, which we came to understand as a worry that a vital part of me, present before his leave taking, was now absent. Like mother, I might be unable to provide the supplies he required for emotional survival. He feared returning to find me decimated by his abandonment, the empty depressed mother in need of his rehabilitative efforts. If I faltered in my understanding of this process, his frustration assumed a paranoid cast; I was a fake; I had gotten my degree off a matchbook cover; I was an exploiter, unethical, out to take his money and leave him with nothing; I should be raped or murdered. Thus we came to understand his rage at his mother when she failed to provide essential functions and the parallel deterioration of his internal representations in the face of his frustration; ergo his paranoid construction of my motivation.

As his wedding approached, his anxiety sharpened. Fears of being usurped and absorbed plagued both Alexander's dreams and waking moments. He was acutely aware of his need for rock-solid steadiness from his fiancée, and for unvarying empathic resonance from me. He was barely able to contain impulses to discharge tension through raw exhibitionistic activity. At the worst possible moment, from his vantage point, I unexpectedly cancelled an hour. He did not return my telephone call but flew into a rage with Mary, then called an old girlfriend with whom he had telephone sex. On his way to the next hour with me, he had a fantasy: "I'm in the hospital in a coma. The wedding's been cancelled. All the guests are there. Mary thinks, `Thank God we're not married yet,' packs her belongings, and moves out. I come out of the coma calling your name, but no one has heard of you. It's like the *Twilight Zone*, like you never existed."

I responded:

> We've been talking about how both relieved and frightened you feel in this deepening attachment to me and to Mary. In the midst of this, I cancelled your appointment, and it was as though you had to put all your tender feelings aside. You found yourself in a coma, back into the land of not feeling, where you resided most of your childhood. And then, because I had let you down, you sought out the solace and comfort of your old girlfriend. It is the woman from the past who is recognizable at these moments, the one who cannot be trusted and over whom you must exercise complete control, the sex slave who does your bidding in such an admiring way.

His need to enact his feelings erupted in the last hour before his wedding. Thanking me profusely for all I had done, he reached out to touch my hand as he walked through the door, seemed to change his mind at the last minute, seized my arms and literally crushed me against his chest. Then, grinning triumphantly, he bade me goodbye. I stood in the doorway dumbfounded, stunned and silent. His "hug" had the quality of an assault, unexpected and violent, and I sampled the paralysis he must have felt in his mother's suffocating embrace. And, like him, I was filled with the wish for revenge. I had a palpably physical sensation/memory of his arms like steel bands cutting into me, which I wanted to erase through some form of counterattack. I lost all empathy for the frightened boy within this frightening man, who again, as he faced a separation from me, lost faith in my staying power, lost track of the relationship that existed between us, and moved back into his own private twilight zone of sadistic action.

Alexander's own memory of our physical encounter sustained him through the prenuptial parties, his wedding, and his honeymoon. At last he had an experience of me he could literally hold onto. On his return, smiling broadly, he said, "Hugging you felt like a victory, like the achievement of a goal. I felt euphoric when I left. I was in charge!"

In fact, he continued, he was flying so high that he had taken the initiative and hugged one of his female associates goodbye as well. When I inquired as to her response, he chuckled and said she seemed as surprised as I had been. He paused, looking doubtful. Since then she had been stiff and distant and had avoided him as much as their work permitted. Hesitantly now, he asked about my reaction to his hug. I told him I had given it a great deal of thought, particularly in relation to his mother and her lack of enthusiasm for his marriage, how that had reawakened his disgust with her ownership of him as a boy. "Your hug," I continued,

> brought all that insecurity and frustration into the room between us. I think it stemmed both from your wish to be immersed with me in a stimulating way, your need for me to admire how masculine and powerful you can be, and from your need for reassurance that I would not abandon you if you chose another love object. Your anger with me for seeming to withhold all of this comfort motivated your "theft of love" both from me and from your colleague.

My interpretation of Alexander's theft of love attempted to

address both the vertical and horizontal barriers in his psyche. What had been repressed was, literally, his right to a life as a functioning man, one who could, like father, marry and someday have children, who could sustain a meaningful and intimate relationship with a woman. His own efforts in that direction had been repeatedly squelched by his mother's withdrawal or indirect criticism via her attacks, first on his father, then on his girlfriend. On the eve of his wedding, as Alexander contemplated an actual and symbolic separation from me, he regressively reconstituted the defense that had served him well as a child: he disavowed his need for confirmation of this step forward, one of independent initiative in which he could live his own life as a man, and retreated to the narcissistic union with mother in which he demanded a response to his primitively displayed power. With this, he also "undid" his knowledge that these were symptomatic actions, and treated them as once again entirely reasonable. In this patient, the vertical split sometimes narrowed to an infinitesimal seam as the antisocial sector expanded and threatened to engulf his entire personality. Relocating the reality sector was no small task. The tiny fissure was found in this instance in his concern over the repercussions of embracing his colleague; this opened the door to self-observation.

Much later, when the transference had stabilized, his newfound capacities to observe and reflect on his emotional life had solidified and he was able to affectively link his sexual interest in me to separations from me, he commented: "You know, you always look more attractive to me right before you go away. I get especially preoccupied with your breasts. It's my way of intensifying things before you leave so I can have a stronger picture of you while you're gone." He shook his head, then added with a wry smile, "With me, there's never a dull moment. But it bothers me. This need to control. It's like I seize images of you that I can hang onto—a way of remembering there's something good enough to keep me here."

Alexander was outlining his recognition of the structural defect in his self with these reflective, occasionally humorous comments. He was describing the manner in which he used the relationship with me to fill in these gaps as well as the fragility of his evocative memory during my absences. Although the sadistic elements of his sexualization were growing egodystonic, he nevertheless continued to seek intense momentarily cohesion-promoting stimulation through sexual enactment and fantasy. This was most pronounced during the times we were apart; he flirted with coworkers; he cruised singles bars and engaged in suggestive conversations; he frequented pornographic bookstores and strip joints. If his behavior stopped short of actual sexual encounters, it was a thin and fading line he trod between fantasy and action.

Midway through our work, Alexander experienced a traumatic event that he likened in magnitude to the birth of his brother. Basking in the glow of his burgeoning success, he neglected to prepare for a presentation of his work and, consequently, did poorly. He lost a highly lucrative contract and felt shamed by his client, an international conglomerate eager to have his mathematical models marketed far and wide. He entered a state of shocked, nearly catatonic immobilization that lasted for several weeks; then he grew incoherently enraged. His failure had now become a deliberate rejection on the part of the decision makers, some of whom he knew personally and had admired for years; he had been refused recognition and membership in the inner circle of elitist consultants. He told me, "It feels like I lost a part of myself. As though I have no worth as a human being." In a strikingly parallel fashion, he once again employed, at age 45, the solution he had grasped at age 5; he turned away from the idealized men in his life to embrace me as the feminine embodiment of support for his crumbling self. Loudly he proclaimed his intention to leave his field and pursue a career in psychology. "I'll show those fuckers I don't need them" he shouted. "They're nothing but a bunch of charlatans!"

His idea of eschewing his professional identity in favor of mine was relatively short-lived. Though he considered registering for a few psychology courses, he did not actually carry through. His work with me now focused on how, in the face of his disappointment, he catastrophically devalued all he had created. In essence, I sensed he needed me to remember who he had been before this failure, in order to help him seize once again the affective tone of his goals and ambitions. Our interpretive work centered on the depth of his need for an idealized father and the terrible, painful anomie he suffered when rebuffed.

He grew depressed and, from time to time, grief stricken. He recalled an endless series of disappointments as a boy, yearning for his father's love but finding it to be illusory, like smoke— dispersing as soon as he reached out to touch it. He also remem-

bered moments of real affection shared with his father, memories that like glowing embers unearthed beneath the ashes of his
despair, did not fade away. He tearfully recalled his father's mad
dash onto the football field following a brutal concussive tackle,
the rush to the hospital, his father's calming words. He remembered his father's eyes filled with tears when they said their good-
byes at summer camp. He recollected the occasional embrace,
kindly looks, proud smiles. We realized he had never fully given
up on his father, despite his conscious depreciation of him.

When he decided not to attend the annual meetings of his scientific group, planning instead to visit his greatly admired elderly
cousin, he dreamed: "I'm running away from an old high school
friend who has suddenly become psychotic. I take a dive—to
escape—thinking I can fly—but I crash on the concrete instead.
I end up paralyzed and crying for help. A man is bending over
me."

We discussed the dream's poignant characterization of the
crushing blow he suffered at the hands of men who seemed oblivious to his needs, his effort to flee these feelings by once again
taking refuge in a magically grandiose solution (flying), and his
newly awakened recognition that this strategy would fail; indeed
it had contributed to the disaster he now faced. It was his self
that had been shattered. His pain was agonizing and he felt helpless to assuage it. He asked if we might meet more often.

Alexander's wholesale incorporation of me as therapist,
attempted in the depths of his regression and temporary loss of
self-cohesion, was abandoned. In its place, in a quiet unobtru-
sive manner, beginning as a delicate counterpoint to his noisy
narcissistic displays, an idealization of the therapeutic relationship emerged. Small gestures—he liked my arrangement of fall
flowers, he had made one too—softened his demeanor during
the hours. He expressed gratitude for my devotion. "You were
there for me when I really needed you. You've become very special to me. I want to give you something." Would I accept a gift
from his foreign travels? He brought me a book, a fictionalized
account of two great men analyzing each other. His therapy, he
said, had awakened the "lad of infinite promise" within himself
and, as a tribute to me, he wanted to write the story of his treatment. He wished to know more about me as a person, my political beliefs, family life, and more. He once wept, in the throes of
his admiration, "No matter how hard I tried, I'd never be as good

as you. I feel like I'm drowning in your eyes. Your concern. I love you. I want to emulate you, follow in your footsteps."

Although the shift in Alexander's demeanor sharply contrasted with his earlier depreciation and was a welcome relief, his loving gaze sometimes felt like a spotlight shining unremittingly on me and all that I did. His adoration was discomforting and resulted in several missteps on my part. For example, on one occasion I misinterpreted his idealizing wish to merge with me as compliance and submission to what he perceived as my agenda. I did not realize that he was delighting in our seeing things the same way. He left that particular hour, and in a fit of frustration with his wife, called her stupid, useless, and uninteresting; he then found his way to a neighborhood bar where he flirted with the bartender for hours. Afterward, he saw a movie in which a woman was dismembered, her torso kept alive in a box. When he reported these events in his next hour, I wondered with him whether the fascination with the bartender and need for a response from her had to do with his feeling less lovable with me, that I had failed to grasp what he was telling me, his tender feelings for me, and that it was I, not his wife, who was stupid. (Once again he had sought to resolidify his shattered self-esteem via sexualization and sadistic control of his faltering selfobjects.) He said, "It's like there's a river of discontent raging inside of me. It really depresses me. Things are catching up with me. I can't delude myself that I'm okay anymore. This stuff really bothers me." He wept.

His capacity to reflect on his sexualized and delinquent behavior had deepened immeasurably as exemplified in his recollection that

> I always used to make you a cunt in order to control you. It had a real aggressive tone. I was manipulating you with all those fantasies. It's taken me this long to really talk about sex (by this he meant intimacy). Before I'd talk about it just to win women over, impress them, so I could control them or fuck them.

Failing to win the business contract seemed to recapitulate experiences, not only of his father's rejection, but of his father's love as well. These memories emerged from repression to imbue the analytic relationship with a healthy glow of intimacy, providing it with forward momentum. Alexander, in his depression, searched for explanations of his feelings; his need to enact them was diminished. He had finally encountered, in an emotionally relevant way, vast reserves of sadness, depletion, and helplessness. His reliance on me for affect containment, regulation, and soothing had in part replaced his need for me to observe and affirm his grandiose displays. At one point he said "I feel like we have deepened. The difference for me now is that I feel understood. You are constant. You don't get defensive. You keep your focus on me, even when I'm angry."

In the context of this newly awakened trust, he disclosed, a year after the event, that he had cheated in his presentation, which was why he had failed to win the contract. As part of his talk, he had presented a colleague's data as his own. He said, "I didn't feel bad about doing it at the time. I felt it would help me. Especially since I hadn't prepared. Now I feel ashamed." We addressed his lack of confidence in himself, its sources and repercussions, in that the prospect of failure literally dogged him every minute of his life, simultaneously spurring him to greater achievement and undermining him the moment success was attained. He began to realize that he was actually anxious when he broke rules, and it was this anxiety that his clients had perceived, prompting their closer scrutiny of his ability to manage their project.

Several months later, we had a lively interchange about his dishonesty. Having suffered another slight at the hands of the senior clientele in his field, Alexander toyed with the idea of writing an anonymous letter charging one of them with unethical conduct. One of these senior executives, Alexander learned, had indulged in an exploitative affair with an underage girl. Alexander viewed himself as an avenging angel, with every right to retaliate for the mistreatment he had suffered at the hands of this man. Astounded by this plan, I reacted unthinkingly, exclaiming "But you cheated! You plagiarized the data!" to which he responded with incipient, fiery self-righteousness, "But they don't know that!" "Yes," I replied, "but you do!" He paused, looked perplexed, disoriented, and then began to smile with genuine warmth. "I suppose I do," he said, "I just hadn't realized it."

I persisted in my comments:

These men never grasped the esteem in which you hold them, nor the depth of your appreciation, when they invited you to compete for that contract. You worked very hard to earn their admiration, but too often it's been too little, too late. I think that when you were faced with that presentation, all these feelings surfaced: your wish to shine, your anxiety about not being good enough, and your anger at being overlooked. Thus, in your anxiety, the temptation to use the additional data was irresistible—both as a shortcut to success and as a way of thumbing your nose at their stultifying rules and regulations. It's understandable then, that the logic you apply to them—that they did something wrong and should be held accountable—doesn't apply to your own actions, because yours were the actions, at heart, of a despairing child, and as such you wish to lash out at the one member of the committee you can hurt.

He returned the next hour stating that my emotional outburst (I had been flabbergasted) constituted a turning point for him. He had seen the division within himself in action and he, too, had begun to feel surprised by his capacity to disavow his own knowledge in the pursuit of revenge. Before his eyes, he said, the righteous rage building a head of steam, first in response to the perfidy of his clients, and then in regard to my criticism, melted away. His appropriation of the data, he realized, explained his failure, and this was in an odd way comforting; he was no longer the injured party, disdained by his business associates, helpless to right a wrong. The fact that he could experience his own actions as having brought about this catastrophe seemed to detoxify the utter failure. He embarked on a detailed exploration and recollection of his response to the clients' increasingly pointed questions. As his associations unfurled, it became clear to both of us that the regression he experienced during the presentation had led him to sabotage it in his old misbehaving ways.

He had one last halfhearted fling with Bruce after which he reached two conclusions: the reality of his relationship with Bruce could harm him; and the fantasy of a sadomasochistic partnership in which women were controlled and rejected was no longer the only basis on which he could construct his masculine self. Although he continued to require a selfobject to support this masculine aspect of his self, the foundation upon which mutuality could be established shifted toward the attainment of ideals rather than grandiose displays. I was perceived in progressively more idealized terms and Alexander began to entertain the desire for a child—for whom he could be a guiding and mentoring parent.

The final year of Alexander's psychotherapeutic work was marked by expansion of his self-understanding paralleled by changes in his life that reflected these insights. He left the organization with which he had been affiliated for the past several years to launch his own business, enduring the ambiguity and loneliness this entailed because he wanted to follow his own program of development. Alexander continued to write but in a more personal vein, keeping a journal of his dreams and inner experiences; he was less focused on publication and self-promotion.

A baby boy was born. Alex flourished in his role as parent, eschewing much of his foreign travel to stay home with his wife and son. Though burdened at times by fleeting fantasies when he saw a pretty woman, he had little inclination to act on his impulses; indeed, his sexual desire in general diminished as did his addictive sexual behavior with his wife. He said, "Sex is pleasant but I can take it or leave it—there's no longer the charge." He felt a little melancholy about the loss of passion in this sphere but was more concerned with other areas of his life: building a home and family, managing his frustration and bouts of low self-esteem when friends or business associates were unavailable or unresponsive.

He eased into termination with the idea of taking a break rather than ending the relationship. He had fantasies of having lunch with me, visiting informally, calling to tell me about milestones in his life. At our last meeting, he brought me a gift—a favorite compact disk; the soft melodies, he hoped, would recall for me his voice, the music we made together. Not surprisingly, he ended his therapy with an action, the gift itself a communication in the nonverbal realm.

Almost a year later he returned for a single visit. Planning to have surgery for a long-standing ailment, he had cancelled the procedure at the last minute due to mounting anxiety. He said, "I thought of calling you, but toughed it out instead. I decided, if I'm this anxious, what's the rush? I can wait awhile." His inclination to dash into a confrontation with his fears had been replaced by a gentler approach to himself, he felt, an approach highlighted in his relationship with his little boy, with whom he felt quite protective.

He talked about the ups and downs of his business, the loss of another important contract, difficulties he'd had with a client. Reflecting on his long-standing vulnerability to criticism he said, "You know how I am—I ruminate. Is it that I'm not valuable enough to them? Is that why they treat me this way? I was able to put it in a context, but not without a struggle."

He then proceeded to his central reason for making the appointment. He had decided to once again apply for work with the prestigious client who had earlier crushed his confidence, a decision reached by putting aside his residual anger and fear in the service of a realistic desire for professional recognition. He had resumed attending his national meetings and no longer felt excluded from the old boys' network. Actually, he said, his desire to belong had diminished. Nevertheless, he felt uneasy as he faced this challenge and wanted to talk over his concerns beforehand.

At the end of the hour, I inquired about his relationship with a friend and colleague, on whom he had relied for emotional sustenance; his "idealized" replacement for Bruce at the end of our work together. He smiled wryly and said that he had not seen much of him lately, they seemed to have drifted apart. His mood on leaving was friendly but subdued.

Discussion

Alexander represents a departure from the dynamic interplay depicted in other cases presented in the behavior disorders workshop. The pattern of mutual enactment and parallel splitting in the therapist did not unfold with the drama and immediacy noted elsewhere, possibly because Alexander's treatment was confined to a once-weekly format. The infrequent schedule may have permitted both of us the time and space to recover from the potentially disintegrative regressive process that threatened our early hours together. Enactments tended to fade in their intensity with the passage of time. Significantly, Alexander did not request more frequent meetings until my unifying selfobject functions were solidly established within the idealizing transference of the later years.

Although Kohut (1971) included delinquent behavior in the category of analyzable self-disorders, he left it virtually untouched in his later writing. With the exception of brief references to lies, plagiarism, or minor rule-breaking activities—misbehaviors that happened to catch his clinical eye from time to time—delinquency faded into the background and was largely neglected in the subsequent self psychological literature.

On the rare occasions *delinquency* reappeared as a distinct nosological entity, it was often conceptualized as a deficiency in the idealizing pole of the self, leading to insufficiently internalized values (Elson, 1987; Ornstein, 1983). The enactment aspect of the disorder was often linked to problems in tension regulation and impulse control stemming from selfobject failures very early in development. The "machismo" and exhibitionistic features, when in the service of propping up an insecurely established gender identity, were construed as originating in a compromised relationship with the homogenital oedipal parent (Ornstein, 1983).

This case describes a delinquent young man whose narcissistic vulnerability, expressed through his addictive search for tension-regulating, containing, and unifying selfobjects, originated in repetitive failures of his early caretakers to engage with him in depth. These early misconnections were recapitulated in the transference when I became the target of perverse fantasy and delinquent enactment. Now as I became the new edition of the despised maternal object, my every word and deed seemed to remind him of an emotionally compromised mother whose unresponsiveness was predicated on her own needs for affirmation, a distracted mother whose attention was claimed by his siblings, a depressed mother preoccupied with a mortal illness, and a seductive mother who failed her oedipal child by presenting him with the archaic idealization of her own father as the standard to which he should aspire. At the same time, she devalued his father, especially those dimensions of his father's self that expressed masculinity and aggression.

His father, discomforted by his young son's intense neediness, emotionalism, and overly close (effeminate?) allegiance to the mother, did not welcome his son's overtures. Alexander's efforts to escape his mother's misuse and entrapment by seeking refuge in the protective embrace of a strong father to whom he could look up were rebuffed. Infuriated, depleted, and rejected, he was thrown back onto the relationship with a mother who expressed her own pathological docket by distortedly mirroring her son's alienation from and revenge on his father.

Thus a split-off delinquent sector of his self originated not only in deficiencies in idealization stemming from his father's unavailability, but also in his mother's selective mirroring of the grandiose and antisocial aspects of his behavior. I experienced a similar dissociation in my responsiveness to Alexander, his delinquent self-organization foreclosing awareness of my deepening attachment to him, and his to me.

Kohut (1971) described the delinquent's "flaunting of omnipotent unrestricted activities" and "pride at ruthlessly manipulating his environment" as reinforcing his defense against awareness of a "longing for the lost idealized object" (p. 163). It is my experience that the therapist may also remain unaware, sometimes for a prolonged period, of the patient's silent, submerged idealization, focusing instead on his noisy, exhibitionistic displays. This unawareness may be multiply determined, stemming first from the need to privilege integrative work at the vertical barrier (i.e., understanding the meaning and function of upsurges of misbehavior as indexing dislocations in the selfobject transference) as well as to protect the analytic couple from premature engagement with the potentially disintegrative affect states embedded in these archaic longings for an idealizable figure. As Alexander stated when he read this report, prior to publication, "I had the feeling of knowing all this, about both of us. But I couldn't have said it in the beginning. And I couldn't have felt it until now."

References

Arlow, J. (1954), Panel on perversion: Theoretical and therapeutic aspects. *J. Amer. Psychoanal. Assn.*, 2:336–345.

Chasseguet-Smirgel, J. (1984), *Creativity and Perversion*. New York: Norton.

Elson, M., ed. (1987), *The Kohut Seminars on Self Psychology and Psychotherapy with Adolescents and Young Adults*. New York: Norton.

Freud, S. (1927), On perversion. *Standard Edition*, 21. London: Hogarth Press, 1961.

Glover, E. (1933), The relation of perversion-formation to the development of reality-sense. *Internat. J. Psycho-Anal.*, 14:486–504.

Goldberg, A. (1995), *The Problem of Perversion*. New Haven, CT: Yale University Press.

——— (1999), *Being of Two Minds*. Hillsdale, NJ: The Analytic Press.

Hesse, E. & Main, M. (1999), Second-generation effects of unresolved trauma in non-maltreating parents: Dissociated, frightened and threatening parental behavior. *Psychoanal. Inq.* 19:481–540.

Kael, P. (1989), Out there and in here. In: *Hooked*. New York: E. P. Dutton, pp. 202–209.

Kernberg, O. (1967), Borderline personality organization. *J. Amer. Psychoanal. Assn.*, 15:641–685.

Kohut, H. (1971), *The Analysis of the Self*. New York: International Universities Press.

Main, M. (1995), A move to the level of representation in the study of attachment organization: Implications for psychoanalysis. In: *Research in Psychoanalysis: Process, Development, and Outcome*, ed. T. Shapiro & R. Emde. Madison, CT: International Universities Press.

Ornstein, A. (1983), An idealizing transference of the oedipal phase. In: *Reflections on Self Psychology*, ed. J. Lichtenberg & S. Kaplan. Hillsdale, NJ: The Analytic Press, pp. 135–148.

——— Gropper, C. & Bogner, J. (1983), Shoplifting: An expression of revenge and restitution. *The Annual of Psychoanalysis*, 11:311–334. Madison, CT: International Universities Press

Racker, H. (1968), *Transference and Counter-Transference*. New York: International Universities Press.

213

Stoller, R. J. (1988), Patients' responses to their own case reports. *J. Amer. Psychoanal. Assn.*, 36:371–392.

Zizek, S. (1992), *Enjoy Your Symptom!* New York: Routledge.

Contributors

Barbara Fajardo, Ph.D., Faculty, Training and Supervising Analyst, Institute for Psychoanalysis, Chicago.

Harvey M. Freed, M.D., Associate Professor of Clinical Psychiatry, Northwestern University Medical School, Chicago.

Arnold Goldberg, M.D. (editor), Cynthia Oudejans Harris, M.D., Professor, Department of Psychiatry, Rush-Presbyterian-St. Luke's Medical Center; Training and Supervising Analyst, Institute for Psychoanalysis, Chicago.

Salee A. Jenkins, Ph.D., Faculty, Northwestern University Medical School; Faculty, Institute for Psychoanalysis, Chicago.

Caryle Perlman, M.S., Faculty, Institute for Psychoanalysis, Chicago; Faculty, Institute for Clinical Social Work.

Brenda Clorfene Solomon, M.D., Faculty, Training and Supervising Analyst, Institute for Psychoanalysis, Chicago; Clinical Assistant Professor of Psychiatry, Abraham Lincoln Medical School, University of Illinois, Chicago.

Jeffrey Stern, Ph.D., Advanced Candidate, Institute for Psychoanalysis, Chicago; Lecturer in Psychiatry and Humanities, The University of Chicago.

Index